HOLD SKYLINE

Our plans were to hold Skyline by using the Hmong on the flanks as ground maneuver elements and reserves. A 105-mm howitzer was moved out to LS 15, and the Hmong began to fire their own close support—mostly by dead reckoning. Thai mercenaries came out and helped set up a fire direction center and patiently taught the Hmong the concept of indirect fire. When the Thais left, the Hmong took their own bearings and used sticks and knotted string to align the gun when they fired . . .

From LS 15 down to the river valley was a tiny theater of war within the little Lao theater of war. The U.S. Army might be pulling out of South Vietnam, but we were still fighting and holding on.

The Special Warfare Series
from St. Martin's Paperbacks

COVERT OPS

THE CIA'S SECRET WAR IN LAOS

James E. Parker, Jr.

Published in hardcover as *CODENAME MULE*

St. Martin's Paperbacks

Published in hardcover as *Codename Mule*

Published by arrangement with Naval Institute Press

COVERT OPS

Copyright © 1995 by James E. Parker, Jr.
Foreword copyright © 1995 by William M. Leary.

Cover photograph by UPI/Corbis-Bettmann.

Library of Congress Catalog Card Number: 94-48538

ISBN: 0-312-96340-8

Printed in the United States of America

Naval Institute Press hardcover edition published in 1995
St. Martin's Paperbacks edition/November 1997

St. Martin's Paperbacks are published by St. Martin's Press, 175 Fifth Avenue, New York, NY 10010.

10 9 8 7 6 5

To my mother, Vera Edwards Parker,
who died on the Island of Martinique,
11 March 1994

She was a strong, Christian woman,
and I loved her very much.

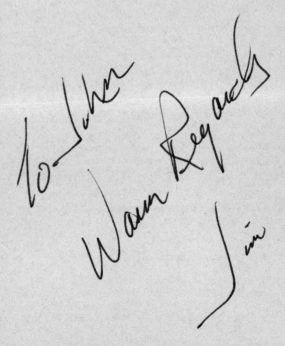

CONTENTS

FOREWORD

The largest paramilitary operation ever conducted by the U.S. Central Intelligence Agency (CIA) took place in the lovely Kingdom of Laos. It was, in many ways, an unlikely location for such activity. Oden Meeker, a government official who was assigned to the administrative capital of Vientiane in the mid-1950s, found a sleepy country with a tranquility "just this side of Rip Van Winkle." The people, he noted, were unambitious, unmechanical, gentle, courteous, and always smiling. Inefficiency was a way of life that seemed to bother only foreigners.[1]

Yet beyond the sleepy surface lay a geopolitical reality. In an age of Cold War, Laos happened to be in the wrong place at the wrong time. To Assistant Secretary of State Walter B. Robertson, Laos was "a finger thrust right down into the heart of Southeast Asia. And Southeast Asia is one of the prime objectives of international Communists in Asia because it is rich in raw materials and has excess food." Robertson painted a grim scenario for a House subcommittee in 1959. Should the Communists gain control of the resources of Southeast Asia, then combine this prize with the manpower of China and the industrial capacity of Japan, he warned, "We will really have to pull up stakes and come back home, because the battle will be lost."[2]

The situation in Laos remained fairly stable following the French departure from Indochina in 1955. The United

States established an Operations Mission in Vientiane to help the royal government with its many economic problems, while a Programs Evaluation Office dealt with military assistance. The CIA had only a minor presence in the country during this early period. Station Chief Milton Clark, the senior Agency (CIA) official in Laos, created a small intelligence network and assigned officers to report on the various political and military factions that were constantly jockeying for power.[3]

Henry Hecksher, who replaced Clark in August 1957, had a more ambitious agenda for the CIA. Resourceful and arrogant, Hecksher disagreed with the policies of Ambassador Horace Smith. Smith wanted to encourage the neutralist stance of Souvanna Phouma, a French-educated political leader, who headed a coalition government that included the Communist Pathet Lao. Hecksher believed that the United States should provide covert financial assistance to anti-Communist and pro-American forces in the deeply divided country. With Washington indecisive, the CIA was able to ignore the ambassador and go its own way.[4]

The quiet in Laos changed dramatically in the summer of 1959 when fighting broke out between the Pathet Lao and the Royal government. As government positions on the strategic Plaine des Jarres (PDJ)—a fifty-square-mile plateau in the mountainous northern part of the country—became endangered, the United States answered a request for assistance and dispatched Special Forces teams (later known as White Star) to train the Royal Lao Army. At the same time, the CIA increased its logistical support to the army by using the transports of Air America, an airline that it secretly owned. Thanks in large part to Washington's vigorous response, the crisis soon passed and the Pathet Lao faded into the jungle.[5]

In late July 1960, Winthrop G. Brown arrived in Vientiane to replace Ambassador Smith. Aware of the problems that Smith had encountered with Hecksher, Brown had visited CIA headquarters prior to leaving Washington in an attempt to clarify the role of the intelligence agency in Laos. CIA Director Allen W. Dulles had assured Brown that all CIA personnel in Laos were subject to the ambassador's authority. Anyone not loyally carrying out Brown's instructions or who failed to work harmoniously with the country team, Dulles told Brown, would be removed within twenty-four hours.[6]

A few days after Brown took up his duties, Laos erupted in crisis. Kong Le, American-trained commander of the Second Parachute Battalion, seized control of Vientiane. Complaining about the corruption of the pro-American conservative government that had come to power following fraudulent elections in April 1960, he called for the creation of a coalition government, which would include the Pathet Lao, and a return to strict neutrality.

Ambassador Brown believed that Kong Le's charges of corruption had merit. When the National Assembly asked Souvanna Phouma to form a new government, Brown recommended that Washington accept the situation. The Eisenhower administration took the view, however, that Kong Le was certainly pro-Communist and possibly another Fidel Castro. A neutral government for Laos seemed a step backward.[7]

Brown's superiors favored Gen. Phoumi Nosavan, a right-wing military leader with a power base in southern Laos. As Adm. Harry D. Felt, commander-in-chief of the Pacific fleet, explained: "Phoumi is no George Washington. However, he is anti-Communist, which is what counts most in the sad Laos situation."[8]

Despite Brown's misgivings, General Phoumi soon became the recipient of substantial American assistance as he prepared to engage Kong Le's forces. Air America transports ferried military supplies from Bangkok to Phoumi's headquarters at Savannakhet, while U.S. Special Forces personnel assumed an advisory role with his army. In November, the rebel army set out for Vientiane, two hundred miles to the north.[9]

Heavy fighting took place in December when Phoumi's troops reached the capital. By the end of the year, Kong Le—who was now receiving support from a Soviet airlift—had retreated to the Plaine des Jarres and secured the vital airfield complex in the area. The appearance of the Soviets alarmed American military authorities. Admiral Felt cabled the Joint Chiefs of Staff on 29 December: "With full realization of the seriousness of the decision to intervene, I believe strongly that we must intervene now or give up northern Laos." Adm. Arleigh Burke, chief of naval operations, agreed. "If we lose Laos," he told the Joint Chiefs on 31 December, "we will probably lose Thailand and the rest of Southeast Asia. We will have demonstrated to the world that we cannot or will not stand when challenged." The effect, Burke warned, would soon be felt throughout Asia, Latin America, and Africa.[10]

President Dwight D. Eisenhower, in his last days in office, rejected direct military intervention. The administration, however, did approve a recommendation from the CIA that had been endorsed by Admiral Felt and State Department officials to arm and train Hmong tribesmen in northern Laos. In January 1961, CIA paramilitary specialist James W. "Bill" Lair met with Hmong leader Vang Pao. He found Vang Pao eager to obtain modern arms and training for the Hmong, who already had suffered at the hands of the better-armed Pathet Lao. As the CIA wanted to maintain a low profile in Laos, Lair arranged to have the Thai Border Police train the first 1,000 Hmong recruits. A special three-day course was set up, with intensive work in map reading, tactics, demolition, and the use of World War II-era American weapons.[11]

With the Hmong scattered on mountainous terrain surrounding the Plaine des Jarres, Lair recognized from the beginning that communications was the key to effective operations. To provide both communications and logistical support, he turned to Air America.[12] In the early months of 1961, Air America had only a handful of helicopters and short-takeoff-and-landing (STOL) aircraft available for the task of supporting CIA operations in Laos. This changed in early March, when the new Kennedy administration became alarmed after Kong Le and the Pathet Lao captured a key road junction and threatened Vientiane and Luang Prabang. President John F. Kennedy not only placed U.S. military forces in the region on alert, but he also authorized the transfer of fourteen helicopters from the Marine Corps to Air America. This marked the beginning of a major expansion of the CIA-owned airline in Laos.[13]

By early June 1961, both the United States and the Soviet Union had decided to defuse the dangerous situation in Laos. At a meeting in Vienna, President Kennedy and Prime Minister Nikita S. Khrushchev issued a joint statement reaffirming their support for "a neutral and independent Laos." At the same time, negotiators met in Geneva, Switzerland, to work out a settlement to the thorny problem.[14]

While the diplomats maneuvered, the CIA continued to supply arms and ammunition to the 9,000 Hmong tribesmen, who, by the summer of 1961, had been trained and equipped under its auspices, and to transport rice to tens of thousands of Hmong refugees displaced by the fighting. Most items came by airdrops, but Air America also began to develop a series of airstrips, many on mountaintops or mountainsides, that would form a key element in Lair's transportation infrastructure for the Hmong. As Air America pilots located suitable landing areas, they arranged to have local villagers cut down trees and level the ground as best they could with their primitive equipment. From less than a dozen Victor Sites, as they were known in 1961, the program grew to encompass more than one hundred Lima Sites by late 1964 and more than four hundred by the early 1970s.[15]

In May 1962, the fragile truce in Laos was shattered when Communist troops attacked and quickly seized the provincial capital of Nam Tha in northwestern Laos.

President Kennedy ordered 3,000 American military personnel into Thailand, and for a time it appeared that full-scale fighting would break out. Kennedy and Khrushchev, however, reaffirmed their support for the neutralization of Laos. Two months later, on 23 July 1962, a formal "Declaration on the Neutrality of Laos" was signed in Geneva. It provided for a coalition government and the withdrawal of all foreign troops from the country by 7 October.[16]

In complying with the agreement, the United States pulled out its 666 military advisers and support staff. Also, Air America arms drops ceased. Assistant Secretary of State Averill Harriman, who was intent on ensuring U.S. compliance with the Geneva accords, allowed the CIA to retain only two men in Laos to monitor Communist compliance with the agreement.

Reports reaching CIA headquarters from its two officers soon made clear that 7,000 North Vietnamese troops had not left the country. In fact, the Army of North Vietnam (NVA) was expanding its area of control and attacking both neutralist and Hmong positions throughout Laos. As Hmong ammunition stores became depleted, William Colby, head of the CIA's Far East Division, pleaded with Harriman to allow the resumption of arms shipments. "My arguments became more forceful," Colby recalled, "reflecting the intense cables I was receiving from the two CIA officers who were still up in the hills observing and reporting on what was happening." Harriman, with great reluctance, finally approved the shipment of a small quantity of ammunition—along with strict instructions that it be used for defensive purposes only. Further shipments followed. Colby points out, however, that Harriman personally approved "each and every clandestine supply flight and its cargo."[17]

As Hanoi sent additional troops into Laos during 1963, the Kennedy administration authorized the CIA to increase the size of the Hmong army, which reached 20,000 by the end of the year. The Hmong acted as guerrillas, blowing up NVA supply depots, ambushing trucks, mining roads, and generally harassing the stronger enemy force. By the end of the year, Hanoi was deploying four battalions to counter Hmong guerrilla activity.[18]

Full-scale fighting broke out in Laos in February 1964, when North Vietnamese and Pathet Lao forces threatened Thakhek, a town on the Mekong River north of Savannakhet. This action, Assistant Secretary of State Roger Hilsman informed Secretary Dean Rusk, went far beyond the level of military activities that had been "tacitly accepted as permissible" under the Geneva accords. It should be viewed as an effort to test the limits of the accords. Hilsman recommended that the United States respond "promptly and firmly," including "visible preparations" to introduce U.S. Marine Corps ground and air units into Thailand.[19]

While the United States considered its options, the situation in Laos deteriorated. In March, the Communists attacked across the Plaine des Jarres. By mid-May, they had taken control of the strategic region and succeeded in bringing an end to the already shaky coalition government. Washington considered reactivating the Military Assistance and Advisory Group that had been withdrawn from Laos after the signing of the Geneva accords but decided instead to expand the role of the CIA in an effort to avoid a major confrontation with North Vietnam in an area of secondary importance.[20]

The year 1965 marked the beginning of what became known as the "secret war" in Laos. Although the full extent of the conflict was not revealed to the American people until 1969–1970, the war really was not all that secret. News of the fighting frequently found its way into the pages of the *Bangkok Post, The New York Times*, and other newspapers.[21] Congress certainly was kept well informed. As former CIA Director Richard Helms has pointed out, the appropriations subcommittees that provided the funds for the war were briefed regularly. Also, a number of Congressmen visited Laos and gave every indication of approving what was happening. They believed, Helms noted, that "it was a much cheaper and better way to fight a war in Southeast Asia than to commit American troops.[22]

It should be emphasized that, although the CIA was largely responsible for conducting military operations in Laos, the American ambassador was the man in charge. "The secret war in Laos," writes author Charles Stevenson, "was William Sullivan's war." Ambassador from December 1964 to March 1969, Sullivan insisted on an efficient, closely controlled country team. "There wasn't a bag of rice dropped in Laos that he didn't know about," observed Assistant Secretary of State William Bundy. Sullivan imposed two conditions on his subordinates. First, the thin fiction of the Geneva accords had to be maintained in order to avoid possible embarrassment to the Lao and Soviet governments; military operations, therefore, had to be carried out in relative secrecy. Second, no regular U.S. ground troops were to become involved. In general, Sullivan, and his successor, G. McMurtrie Godley, successfully carried out this policy.[23]

The early years of the war took on a seasonal aspect. During the dry period, which lasted from October to May in northern Laos, the North Vietnamese and Pathet Lao went on the offensive and applied pressure on Hmong and government forces. During the monsoon, lasting from June to September, the anti-Communists took advantage of the mobility provided by Air America and struck deep into enemy-occupied territory. The situation was a mirror image of Vietnam. In Laos, the Communists acted as conventional military forces and were tied to roads and supply lines. The Hmong, at least at first, countered with guerrilla tactics.

Events in Laos were soon overshadowed by the expanding conflict in South Vietnam. As national security adviser Walt Rostow wrote to President Lyndon B. Johnson in August 1966, "We often forget there is a significant—secondary—war going on in Laos." He passed along to Johnson a memorandum by Emory C. Swank, deputy chief of mission on Vientiane, that detailed the fighting in Laos in recent months. Enemy losses between November 1965 and June 1966 in 952 ground clashes— "a grinding guerrilla campaign of ambushes, small unit actions, etc."—amounted to 1,359 killed and 783 wounded. This compared to friendly casualties of 517 killed and 678 wounded. In addition, Swank noted, a "conservative" estimate of enemy losses from air strikes stood at 4,300 killed and 700 wounded.[24]

The character of the war began to change in 1968. The North Vietnamese, apparently impatient with the progress of the Pathet Lao, introduced major new combat forces into Laos and took control of the year's dry season offensive. By mid-March, they had captured the strategic valley of Nam Bac (north of Luang Prabang), successfully assaulted a key navigational facility at Phou Pha Thi that was used by the U.S. Air Force for bombing North Vietnam, and threatened to push the Hmong out of their mountaintop strongholds surrounding the Plaine des Jarres. On 21 March, the CIA issued a Special National Intelligence Estimate to top-level policymakers in Washington on "Communist Intentions in Laos." Despite the presence of 35,000 NVA troops in the country, the CIA's analysts were relatively sanguine about the situation. Although the North Vietnamese had the capability of overrunning most of Laos in short order, the analysts concluded that Hanoi was mainly interested in protecting its supply routes to South Vietnam and did not wish to destroy the general framework of the 1962 Geneva settlement.[25]

Events soon proved the CIA estimate to be correct. The NVA offensive ended with the onset of the monsoon in May. The Hmong, however, had suffered heavy casualties, losing over 1,000 men since January, including many top commanders. A recruitment drive turned up only 300 replacements: 30 percent, between the ages of ten and fourteen; 30 percent, ages fifteen and sixteen; and the remaining 40 percent, all over age thirty-five. "Where were the ones in between?" asked Edgar "Pop" Buell, an official with the U.S. Agency for International Development. "I'll tell you—they're all dead."[26]

As the strength of the Hmong waned, the United States attempted to redress the growing balance of forces in the field through increased use of air power. Between 1965 and 1968, the rate of sorties in Laos had remained fairly constant at ten to twenty a day. In 1969 the rate increased sharply, reaching three hundred per day.[27]

During the wet season of 1969, Hmong leader Vang Pao abandoned the use of guerrilla tactics. Launching a major offensive against NVA/Pathet Lao forces, he utilized the increased air power to support a drive against enemy positions on the Plaine des Jarres. Largely designed to preempt an NVA/Pathet Lao attack, Operation About Face was a huge success. The Hmong reclaimed the entire PDJ for the first time since 1960 and captured 1,700 tons of food, 2,500 tons of ammunition, 640 heavy weapons, and 25 Soviet-built PT-76 tanks.[28]

The victory proved short-lived. In January 1970, the NVA brought in two divisions that not only quickly regained all the lost ground but also threatened the major Hmong base at Long Tieng. Ambassador Godley acted upon pessimistic appraisals of the Hmong's ability to withstand the enemy assault and asked Washington to authorize the use of B-52s against NVA troop concentrations. His request caused considerable soul-searching in the highest echelons of the Nixon administration. No one wanted to disturb the fragile equilibrium in Laos. "It would not make any sense to expand the conflict in Laos," national security adviser Henry Kissinger observed, "except for the minimum required for our own protection, while we were busy withdrawing troops from South Vietnam." Nonetheless, the situation was deemed so grave that President Richard M. Nixon approved Godley's request. On 17 February, shortly after receiving a formal request from the Royal Lao government, Operation Good Look began with the first B-52 strikes on the PDJ. Over the next three years, 2,518 sorties would drop 58,374 tons of bombs in support of U.S.-backed forces in northern Laos.[29]

The hard-pressed Hmong managed to stop the enemy's dry season offensive, thanks largely to air power, but it had been a close call. "The most positive thing that can be said about Laos," the CIA's Office of National Estimates observed in April 1970, "is that it still exists as a non-Communist state." Although NVA strength had now reached 67,000 men, CIA analysts continued to argue that the enemy did not wish to risk a decisive action. "Hanoi quite clearly considers Laos a less important target than South Vietnam," they noted. "The Communists believe that when they obtain their objectives in South Vietnam, Laos will fall into their hands."[30]

While the enemy may have been prepared to devote only limited resources to the war in Laos, the toll on the Hmong continued to rise. Lao authorities, recognizing the declining strength of the Hmong and the poor quality of its own forces, in June asked the Thai government to supply regular troops to fend off the North Vietnamese. While the Thais were anxious to stop the Communists short of the Mekong River, they did not wish to send large numbers of regular army troops into Laos and thereby take a more visible role in the war. Instead, officials in Bangkok agreed to recruit "volunteer" battalions that would be led by regular army officers and NCOs. The cost of these units would be underwritten by the U.S. government.[31]

Thanks to the presence of the Thai troops, plus the transfer of CIA-supported irregular battalions from other sections of the country, the enemy's dry season offensive of 1970–1971 was again stopped short of Long Tieng. The outlook for the future, however, remained grim. The United States was in the process of accelerating its withdrawal from Vietnam. Like Kennedy and Johnson before him, President Nixon wanted a neutral Laos that would serve as a buffer between pro-Western Thailand and the aggressive intentions of North Vietnam and China. Although Nixon was willing to approve the use of B-52s and support Thai "volunteers" in Laos, it was clear that he had no intention of making a major commitment of U.S. forces to assure Laotian neutrality.[32]

The CIA's presence in Laos had grown steadily since the early 1960s, but it still remained small. According to one knowledgeable CIA official, the total number of people connected with the war, both in Laos and in Thailand, never exceeded 225. This included some 50 case officers with Hmong, Lao, and Thai units.[33]

Ambassador Godley, like Ambassador Sullivan, was—by presidential directive—responsible for the "overall direction, coordination, and supervision" of all military operations in Laos. By all accounts, he brought a great deal of enthusiasm to the job. Daily, he presided over "operations meetings," lasting from 9 A.M. to 10:30 A.M. (or later) at the embassy, in order to receive detailed briefings from military and intelligence personnel on the war's developments during the preceding twenty-four hours.[34] During critical periods, Godley attended evening meetings at the Vientiane airport, where he would hear directly from CIA case officers who had just returned from the day's fighting. "Godley was there every night for the briefing," one case officer recalled, "and knew exactly what was going on. He certainly had a 'zest' for the job."[35]

Godley delegated responsibility for the tactical conduct of the war to Hugh Tovar. An experienced and respected intelligence officer who had served with the Office of Strategic Services (OSS) during World War II, Tovar had been a member of a small OSS team operating in Laos at the end of the war. As the CIA station chief, he preferred to exert a general supervision over military affairs and allow his subordinates to handle the operational details.[36]

The primary CIA headquarters responsible for the con-

duct of the war—in effect, Tovar's "executive agent"—
was not in Laos but in Thailand. Located in a two-story
block building adjacent to an aircraft parking ramp at
Udorn Royal Thai Air Force Base, the 4802d Joint Liaison Detachment was the CIA's command center for
military operations in Laos. In charge of the 4802d was
Lloyd "Pat" Landry, a paramilitary specialist who had
been involved in Laotian affairs for more than a decade.
Landry had especially close rapport with the Thais,
whose close cooperation remained crucial to the conduct
of the war.[37] He had a small but talented staff to deal
with the complex details of managing the war. His chief
deputy, James N. Glerum, handled administrative chores
with cool efficiency and looked after relations with Air
America. The Princeton graduate (class of 1952) also was
known as a superb briefer.

A retired Green Beret colonel, who earlier had been
prominent in laying the foundations for the Special
Forces effort in Vietnam,[38] served as chief of operations.
By the early 1970s, all operations involving more than
one battalion required Washington's approval. The colonel became especially adept at drawing up military-type,
five-paragraph field orders that invariably won the
approval of higher headquarters. "Of course," Glerum
recalled, "any resemblance to the field order and what
actually happened was purely coincidental." Weather,
the reaction of the North Vietnamese, and, above all, decisions made by Vang Pao and other local commanders
were beyond Udorn's control.[39]

Other CIA officers at Udorn oversaw air operations,
photographic and signals intelligence, order-of-battle as-
sessments, and coordinated military operations and re-
quirements with 7/13 AF headquarters, also located at
Udorn. There was constant communication with Gen. Vitoon Yasawatdi ("Dhep"), who commanded the nearby
"Headquarters 333," the Thai organization in charge of
Thailand's forces in Laos.[40]

Lines of authority ran from Udorn to CIA regional

headquarters in Laos at Pakxe, Savannakhet, Long Tieng, Luang Prabang, and Nam Lieu. The most important of the five subunits was Long Tieng, the major logistical and operations base in Military Region II. Joseph R. Johnson, the CIA's chief of unit at Long Tieng, directed some 20 or so paramilitary and support personnel who advised Hmong and Thai units. His chief of operations, a former Forest Service smoke jumper who had the confidence of Vang Pao, was responsible for coordinating military activities in the Region, especially those relating to the Hmong. At Long Tieng, the U.S. Air Force had an Air Operations Center that housed the ten forward air controllers who used the radio call sign "Raven."[41]

James E. Parker, Jr., arrived in Laos in late 1971 as the North Vietnamese geared up for another major dry season offensive, this time with greater military strength than ever before. Whether the CIA-supported forces in the country would be able to withstand the enemy attack remained an open question. The young CIA officer and his band of paramilitary case officer brothers at Long Tieng faced an uncertain but surely violent future as the war in Laos reached its climax.

William M. Leary
Professor of History
University of Georgia

NOTES

1. Oden Meeker, *The Little World of Laos* (New York, 1959), 35-39.
2. Robertson testimony, U.S. House of Representatives, Subcommittee of the Committee on Government Operations, *Hearings: United States Aid Operations in Laos*, 86th Cong., 1st sess., 1959, 184-85.
3. Charles A. Stevenson, *The End of Nowhere: American Policy Toward Laos Since 1954* (Boston, 1972), 62.
4. Ibid., 61-62.
5. Arthur J. Dommen, *Conflict in Laos: The Politics of Neutralization*, rev. ed. (New York, 1971), 119-25; Stevenson, *End of Nowhere*, 72-91; Edward J. Marolda and Oscar P. Fitzgerald, *The United States Navy and the Vietnam Conflict: From Military Assistance to Combat* (Washington, 1986), 24-25.

6. Winthrop G. Brown, recorded interview by Larry J. Hackman, February 1, 1968, John F. Kennedy Library Oral History Program.

7. Stevenson, *End of Nowhere*, 92-113.

8. Quoted in Marolda and Fitzgerald, *United States Navy and the Vietnam Conflict*, 47.

9. Dommen, *Conflict in Laos*, 154.

10. Quoted in Marolda and Fitzgerald, *United States Navy and the Vietnam Conflict*, 55.

11. See Theodore Shackley, *The Third Option* (New York, 1981), 122, and Douglas S. Blaufarb, *The Counterinsurgency Era* (New York, 1977), 141-47. Both Shackley and Blaufarb served as chief of station in Vientiane during the 1960s.

12. James W. Lair, interview, 8 July 1988.

13. Timothy N. Castle, *At War in the Shadow of Vietnam: U.S. Military Aid to the Royal Lao Government, 1955–1975* (New York, 1993), 29-30, 43-44.

14. Michael R. Beschloss, *Crisis Years: Kennedy and Khrushchev, 1960–1963* (New York, 1991), 231.

15. Edward G. Lansdale, memorandum to Maxwell D. Taylor, "Resources for Unconventional Warfare in S.E. Asia," n.d. [July 1961], in *The Pentagon Papers—New York Times Edition* (New York, 1971), 130-38; William R. Andresevic, interview 19 June 1987. Andresevic was Air America's chief pilot for STOL aircraft in Laos during the early 1960s.

16. Dommen, *Conflict in Laos*, 200-22.

17. William Colby and Peter Forbath, *Honorable Men: My Life in the CIA* (New York, 1978), 192-95.

18. Jane Hamilton-Merritt, *Tragic Mountains: The Hmong, the Americans, and the Secret Wars in Laos, 1942–1992* (Bloomington, Ind.: 1993), 113-26.

19. Memorandum, Hilsman to Rusk, 15 February 1964, Country File, National Security Files, Lyndon B. Johnson Presidential Library, Austin, Texas.

20. Ambassador Leonard Unger, cable to Secretary of State, 21 March 1964, Country File, National Security Files, Johnson Library; William L. Sullivan to author, 17 April 1994.

21. For example, see the feature article by Seymour Topping on "The 'Twilight' War in Laos," *The New York Times*, 25 January 1965.

22. Richard Helms, interview by Ted Gittinger, 16 September 1981, Oral History Program, Johnson Library. For an early example of a congressional briefing, see William L. Sullivan to Secretary of State, 15 January 1966, Country File, National Security Files, Johnson Library, reporting that Senator Stuart Symington had received "a thorough briefing" during a recent visit to Southeast Asia.

23. Stevenson, *End of Nowhere*, 208-18. See also, Castle, *At War in the Shadow of Vietnam*, 67-71, and William L. Sullivan, *Obbligato* (New York, 1984), 196-235.

24. Note, Rostow to Johnson, attached to cable, Swank to Secretary of State, 3 August 1966, Country File, National Security Files, Johnson Library.

25. CIA, Special National Intelligence Estimate 58-68: "Communist Intentions in Laos," 21 March 1968, Declassified Documents Reference System (DDRS), 1989: 1865.

26. Robert Shaplen, *Time Out of Hand: Revolution and Reaction in Southeast Asia* (New York, 1968), 347-48.

27. Raphael Littauer and Norman Uphoff (eds.) *The Air War in Indochina* (Boston, 1972), 79. See also, Earl H. Tilford, Jr., *Crosswinds: The Air Force's Setup in Vietnam* (College Station, Texas, 1993), 119-24.

28. CIA, Special National Security Estimate 14.3-1-70: "North Vietnamese Intentions: Indochina," 3 June 1970, DDRS 1980: 324.

29. Henry Kissinger, *White House Years* (Boston, 1979), 448-57; U.S. Department of Defense, "Report on Selected Air and Ground Operations in Cambodia and Laos," 10 September 1973.

30. CIA, Office of National Estimates, "Stocktaking in Indochina," 17 April 1970, DDRS 1977: 270C.

31. Kissinger, *White House Years*, 448-57; Shackley, *The Third Option*, 122-24.

32. William W. Lofgren and Richard R. Sexton, "Air War in Northern Laos, 1 April–30 November 1971," U.S. Air Force CHECO Report, 22 June 1973, U.S. Air Force Historical Research Center, Maxwell Air Force Base, Ala.

33. Information from a retired intelligence officer who was in a position to have an accurate count on CIA presence in Thailand and Laos. William Colby, *Lost Victory* (Chicago, 1989), 198, gives the number as "between 300 and 400." This estimate is too high.

34. A profile of Godley appeared in *The New York Times*, 12 July 1973. See also, the informative staff report of visit to Laos by James G. Lowenstein and Richard M. Moose: U.S. Senate, Subcommittee on U.S. Security Agreements and Commitments Abroad of the Committee on Foreign Relations, *Laos: April 1971*, 92d Cong., 1st sess., 1971, 2.

35. George W. T. O'Dell to author, 5 January 1993.

36. B. Hugh Tovar, interview, 13 March 1992; Arthur J. Dommen and George W. Dalley, "The OSS in Laos: The 1945 Raven Mission," *Journal of Southeast Asian Studies* 22 (September 1991): 327-46.

37. Lloyd Landry, interview, 3 July 1993. As noted by Senate staffers Lowenstein and Moose, following a visit to Southeast Asia in January 1972, Udorn Royal Thai Air Force Base was "the most important operational military nerve center in Thailand." U.S. Senate, Subcommittee on U.S. Security Agreements and Commitments Abroad of the Committee on Foreign Relations, *Thailand, Laos, and Cambodia: January 1972*, 92d Congress, 2d sess., 1972, 12.

38. See Shelby L. Stanton, *Green Berets at War: U.S. Army Special Forces in Southeast Asia, 1956–1975* (Novato, Calif., 1985), 48, 52-53, 62.

39. James N. Glerum to author, 20 February 1993.

40. General Vitoon Yasawatdi's activities are discussed in Rueng Yote Chantrakiri, *The Thoughts and Memories of the Man Known as Dhep 333* (Bangkok, 1992). The author is indebted to the Office of the Vice President for Research at the University of Georgia for a grant to have this volume translated from the Thai by Kris Petcharawises.

41. On the forward air controllers, see Christopher Robbins, *The Ravens* (New York, 1987).

PREFACE

High within the rugged Annamese mountain chain that divides Laos from Vietnam is a grassy plateau with gently rolling hills, fifty square miles in size. The French named it the Plaine des Jarres for the hundred or so large stone jars, some ten feet tall, scattered helter-skelter across the landscape. No one knows the history of the jars, and the stone is not indigenous to the area. According to one legend, the plateau itself was formed when slaves leveled the tops of several mountains to make the palace grounds for an ancient Oriental warlord. Over the centuries, the area (commonly referred to as the PDJ), became a farming region and trading center. The French foreign legion had garrisons there for fifty years and regulated trade along the road that ran from the Plaine through the mountains to North Vietnam.

The PDJ was also critical, strategic military terrain and, during the mid-twentieth century, often a battlefield. On the one side were the forces of North Vietnam, who supported the Communist Pathet Lao movement of Lao Prince Souphanouvong, and on the other were poorly organized forces supporting the pro-Western Lao government of Souvanna Phouma.

In the early 1960s, as the war in Vietnam began to take shape, the U.S. Central Intelligence Agency (CIA) was given the mission of providing military support to Souvanna Phouma to counter the overwhelming influence of the opposing North Vietnamese military. Part of the mission was also to attract as many North Vietnamese troops as possible to the Lao theater to keep them from South Vietnam, where they would be used against American soldiers. CIA agents made direct contact with General Vang Pao (V. P.), the leader of the largest tribe of Hmong hill people near the PDJ, and enlisted his assistance. V. P. was a staunch anti-Communist; he had previously worked for the French and, in fact, had lead a relief column to Dien Bien Phu in 1954. The Hmong irregulars under his command, supported and advised by CIA paramilitary officers, fought bravely through the early and mid-1960s, but they were outnumbered by the North Vietnamese and took severe casualties. To fill the ranks, the government of Thailand began to recruit and train Thai volunteers, or mercenaries, under the auspices of the CIA. It was in Thailand's best interests to keep the North Vietnamese as far from its borders as possible. The Hmong and the Thais working together—the Hmong as the maneuver element and the Thais as the "hill sitters" who occupied and controlled ground—subsequently held the North Vietnamese to a draw, with each side giving and taking back land in a seasonal ebb and flow of control.

By 1970, the CIA forces controlled the PDJ, but in December of the following year, with the Thai mercenaries in defensive positions along the western edge of the Plaine, two reinforced divisions of North Vietnamese attacked, rolled across the PDJ, and killed and scattered the mercenaries. The North Vietnamese force continued to advance south until it was stopped at Skyline ridge, which protected the northern edge of the Long Tieng valley, location of the CIA headquarters in the region. The North Vietnamese fell back and, in the fall of 1972, were positioned on and around the PDJ, as they waited for counterattacks by CIA forces.

They were not to be disappointed.

James E. Parker Jr.

COVERT OPS

THE CIA'S SECRET WAR IN LAOS

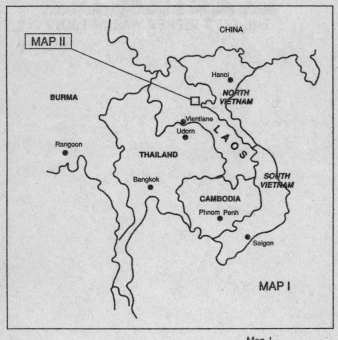

Map I.
Laos and Southeast
Asia, 1971

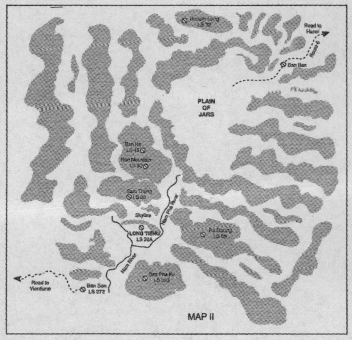

Map II.
The Plain of Jars, surrounded by rugged mountain ridges, in the Long Tieng valley, Military Region II, Laos, 1971.

1

WHAT'S A WAR WORTH?

The buildup of the CIA irregular forces to drive the North Vietnamese from the PDJ plateau began in the early fall of 1972. A Groupe Mobile (GM) battalion of approximately eight hundred Lao irregulars from western Laos, flown into the Long Tieng valley on Air America C-130 aircraft, set up a temporary camp near the old hospital at the east end of the runway. The GM was led by an American, a CIA paramilitary officer. Tahn was his call sign. The Bear, another CIA officer, came in with his unit from south Laos. Digger and I (my call sign was Mule) returned from training camp with our two Hmong GMs. Kayak and Clean, each with two GMs, and Bamboo with the Hmong commandos, plus all the Thai mercenaries, were already in position around the valley.

The muddy Long Tieng marketplace was suddenly crowded with hundreds of armed Thai, Lao, and Hmong irregulars drifting in from their various camps to drink warm beer in thatched shanty bars operated by enterprising Hmong women. The Thai mercenaries, taller than the other nationalities, were heavily tattooed and wore distinctive unit scarves; the Lao forces looked like the French foreign legion with their berets and camouflage tunics; and the Hmong, the smallest and the youngest, looked like dirty mountaineers. There was no friction or fighting between different groups; they were soldiers

1

marshaling for battle. They were restrained and unsure about what lay ahead—fighting around the PDJ always had been fierce.

Three days before the launch of the offensive, Kayak's two GMs were assembled, issued extra ammunition, and moved out of the valley to the east. The next day, my GM was moved by Air America helicopters and C-123s from the valley north to an abandoned airstrip. The following day, Bamboo's commandos were moved southeast of Long Tieng to a staging area.

The lead element in the offensive, a small pathfinding unit of the commandos, remained behind at the Long Tieng airfield ramp near two Air America choppers that were scheduled to insert them on a narrow, deserted mountaintop in the northwestern corner of the PDJ. As night fell, it began to rain, keeping most of the Hmong villagers, who usually congregated around the ramp, under cover and out of sight. Near midnight, the pathfinders climbed aboard the helicopters. As the pilots warmed their engines and went over the final checklist, only two CIA officers stood by under the protecting eaves of the concrete Air Operations (Air Ops) building. One gave a thumbs-up to the lead pilot, and the heavily loaded helicopter lifted off, skimmed along the ramp, and began gaining altitude as it flew down the airfield. The second helicopter followed, and both were soon out of sight.

Flying by instruments, the pilots circled to the west, high and lonely over the rugged mountains—there was no protecting air support—and eventually came down through the weather to locate the target mountaintop. There was little margin for error. As they broke through the clouds, the PDJ was to their right front and ahead, clearly defined by recently made B-52 bomb craters, was their mountain. With all lights off, the helicopters descended. The flight mechanics (kickers) in the back opened the doors, leaned out into the driving rain, and helped guide them to the ground.

The pathfinders quickly jumped out, and the helicopters lifted off. Within minutes, they transmitted a coded radio message to the commandos, waiting at the staging area, that a landing zone (LZ) had been marked with lights and the commandos could jump in.

Shep, a lean former smoke jumper from the hills of Montana on contract to the CIA, ran the rigging shop and had helped give the seventy commandos parachute training. He was standing in front of them at the end of the dirt airfield near the back of an idling Air America C-130 when someone yelled from a nearby shelter that it was time to go. A dark, swarthy group, the commandos were hunched forward in their parachute riggings, their helmets tied down with strips of old sheets Shep had found in the back of a warehouse earlier in the day. They were wet to the bone, some less than fifteen years old and none much taller than their M-16 rifles. Shep walked up to the first man in line and peered in at him under his helmet. The Hmong looked up and smiled. Shep checked his equipment and continued down the line to check parachutes and count off the men.

There were seventy-seven.

"Hold it, goddamit to hell. Just wait a damn minute here," he yelled, arresting the movement of the first man, who was edging toward the dry interior of the plane.

Shep knew that there were only seventy commandos with parachute training scheduled to make the jump. He went back up the line and counted again.

Seventy-seven!

Seven Hmong, most of whom had probably been assigned support functions at the airfield, had picked up extra parachutes and intermingled with the others. The Hmong commander came up, and Shep yelled, "Buddy, we got seven people here who don't know how to jump, and they ain't supposed to go. I don't know what they're trying to prove, but it didn't get by me."

The commander, unsure of the problem, shrugged. The Air America C-130 had fired its engines, and the wind from the props was blowing the rain back hard at the group. There was no way to determine who the seven interlopers were. The commander didn't seem concerned, so Shep stepped aside with an angry look and watched as all seventy-seven of the Hmong soldiers boarded.

"They don't know how to jump. Ain't never had any training," Shep said to no one in particular as he pulled his old cowboy duster together against the weather and watched the back of the plane close. Within minutes, the plane took off, barreling down the dirt mountain strip lit on both sides by oily rags burning in No. 10 cans.

Twenty minutes later, all seventy-seven men ran out the back of the C-130 and parachuted without injury on top of the pathfinders' lights at the edge of the PDJ.

The next day, Digger's GM was lifted by helicopters into the LZ, now firmly secured by the commandos. There had been no reaction from the North Vietnamese.

Late that same morning, my GM began moving toward the PDJ. The troops launched with no precision whatsoever, at odd intervals, in small groups, in fits and starts. I was standing near a forward outpost with one of the commanders. Nhia, my Hmong interpreter, was lounging nearby with the radios. Groups of Hmong were milling around. A couple of the younger boys moved off down a mountain trail, one with his M-16 over a shoulder and the other carrying a box of grenades, with cooking pots strapped to the outside of his pack. Then, a few more of the older boys followed and then several more.

Kayak's GMs from the south also began heading north toward the PDJ. Tahn's and Bear's GMs from the other regions were held in reserve in the valley. Clean's forces and all the Thai mercenaries were to remain behind in Long Tieng defensive positions.

There was no contact for the first few days. I spent most of the time sitting by the radios at the launch site. Occasionally, I called in an Air America helicopter for a recon (reconnaissance) high over my advancing GM out to the edge of the PDJ.

On the third day, as Kayak's forces came close to a river valley that led down to Skyline, they had a violent clash with North Vietnamese regulars. Kayak's forces pulled back. Tahn's GM was heli-lifted in near the original contact. Because of some confusion during the last couple of shuttles, Tahn was left on the position. Moving an element of his people to some high ground as the sun went down, he was not near a radio to tell any of the last helicopter pilots that he was still out.

Only when the case officers gathered that evening in the CIA headquarters bunker in Long Tieng did anyone realize that Tahn had not returned. He was contacted through a radio relay on Skyline, and he gave assurances that he was fine. He said his men were still digging in and they didn't expect any action that night. It would take the Vietnamese a couple of days to react.

But, it didn't happen that way. During the night, his position was overrun and Tahn was killed, his face blown away by a grenade blast. General Vang Pao and Hog, the chief CIA case officer, went out at first light with a company of V. P.'s personal guards to retake the position and bring back Tahn's body.

Greek and I watched from Air Ops as other case officers took the limp body from the helicopter, placed it tenderly in a body bag, and put it on a plane for the rear CIA base at Udorn. Tahn was a friend; we had trained together in the States. After graduation from the University of Washington, he had served as a U.S. Marine combat engineer in South Vietnam. He was very adept at leading the Lao irregulars—intelligent, unassuming, liked and respected by all the Agency (CIA) officers who worked up-country. He never said much, but he had strong opinions and people listened when he did talk. Now he was dead.

A steady procession of men in body bags moved through the Long Tieng valley: Hmong, Thai, Lao, Air America, U.S. Air Force.

It was part of the job, handling our dead. Earlier in the

year, when the North Vietnamese were attacking Long Tieng, I had taken a fixed-wing Air America plane down to Udorn, Thailand, every night. The bodies of Thai mercenaries were always the last to be loaded. It was a gruesome sight as the body bags were being tossed on board, often a dozen or more. As I sat through the many flights south, I looked at the bags and wondered about the men inside, about their families and their past and what they had planned for the future. But that was horrible, unnecessary imagery, and it did not take me long to accept the body bags. After a while I was happy to see them loaded because it meant we soon would be heading south.

War forces that on people—makes us insensitive to the suffering and dying of others. Searching for moral justification each time a man dies in war is futile and hurts the soul. If we dwell on it, the hurt makes us crazy or turns us into drunks. The sane alternative is to put it out of our minds and resist introspection and grief. I could understand how people, such as the Air America pilots, who had worked for years in the Indochina War were able to develop detached, unemotional attitudes.

But I could not ignore the loss of my friend.

Sitting with Greek in Air Ops I hurt. A tear ran silently down my cheek. Was this "secret" CIA war in Laos worth Tahn's life? Was all of Indochina worth the life of any of the men I knew? What's a man's life worth, anyway? What's a friend's life worth?

In war, it's only worthwhile if you win, I thought. Don't fight a war if you're not going to win.

We were intent on what we were doing in Laos in 1972. We were going to retake the PDJ, and we were going to continue to win here, regardless of the outcome in South Vietnam.

I would see the fighting in Laos and in South Vietnam to a conclusion. I was around when it all really started in 1965. What I know most from those experiences is that war hurts, good men die, and it's only worthwhile if you win.

2

CIA RECRUITER

I grew up in a large white house on a hill overlooking the town of Southern Pines, North Carolina. My best friend was Cottonpicker, an army staff sergeant who lived nearby. He taught me how to hunt deer during the winter and gig for frogs in the summer. I was not an all-round, prizewinning child. My school friends tended to be the class rowdies, and we had little interest in academics. I ran away from home after my freshman year in high school and went to Havana, Cuba. It was the summer before Fidel Castro came to power. Although the country was caught in a revolutionary fervor, the bawdy, spirited nightlife in the area by the Havana harbor where I stayed was unaffected. At 3 A.M. one morning not long after my arrival, I was sitting on a curb beneath the flickering light of a neon bar sign—Cuban music coursed the air, people around me were yelling in different languages, street vendors hawked strong-smelling coffee. Up the street, a fistfight broke out and no one tried to break it up. Longshoremen, seafaring men, whores, musicians, and con artists meandered along the street. It was as exciting as anything a fifteen-year-old from a small southern town could have ever imagined. I never forgot that scene or how much I enjoyed being there.

When I returned home I dreamed of future travel to more places like Havana and talked about it with my parents. They did not want to hear this. They expected me to be more involved in traditional southern pursuits, and I was eventually enrolled in a local military school. I went on to the University of North Carolina at Chapel Hill, worked summers as a lifeguard at Myrtle Beach, South Carolina, and left school one fall to travel through Central America in search of Havana-like places—a trip that ended when my two traveling companions and I ran afoul of what were to become the Nicaraguan Sandinestas. I returned to Chapel Hill but dropped out and joined the army in 1964.

Basic training was a sobering experience—my life's wake-up call. Although I had had a privileged adolescence in a small southern town, I soon discovered that I was no one special as a private in the U.S. Army. Basic training was a tough, profane, demanding experience. As a result of the soldiering skills I had learned in military school, I was selected the outstanding trainee in my basic training course and went on to Officer Candidate School (OCS) at Fort Benning, Georgia. When I received my commission as an Infantry second lieutenant in the spring of 1965, particularly while my father and mother were pinning on my gold bars, I felt a tremendous sense of achievement and self-worth. In six months, I had gone from a scrawny recruit to the Officers Club. On my own. No one gave me a thing. I had earned my commission.

When I arrived home from OCS, Cottonpicker was waiting in the front yard to give me my first salute.

After paratrooper training, I was assigned as a platoon leader in the 1st/28th Battalion of the 1st Division at Fort Riley, Kansas, just months before the division was deployed to Vietnam.

My regiment crossed the Pacific on a merchant marine ship and went ashore by landing craft near the South Vietnamese village of Vung Tau. Within weeks, we were fighting north of Saigon and then moved on to the tunnels of Chu Chi, down to the Delta, and back up along the Cambodian border. We suffered casualties, got replacements, suffered more casualties, and got more replacements. At first, we fought the Vietcong, but we eventually targeted North Vietnamese units and fought them when we could find them. Fighting a war of attrition, we tried to kill more of them than they could of us, and our field operations were planned to maximize contact. Hardened by the experience of leading men in combat, I came of age at twenty-three.

After being wounded in 1966, I finished the year as a staff officer in the battalion's operations section and then received a Stateside assignment at Fort Ord, California. I left the military in 1967 and returned home to North Carolina, where I worked a year for Dad at his lumber mill and married Brenda Joyce Denton, a local girl of warmth, common sense, and charm. We moved to Chapel Hill so that I could continue my work toward a political science degree in preparation for law school.

One day at school, while waiting for Brenda to get off work, I visited the student placement office and noticed a man leaning on the door to one of the interview rooms. I told him he looked like a prostitute scanning the crowd for customers, and he said he often felt that way—it was a competitive business. I asked whom he represented, and he said the Central Intelligence Agency. One doesn't meet that many CIA people during a normal day and I told him so, guessing that his work must be interesting. It was a good job for some people, maybe me, he said, and we went into an office where I summarized my background. He told me that the Agency had openings for young men who had served in Vietnam and might consider working on contract in Indochina.

Alluding to a recurring media story about a CIA operation to assassinate Vietcong leaders, I asked him if this was the Phoenix program. ''Terminate with extreme prejudice'' was a term I had heard associated with the work. He smiled, shook his head as if he often heard that comment, and said he wasn't at liberty to discuss the particulars of the job, other than to say the work would be interesting and challenging, especially to a person who knew something about fighting. He cautioned that anyone who did drugs, had committed a felony, was a homosexual, or had a disreputable character would not be hired. Scoring well on Agency tests was also necessary. Many applied, but few were accepted.

I filled out most of the twenty-page application that night and sent it in within the week. A couple of days later, I received notice from a CIA administrative office in Washington that my application had been received. That was soon followed by an invitation to take a battery of tests at the university's testing center. I took the tests, then months passed before I received a telephone call from a CIA administrator who said that I was still being considered for contract employment in Indochina. Although I did not have a job offer yet, she said my application looked good.

The CIA.

The more I thought about it, the more it seemed exactly what I wanted to do. I tried to remember everything the administrator had said over the telephone, how she had said it, the inflections in her voice, what she had really meant. Would she have called and said that my application looked good if there wasn't reason to believe I would be hired? The CIA—paramilitary case officer. "That's me," I told Brenda, "that's what we're going to do."

Convincing myself that the CIA was in our future, I did not even send in a deposit for law school. After graduation, I took a series of part-time jobs while my CIA application was being processed. In March, I was invited to Rosslyn, Virginia, for two days of aptitude, psychological, and polygraph tests. I also met with a representative of the CIA office that was interested in me as a contractor. He said, barring unforeseen difficulties, I would know whether I would be hired by early summer.

He told me to hang in; the Agency liked people with "hang," especially for this job.

In the middle of June, I received a telephone call from the CIA offering me a job starting 2 August 1970, ten months after I had happened upon the recruiter in the university placement office. We left North Carolina in late July, found an unfurnished two-bedroom townhouse in Northern Virginia, rented some furniture, and moved in. Two days later, wearing my best suit, I reported to work at the CIA headquarters building in Langley, Virginia.

Guards at the outer gate took my driver's license, checked my name against a list of authorized visitors, and admitted me into the fenced compound. In the front lobby of the main building, I was processed for a badge. The building had a stillness—cathedral-like, holy, mysterious. People looked intense and purposeful, their footfalls echoing down the wide, sterile halls. I was escorted to meet my new boss, chief of the Special Operations Group (SOG) of the Directorate of Operations, in his small, cluttered office in the basement. (The SOG section of the CIA should not be confused with the U.S. Army Special Operations Group, which saw extensive action in Vietnam. They had some similar paramilitary missions but were separate organizations.) The boss welcomed me on board, told me that I would be in training for about a year and, if I successfully completed it, that I would be sent somewhere in Indochina, depending on need, for paramilitary chores. The Agency had been given these types of duties since its inception, and people like myself had been contracted for them. I was following a proud tradition. The boss said to focus on the training, learn Agency rules of conduct and tradecraft, and keep my personal affairs in order. I would be given a cover legend to hide my CIA employment to outsiders and an alias to be used within the Agency. I was not assigned to any class group; SOG training programs were structured individually. "Get to know the training officer," he said, "and help plot a course through the training cycle and get out to the field."

Later, I met other SOG officers hired for assignment to Indochina. Most were athletic and personable, all were intelligent, and all were ex-military officers with Vietnam combat experience. We tended to be older and more earthy than many of the other trainees who had been hired for traditional roles as intelligence officers. Some of the latter were aloof and pedantic, although the SOG officers tried to make the career trainees (CTs) aware that we existed on equal terms. Our efforts were not always well received, and we were referred to as "knuckle draggers," alluding to our possibly close kinship with the gorilla family. An outgoing personality was a common trait among all clandestine service trainees, and repartee between our two groups tended to be lively and caustic.

A story circulated at one of the training sites about an arrogant career trainee who had developed an image in his mind of what a young intelligence officer should look like. This involved a pipe. He brought several pipes and a big tin of tobacco to the training site. He sat at the back of class and worked meticulously to clean the pipe of the day and then fill it, pack it, and light it with a special lighter that fired the flame down. He then leaned back in his chair, drew in slowly and deeply from his bowl of tobacco, and blew the smoke out through pursed lips. Here was an individual who desperately needed to be humanized. One day when he was away from his pipe accessories, some SOG trainees (SOGers) took the shavings from a pencil sharpener and mixed them with his tobacco—not quite half and half, but close. The pencil shavings in the tin were indistinguishable from the tobacco. The next time this young intelligence officer candidate smoked his pipe, he looked like he was firing a little wood stove in the back of the room. Even though he was almost lost in a smoke cloud of tobacco and pencil shavings, he was oblivious to the snickers of those

around him. No one ever told him how foolish he had
looked.

I was scheduled for traditional clandestine service operations training, in addition to specialized SOG nonconventional warfare training. After several introductory
paramilitary training courses that included small arms familiarization and defensive driving, I was assigned to the
intelligence operations (ops) course. This core training
for CIA new hires in the clandestine service got at the
essence of the spy business, which dealt with people's
lives. We were told at the orientation that intelligence
work took nerve and discipline. Professional tradecraft
was complicated. Basic principles applied during most
assignments, but every situation was different. In an im-
perfect world, we must try to make our work exacting
and structured. The intelligence we gathered had to be
reported; it had no value until it was disseminated, ver-
bally and in written reports. Getting the story was only
half the job. Getting it right and getting it to the appropriate U.S. government customers was of equal importance.

The instructors were all experienced field case officers.
Some had been assigned to the training facility to cool
off, having been suspected of or exposed while doing
Agency work abroad. Some were called back from overseas assignments because of threats to their lives. Others
had been living under deep cover overseas and took training assignments to be with their own kind and talk about
their experiences. We learned as much about the intelligence business in casual conversations with the staff as
we did in the classroom. James Bond movies were popular entertainment about this time, and our perceptions
of the espionage business included Hollywood-type vi-
sions of intrigue and dazzling scenery. We learned, however, that the business had its share of drudgery and
bureaucracy. Nothing happened in the field exactly the
way it was planned. Crisis management would be a large

part of our field work because of the capriciousness of agents and counterspy efforts of foreign services. The people we would deal with were often the underside of humanity, and we had to put aside our personal feelings and work with them professionally and dispassionately.

After training, the knuckle draggers would be off to fight the hot war in Indochina. The traditionalists, the CTs, were going to the far reaches of the world to fight the Cold War against the Soviets, Cubans, North Koreans, and East Germans, often in places where CIA operatives were the only U.S. resources. It was a time when thousands of nuclear warheads around the world were aimed at the United States, and the CIA traditionalists in our training course would be sent out there to find out what the people who controlled those weapons were thinking. No simple calling.

We usually worked late into the night on our training assignments. Conversation during our free time, though spirited, was generally serious and dealt with the spy business.

At the conclusion of the course, some trainees were not recommended for field work. Others decided that they wanted to play different roles in the Agency and elected out of the Directorate for Operations. But the majority would go on to field assignments as case officers in the CIA clandestine service.

There was no graduation exercise. During the last hour, a ranking CIA official made some brief extemporaneous comments about the important work that lay ahead of us. This put an appropriate punctuation to the end of the operations course—there is little ceremony involved in spy work.

The next training for me was the SOG escape and evasion (E&E) course, a welcome change out in the sun.

3

KNUCKLE
DRAGGER U.

E&E training was divided into three phases. During phase one, we were taken to one end of a valley in the Sonora desert of Arizona, broken down into teams of two, and released. With no food and only three canteens of water each, we had three days and two nights to make our way to the other end of the valley. We also had to avoid paramilitary instructors who were on patrol in front of us twenty four hours a day.

When we were released, my partner, Ches J., and I decided to sleep for the rest of the day and begin our E&E at night. We sweltered during the day. That night, when we started our trek across the valley floor, we ran into snakes. Every ten steps, it seemed—rattlesnakes.

"Worse than a Vietnam mine field," I told Ches.

We were undetected that night, and we endured the next day in the holes of a dry river gulch. The midday sun was absolute torture. Our eyes hurt, our skin burned, and we were thirsty.

Moving again the second night, we had to go far out of the way at one juncture to avoid an instructor. Once, we were resting by a road that ran through the valley when three Mexicans stopped nearby to pee. At first light the next morning, we arrived at the rally point, the second team to come in.

Ice-cold orange juice, milk, coffee, eggs, and bacon were served by instructors turned cooks. Our hollow-eyed compatriots dragged in throughout the morning.

We slept like babies that night in a Holiday Inn. The following day, we boarded four-wheel-drive vehicles for a ride up into the mountains for the second phase of E&E: mountain survival, rappeling, and land navigation. Escape and evasion in the mountains caused different pain from that experienced in the desert, but pain was pain. E&E training was never comfortable. One evening at dusk, a trainee came in to a group campfire after a long day of mountain climbing in severe weather. He fell to his knees and leaned over the fire to warm his face. The other tired trainees watched quietly as he bowed, with his face in the smoke; he seemed to be genuflecting to the fire gods. He was tall and lanky—a former basketball player for a large western university. Finally, he leaned back on his haunches and looked around. Everywhere he looked, people laughed. His face was black from the smoke.

He kept repeating, "What're you laughing at? What's so funny?"

Sitting around that fire was one of the most intense SOGers in the program. Cuban-born Amado G., who had emigrated to the United States after Castro came to power, had been a soldier in the Bay of Pigs invasion force. He was captured by Castro forces and spent a year in a Cuban prison before being released in exchange for tractors. Once back in the United States, he joined the U.S. Army, served with distinction in Vietnam, and was subsequently hired as an SOGer. He was the intellectual of the group. Even during the mountain phase of the training, he pulled out a dog-eared book on Plato and read it during rest breaks. He was reading his book that night after the black-faced trainee wandered off to find shelter. My good friend, Jerry F., was sitting nearby and said, "Amado, you know you reading that book all the time has come to the attention of the instructors and Joe, the chief instructor, doesn't like it. He doesn't like you.''

Amado looked up into the fire and then slowly around at Jerry. His smirk clearly said that he wasn't going to be fooled into getting angry at the instructors. He knew a setup when he heard one, and he went back to his book. For ten minutes he stared down at the book but didn't turn a page. Finally, looking back at Jerry, he said in his heavy Cuban accent, ''So he doesn't like me to read Plato? I try to improve my mind, to make me a better person and a better Agency officer and he doesn't like this. On my free time, I do what I like.''

At a training session the next day, Amado sat near the front and stared up at Joe, the chief instructor. Then he got up and started walking off into the woods.

''Hey, mac,'' Joe said, ''where do you think you're going in the middle of my class?''

''You have been talking for three hours, three hours and I have to take a piss,'' Amado said. ''I have to take a piss.''

Joe was not intimidated. He said, ''Sit down. Shut up. I'll tell you when to piss and when not to piss.''

Amado glared at him and finally sat down beside Jerry. ''You know,'' he said to Jerry, ''you were right, he really doesn't like me.''

Jerry F. had a talent for identifying and exposing the vulnerabilities of his friends. He was naturally cunning, a lawyer by education. He grew up in a Catholic section of Philadelphia. When he was about seven, he had to take a class on confession. Afterward, the class members lined up in a side aisle of the church to go into one of several booths for their first confessions. Jerry, well back in the line, was waiting for others to find the pitfalls in this exercise. As each boy went into one of the booths, a faint, high-pitched whisper could be heard from the boy's side: ''Forgive me, mumble, mumble, mumble.'' From the priest's side of the booth, there came a lower-pitched, inaudible response, except in the booth of Father O'Riley, who was hard of hearing. After a boy's whispered opening, Father O'Riley said in a loud voice, "You did what? To your mother, you said what? What?" Everybody could hear him.

Jerry prayed that, when he came to the head of the line, he would not have to go into that booth because the good father was responding loudly to every boy who went in: "You did what? You said what?!"

When Jerry's turn came, he was sent to Father O'Riley's booth. It was warm from the last youngster who had been there, and it was dark. He could hear Father O'Riley breathing through the opening of the partition that separated them. He began, "Forgive me, Father, for I have sinned," and paused.

In an even tone, the priest said, "Yes. And?"

Jerry was quiet for a moment. "Actually I haven't sinned," he said.

Father O'Riley yelled, "You what? What?" Everyone in the church must have heard. "You what? Don't lie to me!"

This made such an impression on Jerry F. that he spent most of his life since then trying to embarrass others.

With my group, the four-day mountain survival training was noteworthy because of the beating our hands took. The rocks and ropes, fires and briars laid them open. "Do these look like the hands of government employees?" someone asked.

We eventually came down from the mountains and boarded a commercial flight for Miami, where we were to do the third phase of the training. The jungle phase—in the Everglades.

Ches and I were partners again. This phase had two parts. The first was a two-day simulated "exfiltration" (exfil) through the swamps. Once we reached our objective near the Tamiami Trail, we were to board canoes for the second part, a waterborne exfil down everglade rivers into the Gulf of Mexico and out to an offshore island.

For two days, Ches and I were up to our chests in the

swamp. Holding our handguns and packs over our heads, we trudged along, trying to be quiet as we searched for instructors-aggressors. Late the second day, I was wading along in the lead, the water up to my waist, when I noticed some high ground off to the right.

The bullets issued for our handguns had the projectiles extracted, leaving only the cardboard to hold in the powder. This cardboard, our instructors had promised us, was more than enough to kill a small dog and would certainly kill any animals we might happen upon in the Everglades—except alligators. They didn't tell us what to do if we ran into alligators. Ches suggested that finding the answer was part of the training.

The guns were primarily for signaling. If we came upon something and absolutely had to shoot, we had been told to aim carefully and use only one shot. In a real escape and evasion situation when being hunted, one shot would not give away the location. Without any other warning, the hunter would have no reference point on which to fix the location of a single shot and wouldn't know if it came from the front or rear. It wouldn't help if there were two hunters. But if we were being chased and fired two shots, we would give away our position. The first shot alerts the hunter; on the second shot, he can fix the direction.

So we knew one shot was all we had. With two shots, the instructors would be on our necks. Three shots meant that someone was hurt and the training was suspended until the instructors or other students could get to the area.

One shot—I thought about this as I waded along waist high in the swamp and turned toward that high ground to the right. We were coming out of the water, and it was down to our thighs, when I saw a giant snake coiled on a rock outcropping. He had a pointed head—poisonous. Making eye contact with his dark little eyes, he seemed to be saying, "You don't belong here. This is my place in the swamp. Get out of here."

Lifting my .45, I aimed it at the snake's head. It was disconcerting to discover that, when I extended the gun with my two hands, I covered half the distance to the snake. He could probably strike and get me before I could get my hands away.

But I aimed carefully right between his eyes. I knew that I had only one shot. I squeezed the trigger slowly until the gun fired.

The snake did not move, no flipping and flopping around like I expected from a mortally wounded snake. He laid back a little more in his coil and hissed. That was about it. I looked into his eyes again. He was not happy.

I couldn't fire anymore. The snake seemed to know this, and he started to arch his back, slightly. Time was of the essence.

So I fired again—and again, and again and again and again. That monster snake never flinched.

"O.K., you win. We're gone."

We started running in the water as fast as we could, which was pretty fast. The instructors never did find us. Oh, they fixed the location of the shots, and they were there in a matter of minutes. But we were in the next county. Snakes can do that to people.

Later that day, after we had stopped running, we came to a railroad spur built through the swamp around the turn of the last century. The workers hired to harvest cypress for shipping had been given oranges to eat, and some of the seeds they spit out had taken root and were now orange trees. After getting all the oranges we could carry, Ches and I hid in the swamp and ate every one. We talked about the training, which seemed to be going on without end, and what lay ahead in Indochina. It was a common topic, our anticipated field work, and we tried to imagine what we would be doing, where we would be sent. Ches, looking like a renegade sitting up out of the swamp on a cypress limb, said it didn't matter as long as we had some oranges every once in awhile. They did have oranges in Indochina, didn't they?

We eventually arrived at the rally point near the Tamiami Trail, where the instructors had positioned airboats, and we began classes on survival. Speedy, a part-Seminole Indian instructor, said if we were striking out into the wilderness and had to carry only one item, we should carry a knife. If we could take two items, take matches with the knife. If we could take three items, take a fishing line and hooks. Even in the woods, a fishing line and hooks can be used to snare small game. Around water, of course, they can be used to fish—and to catch ducks.

"Catch ducks?" someone asked.

"Yeap," Speedy said, "You get your pond where you got your ducks and you get a log and you tie one end of your line to your log and you get a rock and you run your line from the log to the rock, leaving a little line free on the other side of the rock to tie your hook. Then you get corn from a field and you put it on your hook. You put the rock on the log, the hook with the corn on the rock, and you push this balanced trap out into your pond where your ducks feed. And some duck will come along and swallow the corn with the hook. When he pulls away, he'll pull the rock off the log, it'll sink, pulling the duck under and he'll drown, quietly. Later, you pull your log in and you've gotten yourself a duck."

I told Ches it wouldn't work. I didn't know why it wouldn't work, but it wouldn't work. It was too clever—sounded like something someone from Newark, New Jersey, would dream up.

"Well," Ches said, "I don't know about them Indochinese oranges, but I know they got ducks over there, so I'm paying attention."

We left later that day on the last phase, the canoe exfiltration down Everglades rivers. And we met the mighty sand fly—the God Almighty, Florida Everglades sand fly.

We had beaten the rattlesnakes and the heat of the Arizona desert, rappeled off the tops of high mountains, walked waist deep through snake-infested swamps, small training challenges that we beat handily—but not the sand flies.

The Everglades sand flies are as small as a grain of dirt and crazy with lust to get up a human nose and into ears. In their own element, they are impossible to get away from with mosquito netting or anything this side of submersion in water and breathing through a straw. That afternoon, unknown to us when we slipped our canoes into the water, there were eight hundred zillion billion sand flies waiting.

We couldn't see them when we were moving. They weren't there. But if we stopped for a second, we were suddenly breathing in sand flies. They were down our shirts, in our eyes, up the cracks of our butts, in our ears, in our food.

In the desert and in the mountains and during the first part of the jungle phase when we had moved overland through the swamps, Ches and I had rarely bumped into the other teams, rarely heard them. But the sand flies changed that.

The second day in the canoes, after thirty or thirty-five hours of total emergence in sand-fly hell, we occasionally heard someone yell, off in the mangroves: "Auggggggggggggg!"

Then, it got quiet as we drifted along, moving slightly above sand fly speed, looking for instructors around a bend, when over some saw grass to one side we heard, "These goddamned, worthless, filthy, insects are driving me crazy. Crazy! I can't breathe!" Then, more quiet and suddenly, off in another direction, "Oh, God, take me now, give me some peace, get me out of here. These flies, these insidious insects are—killing me. They are—everywhere!"

We finally reached the island, and the ocean breeze kept the sand flies away. Oh, it was a wonderful day.

*   *   *

For reasons never clear to me, I had to take three months of French language next. I knew of only one other SOGer who had ever been scheduled for French, and I told the training officer I did not want French. I thought if I spoke English loud enough in foreign countries, everyone could understand me. The instructors were lovable little old French ladies who smothered me in their language. There were so many of them that they reminded me of the sand flies.

Next came a report writing course, and then I rejoined other SOGers at another downstate facility for one of my last courses, special training in interrogation, sabotage, and explosives. I elected myself the bus driver, the de facto leader of the group. I told them, for lack of any other reason, that I drove the bus because I spoke French and they didn't. It was spring and we were in the woods most of the time, so I drove with the doors open, which gave us a nice breeze. I drove too close to some trees once and banged up the doors. Then, I couldn't get them shut. This was all right because, as I said, we liked the breeze and I always left the doors open when the bus was parked.

One Friday morning, we went for training at a site some distance from the main facility. A few of the SOGers drove their cars so that they could leave directly for Washington after the class. We had time to kill because the class was postponed until early afternoon. While driving the bus back to the cafeteria for lunch, I saw a beach along a wide river and asked if anyone wanted to go skinny-dipping. Jerry F. and another man said they'd go. I stopped the bus along the riverbank, and everybody got off. Some grumbled because they wanted to go on to the cafeteria, but I was driving and I didn't care what they wanted—they couldn't speak French. Jerry and I and another guy took off our clothes and waded into the river. And we waded and kept wading. We had gone about the length of two football fields out into that wide river, and the water was still only at mid-calf. Believe me, one can never feel more naked—way out in a river with the water sloshing a bit above the ankles.

We had just turned to look back at the beach as an evil SOGer drove up, jumped out of his Corvette, ran out on the beach, picked up our clothes, ran back to his car, and sped off.

Hot-stepping to shore, the three of us were yelling, "Hey, hey, hey, don't take our clothes. Please, please, don't take our clothes!"

Fortunately, I had the keys to the bus with me so it was still there. I jumped behind the wheel, naked, and started chasing the guy with our clothes. One SOGer on board the bus kept saying, "Oh shit, oh shit." The door to the bus wouldn't close, of course, and we sped through the facility, occasionally having to stop at intersections to let cars pass. When I stopped for traffic at one intersection, a woman in a station wagon stopped beside me on the open-door side. I didn't dare to look in her direction, so I don't know whether or not she noticed that the bus driver was naked.

Catching up with the clothes snatcher as he pulled into the parking lot of our residence hall, I tackled him before he got inside. He was laughing so hard he didn't put up much of a fight. I put on my fatigue pants and drove back to the beach. Jerry F. and the other guy had dug out little holes in the river bottom and were sitting in them, submerged just to the top of their butt cracks.

A gale wind blew through the training facility the next week and forced suspension of training. We battened down the hatches at the residence hall and prepared to weather the storm there. When it hit, however, we decided to go outside and play "hurricane football." Rain came down in sheets, and the wind blew so hard at times that we had to lean into it to stand up, which often made a forward pass difficult. The field was muddy. Deep into the game, the score was something like 6,000 to 4,500—

we had our own scoring rules tied loosely to the force of the hurricane. I went out for a pass to the side of the playing area, got lost in the storm, slipped, fell on a rock, and cut my right knee to the bone. Play did not stop, however. It was only after I began yelling over the noise of the storm that some of the players found me and helped me to a medic inside the hall. I was stitched up and waiting at the "Hurricane Central" bar when the game ended.

"Man has no hang," some of my compatriots said to me, as they walked in from the gale force outside and bellied up to the bar. Covered with mud, they all looked like creatures from the dark lagoon

"How's this individual going to work out in the field if he can't operate in a little bit of rain?" someone asked.

"Think he's heading for indoor work," someone else suggested.

Brenda also had a job with the CIA. Because most of my training took place away from Washington, I was generally home only on weekends. She became friendly with a neighbor whose husband worked in New York City. The neighbor—I called her Silly Susan because she didn't have an ounce of common sense—eventually moved in with Brenda during the week while I was away. I left for training on Sunday afternoon or early Monday morning, and Silly Susan came in from New York on the shuttle early Monday morning and went directly to work. She came to our place each night during the week and, on Fridays, left work and went directly to the airport for her flight to New York. I came in on Friday nights.

This went on for months. I saw Silly Susan no more than a half dozen times.

We bought our furniture at garage sales. We quickly developed a routine and came to know the higher-class neighborhoods where senators and diplomats lived and where we were more likely to find better stuff. We went through the ads on Friday night and were out on the road by 0700 on Saturday morning. We found couches and a breakfast table and end lamps and books and knick-knacks. At one swanky house, I bought a chair for twenty-five cents. A quarter. It was the most comfortable chair in the world. When I sat in that chair, all the troubles of the world went away. Only, it didn't look like much and Brenda made me put it in the basement. Sometimes, I sat in it next to the furnace with Harry, the dog, and read the paper.

One weekend, Brenda and I went to a Washington Senators baseball game at Kennedy Stadium. The game was decided in the last inning, and we left with everyone else. The parking lot exits were clogged. We waited patiently for our turn to move out. As we inched forward, a car on our right was trying to cut us off. Slowly, one turn of the tires at a time, our front bumpers moved toward each other. I tried to intimidate the driver of the other car with a fierce look. He was talking with a man in the passenger seat, looking back at me, and pointing. When our bumpers finally bumped, the other driver gave me the finger.

That was it. This was the time to take a stand. So I got out of the car, walked in front, hiked up my pants, and yelled at the other driver. He got out of his car, so did his passenger, so did his buddies in the car behind him. Six drunk men stumbled in front of my car to challenge me.

Jesus. This was not exactly what I had in mind.

Out of the corner of my eye, I saw our car back up slightly to get around the bumper of the other car. Brenda had gotten behind the wheel. Traffic in front had cleared out. Brenda gunned the car, and the men cleared out of the way. I jumped on the hood and rode along for about a city block before we were stopped in traffic again.

I climbed off the hood and got behind the wheel. "Not bad, hon," I said. "But don't tell the guys, OK?"

*   *   *

In August 1971, a year after I had joined the Agency, I received my overseas orders.

The war in Vietnam continued, but it had exhausted the patience of the American people. We appeared to be losing on every front. Even when we won, such as the Tet offensive, the press put a negative spin on it and we appeared to lose. There were individual, unpublicized CIA victories, however, and the SOGers assigned to Vietnam looked forward to being in contact with the South Vietnamese police forces or working in isolated provinces where they would have opportunities to develop sources that could provide significant information on Vietcong and North Vietnamese plans and intentions. If American forces were withdrawn and the fight was left completely to the South Vietnamese, which looked more and more possible, the Agency would stay and its role increase. There were uncertainties and challenges for the men headed to Saigon station, the destination of the majority of the SOGers with whom I had trained.

On the other hand, Laos was the promised land for SOGers: the best assignment. A country in the shape of a water ladle standing on its end and slightly larger than Utah, Laos had a 1,322-mile border with Vietnam to the north and east. The CIA ran the war there. It had its own Air America fleet of helicopters and fixed-wing planes, got good support from the U.S. Air Force, and employed a variety of indigenous forces. And though there was almost no media coverage, we heard throughout training that we were getting the most out of our resources and were accomplishing our mission there. The CIA's rear base for the Lao program was at the Royal Thai Air Force Base in Udorn (Udon Thani), Thailand, where some contingents of the U.S. Air Force were also located.

My orders were to Udorn.

I took other specialized training and out-processed during the month of September. Brenda took a leave without pay from the Agency, we packed, loaded our dog and some of our favorite plants, and went to North Carolina for home leave during October.

Mom and Dad took us to the airport on a crisp November morning. En route to Thailand, we spent four days in Hawaii at Waikiki Beach. It was Brenda's first trip outside the continental United States, and she was enthralled with the Pacific paradise. Although we had a wonderful time, I was anxious to get it behind us so that I could begin my work as a CIA paramilitary officer.

4

LAOS ASSIGNMENT: INDOOR WORK

We arrived in Bangkok, Thailand, in early evening and took a taxi from the airport to a downtown hotel. Brenda was enthusiastic about the trip and what lay ahead, but she was startled by the chaotic traffic on the ride into town and the earthy evening scent coming in through the open windows of the old taxi. She suddenly realized that this country was not as orderly or as sanitary as the one where she had grown up, and her excitement began to wane.

While walking outside the hotel the next morning, Brenda came across Thai women squatting by their charcoal grills in the shade of alleyways as they cooked meat on wooden skewers. She was further taken aback.

"These people are not clean," she explained to me with her eyes wide. "Their food is out in the open, just a few steps from where people walk, near open car exhausts." Also, the bustling street people in Bangkok tended to have different attitudes about personal space, and Brenda felt crowded. It was very strange, very foreign—much more of a culture shock than she imagined it would be. She was tired and later said that she wanted to go home. After twenty-four hours in Thailand, she was ready to go home.

I asked her to give the country time, to understand that this was Bangkok, as far from the States as you could get without starting to come back. People just did things differently on this side of the world. I asked her for a little bit of "hang," as they said in the Agency. She agreed but continued to be very tentative in her dealings with the Thai people and their food.

Following instructions we received at a small commercial office building in the downtown area, we went back to the airport after two days in Bangkok and made our way to a private terminal used exclusively by Continental Airlines Service (CASI) and Air America. After a short wait, we were called to the ramp and boarded "50-Kip," a regular CIA-chartered CASI flight north to Udorn. The plane, an old C-47 aircraft, would go on to Vientiane, Laos, from Udorn and then down to the two southern cities in Laos—Savannakhet and Pakxe—before returning to Bangkok. The two pilots knew many of the passengers, and the chatter from the cockpit was neighborly as we boarded.

The copilot looked around the cabin after the plane was in the air, and we made eye contact. "Hey," he yelled out, "we've got some folks making their maiden 50-Kip. Welcome aboard."

Although the old plane was noisy, people talked and moved around as if it were a community outing. The plane banked slowly as we approached Udorn, and we could see the air force base south of town. The small commercial downtown district and the airfield—a small urban oasis—stood out in the middle of a vast expanse of sectioned rice fields. Brenda said, "Now, we are as far from North Carolina as we can get."

After landing, the C-47 taxied up to a repair hangar where planes and helicopters with the distinctive Air America logo were in varying stages of disassembly for overhaul and inspection. We walked to a two-story block building off the tarmac and announced ourselves to the Thai receptionist. Jim G., deputy chief of the CIA base, came out of an inner office. A tall, neatly dressed, well-mannered man, he greeted us in a rather formal manner and escorted us inside. We went into the first office off the reception area and were introduced to the Stick, the CIA base chief. A squat, hard, square-jawed ex-GI, the Stick had been in Indochina most of his adult life. He was well liked by the Thais, the Hmong, and the men who worked for him. He lived by himself in the upstairs area, had no known interests outside of work, and was not particularly comfortable in small talk with people he didn't know. As a boss, he had a reputation of being blunt and having the capability to make hard decisions and stick to them. He carried a variety of sticks around with him, thus his monicker. One stick lay on his desk. He welcomed me to the program, said there was a lot of work to be done, and deferred to his deputy to get me settled.

Outside the Stick's office, there was constant movement of people from room to room in the almost windowless building. Radios scratched and chattered in the background. In the center room, maps, hinged on boards, were moved back and forth by a variety of men and women as they plotted positions, posted overhead photography, and added to lists of call signs and other number/name combinations along the sides. No one was idle. Occasionally, someone shouted out to a person in another room or yelled a profanity. Except for Jim G., dress was casual, what one would expect clerks in an army/navy store to wear. The women I noticed were as loud and profane as the men. People looked us in the eye as they passed. Though they seemed friendly, no one stopped to talk.

The general atmosphere inside the base building was that things were happening, and they were being dealt with straight on. It was a lean, no-nonsense workplace, a reflection of both Jim G. and the Stick.

We calmly moved through the flurry of activity. Brenda was introduced to a clerk who answered her questions about housing as they moved off to a side room. George M., chief of operations, was standing in front of the main map board in the center room. I was introduced to him as a new paramilitary case officer. His manner was cordial. He was a retired Special Forces colonel, one of the first U.S. Army officers sent to Vietnam.

His welcoming briefing went something like this: "Our two main jobs here are to engage as many of the 70,000 North Vietnamese soldiers in Laos as we can— to keep them from South Vietnam—and to protect the sovereignty of the country. We divide the country into four military regions, or MRs. MR I is here to the west." He pointed to the map. "There are several Groupe Mobiles—that's French. We call them GMs. They are battalion-size units of guerrilla soldiers, committed to fighting the local Pathet Lao and monitoring the construction of the road the Chinese are building south through Laos. Our officers in this MR just lost their base camp and have pulled back close to Louangphrabang, the ceremonial capital of the country. In the south are MR III and MR IV. They also fight the local Pathet Lao there, plus the North Vietnamese who defend the Ho Chi Minh Trail. They also do road watch work, surveilling the traffic on the trail. There's a lot of seasonal shifts in control. In the dry season, we'll have people in the forward areas, near the border of Vietnam, but when the rains come, and we can't provide resupply or fire support, the irregulars pull back. Those southern MR areas you'll find are quiet most of the time, but during the changing of the seasons when we don't know who is exactly where, there are violent clashes, sometimes hand-to-hand. Often, whole units are wiped out.

"MR II," George M. continued, "is the big show. We have six GMs of Hmong plus Thai mercenaries there. The Hmong are commanded by General Vang Pao, or V. P., as he's called. His Hmong guerrillas work on the ground—patrolling, maneuvering. The Thais sit on mountains and hold ground. Right now, they are defending positions on the PDJ, right here," he said, pointing to a distinctive, well-marked part of the map.

"This is Route 6," he said, pointing to another map, "which runs from North Vietnam down to the PDJ. As we speak, elements of the North Vietnamese 312th and 316th divisions are bringing troops and supplies down this road for what looks like a major push against our Thai positions on the plateau, probably in early December. We know the North Vietnamese are serious about the campaign this year because they have assigned one of their most senior officers to launch the attacks. The PDJ has always been pivotal, strategic terrain, and it will be another battlefield soon.

"We have fought on both sides of the Plaine for several years now, and there are still several friendly Hmong villages there. However, because of this imminent threat of the North Vietnamese attack, most of the Hmong hill tribe people have pulled out and most of the villages are deserted. Only a few elements of the Hmong GMs are in place. The Thais are busy hardening their positions. The job of 'Sky'—the name for the Agency in up-country Laos—is to work these Thai and Hmong and the U.S. Air Force and Air America and CASI to defend the PDJ."

That was where I wanted to go. The big show—the PDJ—with the mountain guerrillas and the Thai mercenaries.

Jim G., standing beside George, told me that I would be working MR II. I smiled and said, "Thank you."

He continued, "You will be working MR II as a desk officer in Udorn."

"What?" I said, "I came out to do paramilitary work. I don't want to be a friggin desk officer."

Jim smiled. "Your duties in Udorn will be to collect the information on the hour-to-hour situation in MR II and collate it for dissemination to our stations in Vientiane and Bangkok and to Headquarters in Washington, D.C. You will make sure the maps and boards are current and you will be prepared to brief. There is a lot of responsibility in this job," he emphasized, "especially with the North Vietnamese offensive about to begin. There are enough Sky officers in MR II at the moment. If you want an assignment up-country after you have done your duty here, then I will try to arrange it. You should know, however, that we rarely send married case officers to MR II. It's very dangerous, and the separation is hard on the wives."

He told me to draw a car from the support officer, check into the hotel on the edge of town, help my wife get settled, and report to work in the morning at 0600.

Brenda took my assignment to Udorn base as good news. I would be around most of the time, and it was safe. She missed the point, I told her. I had come so far, and I wasn't on the playing field. I had to sit on the sidelines, at a typewriter all day. And give briefings. That is no fun. I want to be out there, where the North Vietnamese are massing and our men are digging in—where there is action and adventure.

"In due time, my dear," my wife said in a motherly fashion.

The Charoen Hotel, the best in northeast Thailand, was not luxurious by American standards. Our room was a sparsely furnished twelve-by-twelve cubicle with a bed and dresser, and the bathroom was heavy on white industrial tile and exposed plumbing. The room was oppressive, and we spent the first evening sitting in the lobby. Brenda was feeling unsure of what we were actually getting into, and I was feeling great disappointment over my desk assignment.

I read reports, studied map boards, memorized unit designations and call signs, and acquainted myself with MR II during my first few days on the desk. I sat in on scheduled and impromptu briefings about the developing situation on the PDJ, some delivered by Buck, the officer I was replacing, and others by Jim G. Both had extensive knowledge of the area. Jim was especially gifted as a briefer. He spoke in a low monotone but with authority. A Princeton graduate and former intelligence officer in the U.S. Navy, his reasonable, cultured nature left visitors assured that the prosecution of the war here was in good hands. His briefings were comprehensive, erudite, and well received by Stateside visitors who had spent many hours in U.S. military briefings—probably the types that I remembered sounding like half time speeches by high school coaches.

On 10 December, Buck took me on a familiarization tour of MR II. We left Udorn on an Air America cargo plane while it was still dark, crossed the Mekong River into Laos as the sun was coming up, flew high above the rugged mountains of the northeast, and landed early in the morning on the airstrip in the Long Tieng valley. The airstrip was designated Lima Site (LS) 20A in aviation handbooks, but was known by many names: "The Alternate" in Air America pilot parlance; "Sky headquarters in MR II" by U.S. Embassy staff; "CIA secret base, Spook Haven," by the newspapers; and "Shangri-La" by the Ravens, U.S. Air Force pilots assigned to Laos, who flew small spotter aircraft.

The runway ran with the east-west valley. Tall rock formations, or "karsts" as they were called up-country, dotted either end and were cause for abrupt takeoffs and landings. There was no road south. The only way in was by air or down small foot trails. Its isolation helped to provide the anonymity of the program. Visitors were flown in by invitation only.

To the north, a switchback mountain road led from the valley floor up the side of the towering Skyline ridge. The road was the main artery to Sam Thong, a previously thriving mountain village two ridgelines to the north. The abandoned village overlooked a river valley that snaked its way almost the entire 20 miles from Skyline north-northeast to the PDJ.

Vang Pao's stone house, surrounded by a barbed-wire fence, was on the south side of the runway in the valley, amid the thatched shacks of perhaps twenty thousand Hmongs. The headquarters for the Thai mercenaries was at the east end, along with several batteries of 105-mm and 155-mm artillery. The Sky compound, on the west end, was situated hard against protecting karsts.

Buck said that LS 20A was one of the busiest airports in the world, with more than five hundred takeoffs and landings a day—more than Chicago's O'Hare International. The loading ramp where the planes parked was about the size of a city block, and it was teeming with activity. Supplies were being off-loaded from some planes, riggers were loading other aircraft with bundles to be air-dropped, helicopters were coming from the ammo dump with pallets of ammunition slung below them, hill tribe villagers with animals in bags and baskets were sitting among wounded soldiers and waiting for rides to outlying regions. There were dozens of Hmong and Thai soldiers standing around. Jeeps and trucks moved among the planes, supplies, and people. A few Americans, mostly pilots, sauntered to and from the Air Ops building and to the rigging shed off the ramp in the shadow of Skyline.

Two Sky case officers, whom I had met in Udorn earlier, came out of the Air Ops building and walked across the ramp with a pair of Air America helicopter pilots. They were discussing locations on a mangled map that one of the case officers had extracted from his back pocket. We passed close by, but it was hard to hear what they were saying because of the roar of cargo planes and helicopters taxiing in the area.

A smiling middle-aged man emerged from Air Ops. Buck introduced him as Sky's chief air controller, jokester, and king of the skies in MR II. A Hmong came out of the building and joined us. Throwing his arm around the short Oriental, the large American air controller introduced the Hmong as the chief laugher at jokes in MR II and his able assistant. We joined them in a short Jeep ride around the karst behind Air Ops to Sky headquarters.

The gates, made of cast-iron fencing and barbed wire, were open, and Hmong walked up and down the compound street. It was not necessarily like the guarded field compounds I remembered as a GI in Vietnam.

Past the gate was a two-story block building on the right, the sleeping quarters. To the left was the mess hall and beyond that the bombproof concrete headquarters building. The front and side entrances to headquarters had large bank-vault doors. The Hmong Air Ops officer jumped off the Jeep when we pulled in and walked across the road, past the sleeping quarters, to the Hmong ops assistants building in the rear. As Buck and I went into the headquarters bunker, a 260-pound-plus muscle man introduced himself as Tiny. Buck said that almost everyone who worked up-country had a radio call sign; whether it was for security or just the ways things were done, everyone was addressed by his call sign.

Inside we met Bamboo, Digger, and Ringo, who were finishing a conversation with Dick J., the CIA base chief. With the exceptions of Dick J. and the chief Air Ops officer, all the Sky people were my age. They wore mismatched civilian/military clothing and jungle boots and carried 9-mm pistols, with E&E bags and canteens on their pistol belts. They all had white string tied loosely around their wrists—placed there by the Hmong for luck—and used the palms of their hands for writing down notes. Their faces were weathered, and they had crow's-feet at the corners of their eyes. They greeted me cordially and were surprisingly well-spoken for looking so rough. Like the people at the base office in Udorn, they appeared seriously intent on what they were doing and no one made small talk. Digger and Ringo walked out, Bamboo began to rummage around boxes of supplies, and Dick J. crouched over a typewriter and started pounding on the keyboard. He looked up and, saying he had an immediate precedent cable to respond to, shook hands without getting up. He welcomed me to Long Tieng and suggested that we go out to the PDJ as soon as possible. Turning to the Air Ops officer, he told him to make sure we got a pickup late in the day. I told him thanks, and he said, with a slight smile, that wasn't necessary, he just didn't want to keep up with some "FNG."

Dick J. had had a variety of intelligence postings around the world, including a paramilitary assignment in the Korean conflict, and understood regulations and the moral responsibilities of CIA field work. He was trusted by Headquarters to make sure that the Long Tieng operation did not turn into a rogue elephant, that it maintained Agency standards of propriety.

As Dick was talking, a man had walked into the small office. He was standing silently by the door. Nodding to me, Buck said, "FNG, meet Hog."

Hog looked at me without offering his hand. He had the dark handsome looks of a Valentino, although like the others, he was weathered. With his dusty, dark clothing and his dour expression, he reminded me of cowboys I had seen in black-and-white photographs taken out west a hundred years ago.

All SOGers heard about Hog their first day in the Agency. He was from western Montana and, as a teenager, was recruited by Air America to work as a kicker/flight mechanic on its planes in Laos. He eventually moved into the Sky ranks as a contract employee, like myself. His first Sky job was to monitor an isolated region of MR II and he spent weeks away from other Westerners as he worked with the Hmong. He learned their language and developed special rapport with the tenacious mountain fighters. Because he was a new hire and didn't have an Agency track record, his assimilation into the Hmong culture was looked on with suspicion by his Agency supervisors.

When Hog was reassigned to Long Tieng and stayed in daily contact with other Sky officers, however, his unassuming nature, clear thinking, and devotion to the Sky mission became obvious. He had no pretensions, no rancor. Standing by his word, he expected others—Hmong,

Thai, Sky, Air America—to stand by theirs. He took minimum risks in doing his job, but he ventured daily into the fighting and was often shot at. His manner never changed, and he never became excited. He knew every mile of the area, every commander, and he was eventually appointed chief of operations. Hog seldom left MR II. Every two or three months, he went to Vientiane or Bangkok and stayed drunk for several days. Before returning to the valley, he always pulled back to the Stick's quarters above the office in Udorn to dry out. He had been doing this for ten years.

The Lao word for a resolute spirit or a strong heart was "hang." Hog put the concept of hang into the work of MR II and into the jargon of the Agency. He was the definitive SOGer.

Hog didn't talk to strangers, and, when we met, he didn't talk to me. He just nodded, turned to Dick J. with a comment, and left.

As we drove back to the ramp later, the Air Ops officer radioed a helicopter that was preparing to lift off and asked the pilot to return to Air Ops to take a couple of passengers ("paxs") out to the PDJ.

I asked Buck what an FNG was. He said, "Fucking new guy."

Nice touch, I thought.

The helicopter, configured with twin turbo engines, was colloquially referred to as a Twin Pack. It had more lift than most of the other choppers and was used almost exclusively for heavy resupply. Although it usually lifted its cargo on slings below, this time it was filled with rations inside and Buck and I had difficulty finding a place to sit. The Filipino kicker/mechanic handed Buck a radio headset, the "customer set." As we taxied back out onto the airstrip for takeoff, Buck began what was obviously a friendly conversation with the pilot who sat in front, slightly above us.

We gained altitude as we left the valley to the east and swung back over Skyline for the 20-mile ride to the PDJ.

As we flew north, we passed rows and rows of east-west ridge lines. Sticking my head out the open door, I could see the PDJ in the distance. It looked absolutely level, an incredible sight among the mountains. It was a freak of geography or, as someone suggested, a monument to what ancient slave labor could do, such as building the Great Wall of China.

During our approach to the PDJ, we could see dozens of aircraft—fixed-wing and helicopters buzzing around like bees during pollination season—servicing different sites. At the south side of the plateau were 105-mm and 155-mm artillery gun emplacements. Stretching out in front were a number of defensive positions. As we neared, we could make out the networks of trenches and bunkers and outlying skirts of barbed wire at each site. Each was situated so that it could be protected by two or three neighboring positions.

The supplies on board were destined for the northernmost site. The helicopter descended toward the LZ, marked by white cloth pegged to the ground, for that position. Standing near the open door, we could see the faces of the men on the ground.

The helicopter suddenly dipped to the left, and we were slung up against the far bulkhead. Buck took off his headset and pointed out the open door to one of the artillery batteries behind us. He yelled over the noise of the helicopter that the battery had suddenly started firing, had gone "hot," through our approach pattern.

The helicopter righted itself and came into the LZ low from the west. We jumped off when the wheels hit the ground to get out of the way of the Thais who had run up to unload the supplies.

Greek, a former Marine helicopter pilot who worked Sky air operations in the field, was off in the grass beside the LZ. Yelling into a radio, he told a Thai artillery officer that someone was going to get killed if they continued to fire when aircraft were landing. Greek said he had to know when the guns went hot again. The Thai said quickly, "OK, OK."

As we stood beside Greek, an Air America helicopter pilot came up on another radio and said he was returning to LS 20A until the guns stopped firing. Greek and the pilot argued for several minutes. The pilot said he was dropping off the 105-mm shells he had at a 155-mm position and leaving. Greek said, "If you do that you low life, scum-sucking, asshole son-of-a-bitch, I'll rip your ears off the next time I see you."

As Greek was yelling in the radio, he was looking south in the direction of a helicopter, with ammo crates suspended below, that was hovering near an artillery position. It finally moved some distance to one side and came down gently, released its ammo, put its nose down, and gained altitude off to the west.

The artillery starting firing again. Greek threw down the handset and said everyone tried to make his life difficult. He reached in his pocket for an antacid pill.

Walking up a dirt trail to the position, we were met by the Thai commander. Speaking colloquial American English in welcoming us to his "campus," he said he was the dean of students and led us to the center of the position. Standing on top of his command bunker, we looked out over the defenses. The perimeter had three interconnected rings with firing ports. Well-fortified mortar pits were behind the command bunker. In front for a hundred meters, the saw grass had been burnt to the ground and strands of barbed wire overlapped circling rows of concertina wire. The commander said the whole area to the front was laced with mines; in some sections, mines were two deep.

"Impregnable," the commander said, and I agreed. I had seen nothing like it in Vietnam. He said he slept soundly at night and, although his was the northernmost position on the PDJ and he was probed often, he had not lost a man since the North Vietnamese began their buildup. He considered the probes a welcome diversion, in fact, and did not doubt the ability of his men to hold off any type of full-scale attack. In addition to his own interlocking fire, local artillery could be brought in within seconds, plus flare and gun ships—"Spookies" and "Spectors"—were usually on station. "I can turn the whole area in front into a killing zone. A Coney Island shooting gallery," he said.

Standing on the bunker, I could hear helicopters behind me to the south. In front, there was complete quiet—no bird sounds, no insects humming, nothing. As a youngster hunting with Cottonpicker, I knew, if you listened, that the woods and forest were noisy with the sounds of living things growing and breathing, their sounds carried by the wind blowing in the trees.

But there was no sound in front of me. That was because thousands of North Vietnamese soldiers were hiding out there in the woody ravines and mountains, some less than a half-mile away, as they waited to attack.

The silence was deadly, ominous.

From the reports I had filed in Udorn, I knew that truckloads of new recruits had been brought in to make the attack. The North Vietnamese used the same tactic in South Vietnam—bringing in young recruits for human-wave assaults and holding out veteran units for occupation duty. Hundreds and hundreds of young men hiding in front of me now were going to be cannon fodder within a matter of days.

In my mind's eye, I could see them storming this position, yelling, whistles blowing, artillery landing around them, running headlong into the barbed wire in front of me, through the mine field, until so many had died that they had cleared a path. The Thais would shoot until the barrels of their guns were hot, and they would pick up new weapons and fire until the enemy stopped attacking or they had used up all their bullets.

Were there more North Vietnamese in the woods in front than the Thais had bullets? How strong was their resolve? How much support will we be able to provide the Thais when the attack comes?

Still standing on top of the bunker, I suddenly had the feeling that I was being watched—from the woods ahead. A North Vietnamese staff officer, perhaps, with binoculars.

I climbed down to join Buck and the commander in his bunker, where a feminine-looking young Thai soldier served us hot tea.

In leaving, I told the commander, the dean of students, that it looked like tough exams ahead. "Ah shit, sir," he said, "we'll pass. My people will make the honor rolls."

Greek called in a helicopter working the area to pick us up, and he joined us for the ride to Long Tieng.

We were among the last to return. As the pilot was shutting down the chopper, we walked into Air Ops. Greek dropped off his radios, and Buck and I picked up our overnight bags. Shep came in from the rigging shop and accompanied us as we walked around the karst into the Sky compound. Buck and I put our bags in an empty room in the sleeping barracks and went to the mess hall where the Air America pilots and a few Sky officers were eating. Bag, Hog's deputy, came in and asked Greek if Kayak had come in off the PDJ. Greek said that, as usual, Kayak was the last man out; the last chopper off the plateau had gone into a Hmong position and picked him up. As Greek was saying this, Kayak came walking in with a toothbrush in his mouth.

Lean and hard like the other Sky officers, Kayak was also high energy. He took the toothbrush out and immediately started to explain to Bag about his request to Hog earlier that day to lead a Hmong patrol to cut off a North Vietnamese reconnaissance unit. Bag listened for a few minutes and told him to come into the Sky bunker next door. As they were leaving, Kayak was saying he didn't go on the patrol, but he had waited until it returned before he left the PDJ.

Leaving Greek in testy conversation with an Air America pilot, Buck and I followed Bag and Kayak out of the mess hall. As I watched the other Air America pilots, especially the younger ones, eating with relish, I was reminded of football players at a training table. Most of the pilots were ex-military. They were drawn to Air America because of the money and the action. Primarily, they were mercenaries, but they were also American patriots. They had lost many friends in Indochina over the years and were not a sentimental group. Frenchy, B. K., Cliff, George, Hurbie, Izzy, and Greenway, among others in the mess hall that night, were aggressive, hard-living, gnarled, tough, in-your-face Americans. There was nothing phony about them—in the way that people who constantly make decisions with life and death consequences are not phony. As a group, they were blunt but calculating. They risked their lives every day and wanted fair compensation. And, they might say, "Fuck you if you don't like it."

When Buck and I walked into the headquarters bunker, Dick J., Hog, Bag, and Kayak were talking beside a stack of C-rations in the open bay area. Close by, Cobra, Electric, and Hardnose, three Sky case officers who worked exclusively with the Thais, were talking with two senior Air America pilots.

Dick J. told Kayak that he was never, ever again to think about going out with the Hmong on patrol. "We don't do that here. The Hmong do that, you understand me."

Kayak said, "I know, I know," and went on quickly to add that the Hmong patrol reported that the North Vietnamese were wearing new uniforms. He walked to a map and plotted the route the North Vietnamese had taken along the west side of the PDJ.

Electric suggested they were looking for an approach route to the middle Thai positions. He said another Hmong patrol reported earlier that day that more North Vietnamese troops had been brought in north of the PDJ overnight, plus their convoy included heavy trucks loaded with what might be tanks.

For the next hour, as other Sky officers came and left, the discussion continued about the buildup and ways to blunt the pending attack. Bag suggested that the best defensive was a good offensive and that we should move Hmong north of the enemy to put pressure on its rear and flanks. Because we simply sat and waited, the North Vietnamese were able to mass their forces at will. Dick said the North Vietnamese were being bombed every day and night by artillery and the air force. Digger countered, however, that nothing substituted for the little guy attacking on the ground. He agreed with Bag's suggestion to send the Hmong north behind the North Vietnamese and push them into the Thai defensive positions.

Hog was sure Vang Pao wouldn't go for it. He said that a similar plan had been discussed the previous night and Vang Pao thought there would be too many Hmong casualties. The North Vietnamese could just put in another call home for more replacements, but where was Vang Pao going to get more soldiers? Plus, V. P. was convinced the Thais could hold off anything the North Vietnamese threw at them. Hog said that the good Hmong general has stared at many North Vietnamese forces gearing for attacks over the years.

Cobra and Bag both opined quickly, loudly, that Vang Pao didn't give a hoot about the Thais and he hadn't often faced tanks before. The Thai positions had been built to hold off attacks by ground forces. If the Hmong road watch patrol was right and tanks were being brought down, that altered the balance of power, tilted the advantage to the North Vietnamese.

Hog said that he would talk with Vang Pao about some type of preemptive maneuvers by the Hmong forces, and he left to go to V. P.'s compound. Dutch came in and said it was time for all the good young Sky men to come to Jesus and give him some good coordinates. Dutch, a Texan, had a number of duties, among them to develop target information for B-52 bomb strikes. He pulled out an acetate-covered map that had strike boxes plotted from the previous day, erased them with an old rag, and started to plot new targets. Many of the officers read coordinates off the palms of their hands that they had jotted down during the day. Others pulled out dog-eared notebooks and called out number groups. Dutch plotted them all on the map. After considerable discussion about some of the plots, the ridgeline north of the PDJ was covered with dots—just north of where I had been earlier in the day.

Dutch quickly drew rectangular boxes around the target dots ("Arclight strike zones") and wrote down the corner coordinates for transmission to the air force. They would be hit tonight or tomorrow.

Hog came back. He said that V. P. had taken a hard position against moving the Hmong out on attacks and had said again that the Thais could hold, especially with U.S. Air Force support.

"The Vietnamese will not attack until the whole area is socked in by bad weather," Bag said. "Guarantee it. We don't need a divining rod to predict the time of attack. The weatherman will tell us. And anyone in this room can tell you how effective the U.S. Air Force will be in bad weather in these mountains." Except for B-52s and flare ships that can operate above the weather, close-support fighters didn't go below the clouds because they would hit mountains or run into small-arms fire.

"Nope," Bag continued, "Charlie's going to come when the U.S. Air Force can't. And when he starts coming, it's going to be him and the Thais. When the whistle blows, it's going to be a local affair, hand-to-hand. Forget about the U.S. Air Force."

Bag was another former smoke jumper from the mountains of Montana. Although he had not served in Vietnam, he had many years of experience in the nonconventional warfare of Laos. He knew what lay ahead.

Dick J. said that the Stick also discounted using the

Hmong to go north of the North Vietnamese. Too late. The Stick had said, "We hold what we got with what we got."

As he was leaving, Cobra said that he'd bring in some bulldozers from Udorn at first light the next morning to dig tank traps around the forward positions.

Greek walked in and complained about the Thais shooting through our landing pattern that afternoon. He went to the map board and began discussing his suspicion that the North Vietnamese were going to move all their forces along the west side of the PDJ and attack by coming up on the soft underbelly of the Thai positions, hitting the artillery first, and then working their way back across the plateau from south to north.

Hog, Bag, and Electric joined him at the map and began a debate on ways to protect the west flank.

By nine o'clock that night, most of the men had drifted away from the office, either to the bar in the mess hall or to their rooms.

I turned in around ten but woke up in the middle of the night. Walking out on the balcony of the building I could hear radios squawking in the Hmong ops assistants' building. Buck had said each of the Sky officers was assigned at least one interpreter/ops assistant, a Thai or a Hmong, depending on which unit they worked with. The Hmong ops assistants were among the brightest, best-educated young men in the Hmong nation. They were translators, note takers, liaison officers, gun bearers, and anything else the Sky officers might call on them to be. At night, they also maintained the radio network to the GMs and to some of the outlying Hmong villages.

As I listened to the radios squawking in their radio room below, I heard the unmistakable background sounds of small-arms fire in one of the transmissions. It was a foggy night, and I thought perhaps the major attack had commenced on the plateau.

I walked downstairs and into the building as Glassman, one of Hog's several ops assistants, was yelling into a radio. He looked up and said the caller was a Hmong man, still living with his family on the western edge of the PDJ. Glassman translated the man's message as it came in.

"Flare ship on station."

"Big light."

"Enemy in open! Enemy in open!"

"They're pulling back. Fast. Running."

"Artillery coming in. Spooky working."

Later, "OK now. Everything quiet. Good night."

I walked out into the street of the compound and then around the headquarters building. There was a jail or stockade built into the karst in the rear. My first thought was that it was for prisoners while they were being interrogated, but I had never seen any reports where Sky had personally interrogated any Pathet Lao or North Vietnamese. Maybe it was a holdover from years past.

There appeared to be a freshly beaten path to the front gate. I peered in to see if it was occupied. There was something under a blanket in the corner—as I looked in, the blanket stood up.

Snorting, a bear walked over to the bars.

"Holy shit," I said, jumping back five feet.

In the morning, I found out the bear had been caught as a cub and was a local pet, even though he was never let out of the cage. He liked beer and expected a bottle from late-night visitors. Once during a lull in the fighting, Bag wandered out to the cage and sat drinking with the bear for hours. Late that night, Bag opened the cage and wrestled with the drunk bear. Or, that's what he told people later to explain the scratches all over his arms. Some people thought he had gone in and made love to that bear. He had been up-country for a long time.

The valley was socked in the next morning with low-hanging clouds. Buck and I sat in the mess hall and drank coffee to stay out of the way of the regular Sky officers preparing for the day's work. I had learned in the army that no one liked loud, chatty replacements. This was very select company here. I was the FNG, and my place was silent and to the side. I had nothing to offer; nobody wanted or needed my comments about anything.

The first chopper that got out of the valley left at mid-morning to pick up two Thais wounded the previous night in the probe attack on the PDJ. The Hmong air ops assistant came into the mess hall not long after it left and told Buck and me that we had a ride to Bouam Long, LS 32, with Digger if we wanted to go. We gulped down our coffee and made our way to Air Ops.

Most of the Sky officers were on the ramp when we got there. Some were busy getting supplies together or talking with Air America pilots; others were sitting and waiting. Waiting was part of the job, and all the officers carried paperback books. Most would read a couple of books a week—fiction, nonfiction, the classics. Except Kayak. He read the thickest, dullest tomes ever written, mostly about economics and the stock market, but also books with such titles as *Calculus as Art* and *Labor Union Considerations of Dental Plans*. And financial journals and curious articles, such as "The Effects of the Industrial Revolution on Italian Emigration Patterns." Greek pulled Kayak's book out of his hands as we walked into Air Ops and told him that he was crazy. Either he was crazy for reading stuff like this or this stuff made him crazy—one or the other. Kayak, sitting on the floor, leaning against the back wall with his knees up, reached up, took the book from Greek, and went back to reading without comment as he swirled his toothbrush from side to side in his mouth.

When our Twin Pack was loaded, Buck and I joined Digger and climbed aboard. Several Hmong soldiers were already on board, heading back to Bouam Long with boxes of batteries, cloth, food, and radios. We lifted off and headed north but stayed well west of the PDJ.

Bouam Long was an oddity. In Laos, generally, clearly distinguishable lines separated areas controlled by the Pathet Lao and North Vietnamese and those controlled by the Sky forces. In MR II, the North Vietnamese, with their Pathet Lao hosts, controlled all the area from North Vietnam down Route 6 to the PDJ except for Bouam Long, twenty-five miles north of the PDJ. It was the home place of one of Vang Pao's fathers-in-law, Yer Pao Sher (alias), and he was not moving. The outpost itself was in a valley at the top of the highest mountain in the area. Surrounding mountains were rugged with sheer drops to lowlands densely covered with trees and foliage. The North Vietnamese and Pathet Lao had been trying unsuccessfully for years to dislodge Yer Pao Sher and his people. Bouam Long was even now under siege, with almost daily attacks and casualties on both sides. The Hmong at Bouam Long tended to their wounded and buried their dead in a corner of the compound. Villagers slept in bunkers and were rationed food and water.

We climbed up through clouds west of the PDJ and turned northeast. Digger said that some Air America helicopter pilots wouldn't fly over the clouds all the way to Bouam Long because, if they developed any mechanical problems and had to make an emergency descent through the clouds, there was almost no chance of survival. Chances were not good in any case, but it was possible to bring in a crippled chopper by auto rotation if there was room and time to find a landing spot. Even when the weather was good, flying to Bouam Long was dangerous because all the territory north of the PDJ was controlled by the North Vietnamese and Pathet Lao, in addition to the constant attacks on Bouam Long.

This Twin Pack pilot, one of the best in the business according to Buck, made the trip without argument because Redcoat, the Sky officer assigned to Bouam Long, had been trying to come down for several days but had been prevented by the weather. Digger was going to replace him for a couple of weeks. A former U.S. Marine officer who had led long-range patrols in Vietnam, Digger also had a master's in psychology and was a clear, objective voice in any discussion about tactics in MR II.

He was not as sympathetic toward the failings of the Hmong guerrillas as others and thought the Hmong forces should be more on the move in patrolling and engaging the North Vietnamese. He was frustrated when the Sky forces were outmaneuvered. Bouam Long was a perfect place for him—one of the toughest officers in Long Tieng working with the toughest Hmong.

As we headed northeast, the clouds dissipated. One of the Hmong soldiers recognized a mountaintop, and that helped the pilot to get his position. Spiderman, an LS 32 ops assistant on board, began to get radio transmissions from Bouam Long, and the helicopter was guided in. This was the highest peak in the area. When the helicopter got over the position, it descended in a tight spiral. It was like landing on the head of a needle.

Redcoat was waiting for us as we jumped off the helicopter in the middle of the compound. After introductions, we joined Yer Pao Sher in his bunker for a general orientation briefing, and Redcoat expanded on his radio reports about enemy activities north of the PDJ. Later, Digger and Redcoat went off to work on a generator and Spiderman asked if Buck and I would like to visit one of the outposts around the compound. He pointed to a position on top of a mountain peak to the north that looked like a turret position to a castle.

We walked up a narrow, winding mountain trail north of the runway—up and up and up. I finally had to stop and rest. As I sat gasping for breath, I looked off to the edge of the trail at a defensive way station where seven or eight young boys squatted and stared. They resembled dirty Boy Scouts, but the way they held their rifles, as if they were extensions of their own bodies, they looked like they had been handling weapons all of their young lives. Their smiles were friendly; they apparently thought it was funny that I was so winded.

Getting back to my feet, I caught up with Buck and Spiderman as they approached the topmost position. It was protected by a moat that had been dug out of the mountainside rock. Some ten feet down at the bottom of the moat, I could see concertina wire and clusters of mines tied on the wire, amid bamboo panjii sticks. There were so many mines I thought that, if one went off, there might be a sympathetic explosion of the whole lot.

That moat looked like the valley of death.

Inside the position, a dozen young boys had gathered in front of me. One lowered a hinged drawbridge made out of six large bamboo poles.

"What is this?" I asked Buck. "My initiation rite? You brought me all the way up here to see if I can cross the bridge?"

I weighed 220 pounds, Buck maybe 150, and Spider-man less than 100. The bridge was made for the youngsters inside, smaller than the ops assistant, but certainly not for me, King Kong Junior.

I didn't want to go into the position that badly and I didn't need to prove myself to Buck—hell, he was leaving—so I don't know why I started to follow him and the little ops assistant across the valley of death on that tiny bamboo bridge, but I did. I was the FNG just going along. Tentatively, I put one foot on the bridge and tested its strength. It seemed secure enough, and I put my other foot on the bridge. It swayed slightly but steadied when I stood still. The rope that raised and lowered the bridge was the only thing for me to grab onto, but I couldn't reach it until I got more than halfway across. With my arms out to my sides like a tightrope walker, I took another very small step forward. Behind me, the bamboo bridge began to eat into the side of the moat. Another small step—the bridge began to sway again. I could either stand perfectly still and wait for it to stop swaying or, because my knees were shaking too much to stand perfectly still, I could take one giant step and hope to reach the rope in a lunge to the other side. This I decided to do because the bridge was swaying more, rather than less. Stepping to the middle, I leaned forward, grabbed the rope, and used it to catapult me forward and up so that I jumped to the other side, but not before the bridge dipped very low toward the concertina and the mines. As I landed with a thud, the bamboo bridge bounced up and down behind me several times.

I asked Buck just how the hell he expected me to get back. Going back, I wouldn't have the rope to grab. "Don't worry about it," he said, "you'll think of something."

Here I am, trapped in north Laos not far from China— prisoner in a tiny little outpost way up on top of a mountain. I thought, Brenda, this is the fartherest you can get from North Carolina.

I looked around at the position. It was much more littered, less organized than the Thai positions on the PDJ. The young boys who defended it looked half the age of the Thais I had seen, some not much taller than their rifles.

"Aren't we in violation of some child labor laws here?" I asked Buck.

"Common observation of FNGs," he said. "We gotta fight an unconventional war here with the forces that are available to us. The average life expectancy of a Hmong male is probably not over forty. This is an almost stone age society, you know. People don't live long. They grow up fast. These young men, number one, are older than they look and, two, the Hmong respect their elders and are not the child worshippers we tend to be in the States. The young men around us are fourteen, fifteen years of age and haven't any established value in their society. Now, someone forty or fifty or fifty-five even, he's got experiences and grandchildren and personal debts—substance, respect, value—and they do other things. The young men, these boys here, have to man the barricades. A bullet leaving their guns can do the same job as a bullet leaving the gun of someone older. And we can't change the Hmong culture to fit ours. These boys are all volunteers, ask them. 'Course they don't have many alternatives. Their fathers and their older brothers have defended this little outpost for a long time. In time, their younger brothers will work here and eventually their sons will defend it, God willing, while these boys sit back in the compound by the fire. And if they die before they get that chance, they'll be buried in the corner of the compound and the older people will make another boy.''

''Ah,'' I said, ''you bring all the FNGs up here and tell them the facts of life in MR II and give them the trial by the bridge over the valley of death and then you give them their Sky pin. Very CIA.''

''No,'' he said, smiling, ''it's just the way things are. You'll understand better after you've been here a couple of years. Let's go back down and see Redcoat and Digger.''

He and Spiderman walked back to the drawbridge and crossed it. I walked to the edge and asked the ops assistant to ask the young soldiers around me if they had any more long planks to give the bamboo bridge some support.

They did not.

Was there another way across the moat?

There was not.

Were all the mines below armed?

They were.

Did anyone have any idea how I was going to get across?

They did not, and everyone laughed except me.

I spotted a rope beside a bunker and asked the ops assistant to tell one of the young defenders to take this rope to the middle of the drawbridge and tie it to the rope that lowered and raised the bridge and then to go to the other side and hold the rope. When I got to the middle, the bridge was going to sway down and I had to have something to hold onto.

One of the young defenders walked casually to the middle, nonchalantly tied the short rope he carried to the drawbridge rope, and continued to the other side. The bamboo bridge did not strain to hold him up. On the other side he, Buck, and Spiderman dug in their heels to hold the rope taut.

. I took one step out. And then another. The bridge started to sway down and then side to side. I jumped, landing in the middle of the bridge on one foot and grabbed the rope and pulled as I pushed down on the bridge, which was dropping anyway because I had jumped on it. And I fell off to the side, screaming.

But I did not let go of the rope.

Thankfully, the three people on the other end did not either and they yanked me toward them. I landed with a thud on the rim of the moat, my feet scant inches from the closest mine. I had the breath knocked out of me. As Buck and the others pulled me to the top, I was gasping.

Everyone was laughing as I turned on my belly and peered back over the edge of the moat at the grenades and mines below. When I finally got my breath, I said it wasn't funny.

We walked down the trail to the airstrip and went into Redcoat's bunker. It was a man's place, stark, dirty, drab. In the entrance was a fifty-five-gallon drum filled with water and an immersion heater—the bathing trough. Radios sat on an earthen shelf near the back wall. On a table was a propane gas camp stove, some empty C-ration cartons, and candles. Rifles, pistols, binoculars, and assorted military equipment lay around in disorder. A couple of boxes of books were near a metal wall locker. At the side, steps led down to an underground bunker. We heard Redcoat and Digger talking below and went down. Two cots were in the corner. Digger's duffel bag lay near the steps.

Redcoat was stuffing things into a pack. He said that he was always glad to leave and always glad to get back.

"Tough duty," I suggested.

"Yes indeed," he agreed. "It isn't safe here. Every night I go to sleep thinking this may be it. Look at this," he said, walking over to a piece of plywood leaning against one of the earthen walls. He pulled it away and uncovered a man-size hole that went out and down.

"That tunnel leads out to a rock quarry by the edge of the runway," Redcoat said. "It is my only escape route, and it doesn't even get me out of the perimeter. I spend many of my nights there. I sleep better in the hole because we get rocketed a bunch and you never know where that first round's going to land."

"Why do you stay?" I asked. "What happens if you ask for another job? Not that I'm asking for it, you understand."

"What would these people do if I weren't here? It's my job. It's where they told me to go."

Digger said we needed to get in the air; a helicopter sitting too long on the ground here drew fire.

We walked down to the airstrip ahead of Redcoat. Several Hmong were waiting to board, and others stood around saying good-bye. I asked the pilot if anyone had ever tried to stow away or jump aboard as he was taking off, and he said, "No, this place is where they were born, it's their home."

Buck and I were back in Long Tieng by midafternoon and on a flight to Udorn minutes later. We said good-bye to Dick J. by radio.

Flying south, I thought about the difference in the way the U.S. military was running the war in Vietnam and the way the Agency was handling its task in Laos. Keeping the American army in the jungle of Vietnam required an incredible support structure. I remembered that it took seven Americans to keep one U.S. soldier in the field. By using local forces in Laos, the Agency needed only one Sky man for about every five hundred soldiers in the field. Inverse pyramid. Plus, it was obvious during my orientation visit that there was a bond between the local soldiers and the Agency men. The Hmong were accepted as they were, and there was no effort to make them Oriental Americans. We did not corrupt their values to accommodate ours. The Agency had good men working in the program. No one had rigid, self-serving attitudes;

the whole work force was experienced, intelligent, adaptive, dedicated, with strong work ethics. Everyone was involved and felt they were making a contribution. The impetus for planning and execution came from the field, not Washington. People tended to stay year after year. There was no bureaucracy. The Agency field headquarters in Udorn was away from the politicized centers of government.

With all those positive factors, could Sky keep the PDJ? I didn't know, but then no one working our side of the line seemed to know for sure either. Except the Thai mercenary commander—he was sure we'd hold.

5

BATTLE FOR THE PDJ

The next morning, I went into Jim G.'s office and told him about my trip. I ended by saying again that I wanted to be assigned to Long Tieng, and he told me to talk with the Stick. Later that day as the Stick walked by my desk, I asked him about a reassignment up-country. He stopped, tapped my desk with his stick, and in an even but annoyed voice said, "Hey listen, do your job here. This here is what you're supposed to do right now. This here's your fucking job."

That night over supper at the hotel, I told Brenda that it was like I hadn't learned anything in my trip up north. Nobody gave a damn what I wanted to do. I hadn't earned my spurs, and I was asking for special consideration. Patience, I said. Patience. I had to have "hang," even in Udorn, though it's a more terrible place, in ways, than Bouam Long.

Brenda said she didn't understand me sometimes, why I wanted to go get shot at. Peer pressure, she thought. I looked at her without comment.

Several government and military VIPs visited the base office in Udorn during the next couple of days. In our briefings, Jim suggested several possible tactics that the North Vietnamese might employ to capture the PDJ—from laying siege to methodical moves to capture one position at a time, either north to south or south to north.

By mid-December, he noted, the smoke from slash-and-burn farmers clearing new land from China to the Gulf of Thailand would begin to cover the area and we would find out what the North Vietnamese planned to do. He was confident in the defensibility of the Thai positions and hoped that the impending battle would engage the North Vietnamese for as long as possible. He often made the point that soaking up their resources on the PDJ improved the overall U.S. government position in Southeast Asia.

On 14 December, we received overhead photography of large covered trailers coming down the road toward the PDJ from North Vietnam. In an effort to cut them off, B-52s and U.S. Marine and Air Force jets (fast movers) targeted the road that night and the next day.

There was light ground activity on 15 and 16 December. The Stick often came into the center ops room and stood in front of the PDJ map. Occasionally, he slapped the side of his leg with one of his sticks. Late on the afternoon of the 16th, after he had stared at the map for fifteen minutes, he said, "Come on, come on, you dirty commie shits. Come on."

On 17 December, resupply on the PDJ was cut short when the whole area was enveloped in smoke. The smoky season was starting. Greek was the last American off the plateau that day.

That evening, Brenda and I had just arrived in Buck's compound to attend his going away party when the beeper on my radio signaled me to return to the ops building. Most of the staff was on hand when I got there. The attack on the Thai positions on the PDJ was under way.

We had three radios set to monitor the traffic through the U.S. Air Force ABCCC (Airborne Control and Command Center) radio platform circling high above the clouds over the PDJ, and they chattered in the background. Grabbing a chair, I straddled it backward, leaned up beside a desk near the map board, and started to take notes.

All of the Thai positions were under simultaneous ground and artillery attack. Most were reporting B-52-like bombs and rounds hitting with accuracy. The background noise of the radio transmissions was deafening. One of the northernmost positions went off the air in midsentence. Someone speculated that the command bunker must have taken a direct hit. A neighboring position reported that the North Vietnamese appeared to have breached the perimeter, and enemy ground troops were swarming over the bunkers. All surrounded Thai positions were ordered to fire on the overrun outpost. Artillery was told to fire air bursts over it. A flare ship came on station and began dropping flares through the clouds.

The commander of the northernmost position, the Thai dean of students, came on suddenly to say that tanks were outside his wire. Spookies and Spectors (gunships) arrived and circled the area, but they could not get through the clouds.

North Vietnamese infantry was reported to be following tanks as they plowed through the mine fields and concertina of the two positions beside the northernmost one.

Thai artillery was redirected at the northernmost position. The radio operator there, who had replaced the commander, was too excited to adjust the artillery fire. He kept screaming in Thai and English that Vietnamese sappers were outside his bunker.

The artillery positions began to report that they were receiving heavy incoming rounds. "Big rounds," they said. Two 155-mm guns were knocked out. One 105-mm gun position came on the air suddenly to say that Vietnamese were inside their perimeter. Another 105-mm position reported that large numbers of Vietnamese and tanks were outside their wire. They were going to lower their howitzers and fire point-blank at the advancing waves of enemy.

The radio operator on the northernmost position, now hysterical, screamed that tanks were inside the perimeter and crushing bunkers. He suddenly went off the air.

A 105-mm battery soldier came on and said that hand-to-hand fighting was in progress. Then he, too, went off the air.

The North Vietnamese kept up their attacks throughout the night. Occasionally, we put Xs over positions we thought were lost but received later radio reports from Thai forces still inside.

By the next morning, every position had been breached by North Vietnamese attackers. North Vietnamese tanks and 12.7-mm antiaircraft guns were positioned throughout the PDJ. Enemy troops surrounded or controlled almost all of our positions.

We had lost the PDJ.

The Stick had gone over to the rear headquarters of the Thai mercenaries when the attack began. Downcast, he returned early the following morning.

"What the hell are they shooting at us?" he asked no one in particular. "And what happened to those tank traps?" He was standing in front of the map, angrily slapping the side of his leg with his stick when I left later in the morning.

Reports came in that day that the Thais—those able to get out of their positions—were retreating to the first ridgeline south of the Plaine. A combined reserve force of Thai and Hmong was heli-lifted in to help them regroup.

A U.S. Air Force jet working the area in the smoke was shot down by a North Vietnamese plane. U.S. air support was directed away from the PDJ to aid in the unsuccessful rescue of the pilot.

By late afternoon, only the westernmost Thai position on the PDJ remained in friendly hands. Ed Reid, flying an Air America Twin Pack helicopter, took Hardnose in under the clouds of haze so that the Sky officer could make an on-the-ground assessment of the situation. When they landed, the flight mechanic held off some of the Thai soldiers who were trying to get on board the helicopter, but they did pick up two seriously wounded mercenaries. The position began taking heavy mortar fire soon after Reid lifted off. Inside the command bunker, Hardnose surveyed the PDJ through binoculars. As he looked at one position to his front, it was suddenly hit by a tremendously large round. Hardnose could feel the shock waves from the explosion. Debris was blown out for hundreds of meters, and a huge dust cloud slowly enveloped the area. The few Thais who survived the blast were breaking out of the dust to join clusters of other Thais retreating off the Plaine to the south.

Incoming mortar rounds pounded Hardnose's position. All of the other Thai positions on the PDJ were obviously overrun or completely surrounded by North Vietnamese. There was no hope to marshall the Thais moving south off the PDJ to make a counterattack. Hardnose called in Reid, who carefully picked his moment to land amid the mortar barrage. Hardnose scrambled onto the helicopter as rounds landed around him.

After gaining altitude, Reid flew along the northwestern edge of the PDJ as Hardnose talked with Thai commanders, interpreters, and forward air controllers fleeing the fighting. The Twin Pack suddenly came under heavy 12.7-mm machine-gun fire. Taking evasive action, Reid dipped and slid the helicopter around in the air. Just as suddenly, large bombs started raining down at the end of the rotary props. Reid and Hardnose could see them only for a fraction of a second as they fell by the helicopter. The bombs were coming from a pack of Hmong T-28's, flying overhead, that had seen the 12.7 firing position and were bombing it, despite the fact that the Air America helicopter was between them.

"Jesus H. Christ," Ed Reid yelled, as he continued to slide his helicopter to one side to get out of the line of fire from both above and below.

For three days, Thai stragglers came in off the plateau. B-52 night strikes were ordered to carpet bomb the old

Thai positions in hopes of destroying the ammo and weapons left behind by the Thais. During the day, Hmong T-28s and U.S. Air Force fighters struck the old positions.

General Vang Pao flew down to Udorn from Long Tieng the fourth day after the Vietnamese had launched their attacks. It was our first meeting. He had a warm, wide smile and a more cultured look than most of the other Hmongs I had met. Rather than a fierce mountain man, he looked like a serene Oriental college professor. The Stick was waiting for him. They went into his office with Jim G. and closed the door. Later, they moved to the briefing room and I joined them, along with George M., the operations chief.

V. P. contended that neither his forces nor the Thai could defend the ridgeline south of the PDJ. There were no protected airstrips or landing zones for resupply, plus the big guns of the North Vietnamese could be fired and adjusted from positions across the PDJ.

The place to make our next stand was Skyline, the ridgeline north of the Long Tieng valley.

The Stick thought we would be giving up too much territory without a fight.

V. P. said we could defend Skyline. "We cannot defend that ridge south of the PDJ. How can we? Come up, we go up together, like old times. You see. Cannot defend that position. Skyline. We can fight from Skyline."

The Stick said he wanted to think about it. He wanted to ensure that we could hold the next place where we took a stand, even if the North Vietnamese used tanks and big guns and jets. Skyline was next to our headquarters; it was better to fight some distance away. After V. P. left, the Stick went over to the Thai rear headquarters. Although the Thai commanders regretted the loss of their men and the positions on the PDJ, they were willing to facilitate the recruitment and training of additional mercenaries to stop the advancing North Vietnamese. They said the North Vietnamese should pay for every inch of ground they took during their advance south.

The Thais and the Vietnamese had been fighting one another for centuries. Cambodia had been the most frequent battlefield, but the Thais also had fought the Vietnamese in what is now Laos. Their natural inclination always had been to attack the Vietnamese at the head of their advancing columns. They wanted to hold the ridgeline south of the PDJ. Recruitment and training of Sky mercenaries was in the best interests of the Thai government. Its borders and national security were at risk. The Thais wanted to stop the Vietnamese in the mountains before they got to the Mekong.

Where to take the next stand was decided that night. The big guns opened up again and blew apart the new positions along the first ridgeline.

The North Vietnamese had to be stopped at Skyline, the new line drawn in the mountains—the next battlefield.

As the Sky forces continued to pull back, bulldozers and construction materials were sent to Long Tieng so that Agency engineers could make the bunkers on Skyline as strong as possible. The plan called for Thai mercenaries who had survived the fighting on the PDJ, plus new replacements, to be positioned in the bunkers. The Hmong GMs would interdict the North Vietnamese soldiers and supplies as they moved south down the river valley to Skyline.

6

MARY AND JOSEPH

Brenda was on her own most of the day and early evenings, but we often got together for lunch. She had bought a car and made a trip to Bangkok on 50-Kip to get our dog Harry from quarantine. She did not like the house Buck had lived in and, on her own, located a nice bungalow near the edge of town. Our closest neighbor would be Izzy Freedman, an Air America pilot.

As Christmas approached, we had been in the Charoen Hotel for almost a month and were anxious to move out. Too many things had to be fixed at the house before we could move in, however, and it became painfully evident that we were going to spend Christmas in our twelve-by-twelve hotel room. Along with the presents we received from North Carolina, I bought my wife a dozen gifts, gaily wrapped, and put them around the tiny plastic tree we had bought at the base exchange.

After Christmas breakfast in our room, we exchanged presents on the bed. By midmorning, the temperature outside was 100°F. Brenda didn't want to go to the pool—"indecent on Christmas to go to a swimming pool"—and refused to go to the lobby and read—"I'd feel like a refugee." We finally decided to visit the local Catholic orphanage near the air base. After buying two large baskets of fruit from the open-air market downtown, we headed to Saint Mary's School and Orphanage on the

Sakon Makhon road. Pulling into the parking lot in the back, we were immediately surrounded by dozens of kids in clean, pressed clothes, some excitedly jumping up and down. All this for fruit? We got the baskets out of the backseat and gave them to some of the larger kids, who led us into the building. Some of the children reached up and grabbed our hands; there were many little hands competing for our fingers. Smiling and talking excitedly in Thai, the kids pulled us along. Some showed missing teeth.

We were brought to a sister sitting behind a desk. We apologized because we had brought so little and there were so many children. The sister said it didn't matter, merely coming was the best gift. Besides, she said, the U.S. Air Force would be here soon with bags of toys. She invited us to go in the back, near the picnic tables where the kids ate, and wait for the air force. They had had a wonderful Christmas party the year before.

Brenda was anxious to go inside to see the babies. In the nursery were rows of large bassinets, the ends hinged in the middle so that they could be rocked from side to side. The only child there was a tiny little boy in a very large diaper. Standing on his small legs, his head steady, and gripping the bassinet, he used his weight to sway it from side to side. He wasn't smiling. His sad expression and the metal bassinet made him look like he was serving time in jail. He followed Brenda with his eyes. He looked tough, but mostly he looked alone in that room of empty cribs. Brenda saw one of the sisters and asked if she could take him to the party outside. The sister extended both her hands in the boy's direction as if to say he's yours. Brenda swept the boy up and carried him out to one of the picnic tables. She put him on her knees, bounced him up and down, and said something silly. He stared at her, deep into her eyes, with that tough guy expression, and then he broke into a huge smile.

Suddenly, it seemed there wasn't anyone else around my wife. Sure, the other kids were there, still vying for her attention, but for Brenda there was just this scrawny kid who seemed to respond to her in a special way.

The air force's sweating Santa Claus and attendants arrived with gifts and ice cream to an explosion of noise among the kids. Some of the gifts were simple, yet to the kids they were the most wondrous things. Everywhere we looked, kids were laughing and jumping around. Some of the GIs got on their hands and knees so the kids could crawl over them and ride them like horses. Off to the side, two of the priests were smiling.

Brenda fell in love with the little boy on her knees. When she put him down once, he reached up and extended his hands to be held again. She picked him up. He smiled, and she hugged him.

"Isn't he the grandest thing?" she said. "Oh Jim," she said, "Look at him laugh. Look at him."

She went back to see the boy the next day and every day until we moved into the house.

His mother had left him at the orphanage when he was only one day old. He had been born with a growth on his stomach and the nuns said the mother, an unwed country girl, couldn't afford a doctor. That was why she had brought him to the orphanage. He was sickly, and no one expected him to live. Because they had so many kids, the young boy was placed in a crib in the rear of the infirmary. He didn't die, and the sisters named him Joseph. He lay on his back so much during his first year that the back of his head became flat. When he was one and a half, he was taken to Bangkok for surgical removal of the growth. It left an ugly scar on his tiny tummy. He became sick right after the operation and was again assigned to a rear bassinet in one of the crowded sleeping areas. He pulled through and had been standing up for only a day or so when Brenda and I visited at Christmas.

There was no doubt that Joseph knew Brenda. And he began to know that Brenda came only to see him—no other child, just him. As she walked in, he called out to her and held out his arms. Brenda squealed and ran to him. The first time Brenda was allowed to take him from the orphanage, she cuddled him close to her on the front seat as she drove. At home, she didn't want to put him down.

By early February, Joseph's afternoon outings with Brenda had stretched to overnights at our home and eventually into long weekends. At each visit, it was becoming more difficult for Brenda to return him to the orphanage. One night over dinner, she asked if we could initiate adoption procedures. Because I didn't know what was involved, I went to the judge advocate general's office on base the next morning and spoke with an air force lawyer who had some experience in dealing with officials from the Thai Ministry of Interior, which had partial but not complete responsibility in adoption matters. According to Thai law for an in-country adoption, the lawyer said that adopting parents had to be at least thirty years old, the natural mother had to sign an unconditional release form, and the Ministry of Interior had to do a six-month home study. He added that it was actually a bit more complicated than that. He advised me not to try it, that I was only asking for heartache. Maybe, he said, we should wait until we got ready to leave the country and apply for overseas adoption. It was easier. The Pearl Buck Foundation in Bangkok supposedly helped.

Brenda was crestfallen when I told her that night. We always knew that we would adopt (Brenda could not have children), though we had not talked about that when we went to the orphanage at Christmas. There was something cosmic about Brenda's contact with Joseph that day, and their time together had resulted in a loving bond.

"There are so many kids at that orphanage, no one would miss that scrawny little runt," she said. "I want that boy, and he needs me. And the U.S. Air Force lawyer asked us to wait for a couple of years before doing anything? Come on, Jim, do something."

I told her I'd get a Thai lawyer the following day.

Because I was only twenty-nine and Brenda was twenty-eight, I suggested that perhaps the orphanage would allow us to be foster parents until nearer the end of our tour when we would be old enough, according to Thai law, to adopt.

Early the next day, a Friday, I drove over to the headquarters of the Thai mercenaries and found Boon, an interpreter I had come to know when he had been working as a translator for our office. I asked him to recommend a local lawyer for a personal matter, like adopting a kid. He suggested that we see the province chief. Because the area was under martial law authority, he was the final approving official on something like that. Boon said we ought to ask the chief directly about what we needed to do and not some lawyer. Getting a lawyer was the American way. "Here, you go to the people making the decisions and get the job done yourself," he advised.

Boon and I drove to province administration headquarters and were admitted to the province chief's office after a surprisingly short wait. I sat silently while Boon explained the situation to the province chief, an army colonel. The chief then spoke for a few minutes in fast Thai, stood up, extended his hand, and ended the meeting.

Walking out of his office, I said, "Good? Bad? What?"

"The colonel said to forget the Ministry of Interior's home study," Boon said. "If the orphanage and the natural mother say it is okay for you to adopt the child, then he'll go along with it. He suggested that we check with both the orphanage and the mother and see him again next week."

My first thought was this was better then I hoped. We could get it all done in a week, maybe, rather than the two years we were talking about yesterday. We had something here!

Then I thought, we don't have a chance in hell to find the biological mother. All we know is that the boy was brought to the orphanage when he was one day old, probably not by the mother because she would have been too weak, and that was two years ago.

I expressed these concerns to Boon, and he agreed that we probably had little chance to find the exact person we were looking for but we could hire some lady to sub for her. He said that's the way things like this are done in Thailand. I said I couldn't do that. He said he could and suggested that, if it reached a point where this was our best option, I could back out and he would generate a mother. "Can do easy, GI," he said, mimicking a barroom phrase popular with Udorn Air Base camp followers.

When Boon and I arrived at the orphanage late that morning, one of the nuns said Brenda had been in earlier and taken Joseph for the weekend. We asked if there was an address given for the mother when Joseph had been brought to the orphanage. The sister thought so and led us into the church administrative offices where old orphanage records were kept. The sister rummaged through a file of 5-by-9 cards and finally extracted one for Joseph—Yongyut Daimuphuang, according to his birth certificate that was paper-clipped to the back. The sister said that the bishop was the final authority on adoption; however, if we could find the mother from the address listed on the card and she consented to our adopting Joseph, she was sure the bishop would approve. She handed us the card and wished us Godspeed.

Boon whistled as we walked back to his Jeep. He said the address was in the worst area of town, occupied mostly by squatters in lean-to shacks.

We walked down a dirty alley on the edge of town and entered a maze of shanties. Jumping over open sewer ditches, balancing ourselves on catwalks, and turning sideways at times, we moved toward the center of the area. The smell almost took my breath. The interpreter asked people directions as we walked along. They answered quietly and gawked at me. Possibly, other Americans had been in this part of town before but not many, I would have bet. I was an alien, out of place.

We eventually found the house we were looking for. It was a relatively nicer building than the others we had passed. Perhaps it had been one of the original structures before the squatters moved in.

Standing in front of the house, Boon yelled the mother's name. Neighbors gathered around, but there was no answer from the house. After he called the mother's name again, several people came out on the small front porch. Boon, who had gone to school in Australia and considered himself above the squatters around him, spoke in a condescending tone, noticeable even in Thai, which I did not understand all that well. He talked loudly, and the various people on the porch responded quietly, as if they were guilty of some crime. This exchange went on for several minutes.

Boon finally stopped talking in midsentence and turned to me, ''The short chunky one is the mother, but she said she's leaving this weekend, Saturday, and isn't coming back. She won't be available to go to the province chief's office. But, in fact, she's not going anywhere. She's just saying that because she's ashamed of leaving the boy, of not ever going to see him. She'll just hide the next time we come back.''

I looked at the only stout girl on the porch. She was young and attractive but looked uncomfortable with us standing in front of her house and bringing up something about her past that she certainly wished to forget.

''OK,'' I said, ''tell her she has to come with us now to the province chief's office, he wants to see her. She has to go.''

Boon agreed. As he walked up on the porch, he talked to the girl. He pointed inside the house, looked over his shoulder, and told me to wait a minute—they would be right back. Everyone on the porch went inside, and I was left to look around at the crowd of people.

Boon and the girl soon came out of the house. She had put on a different outfit and some makeup and was accompanied by a friend. Boon told me he had gone into the house with them because he didn't want the girl to run out the back.

The province chief met with the mother alone in his office. When she came out, Boon and I went in. The province chief said that he thought he could finalize everything that afternoon. He said he had the mother's consent. Now, he needed the birth certificate, the orphanage's release, and my wife to sign some forms. Boon handed him the birth certificate and said the sisters at the orphanage had given us approval for the adoption.

"Fine," the chief said, "go get your wife, and we'll have things ready."

Outside the office, I saw the girl and her friend going down the stairs to the front entrance. Asking Boon to follow, I chased after them and caught up to the pair on the street. I told Boon to tell the mother that what she had done, what was happening, was maybe God's will and she should know that Joseph was going to have much love and a good home. Boon repeated what I had said. The girl continued to look away, still very uncomfortable. I asked if I should give her anything, and the interpreter said, "Taxi fare home, that's all. She lives among thieves who would take anything more as a sign of weakness and might come after you for more money. I'll give her taxi fare, that's enough."

Boon gave her some change, and I put my hand on her shoulder as she turned and walked away.

It was only early afternoon when I pulled up in front of our house. Brenda was on the front porch with Joseph and waved as I unlocked the front gate and walked in.

Five minutes later, she was crying and laughing and hugging Joseph so tightly that he cried out. She couldn't talk. Stamping her feet in a little circle, she kept saying, "Woooh, woooh, woooh!"

Leaving Joseph with the maid, we went to the province

chief's office and, within fifteen minutes, signed the forms that had been prepared. Brenda went in and thanked the province chief. I dropped off Brenda at home and then went to the American Consulate, where the papers were authenticated. As far as the Americans were concerned, Joseph was officially adopted and we could request a U.S. passport.

Brenda could not keep her eyes off Joseph. She kept saying out loud, "He's my son. My son." He was almost two but could not walk because he had spent so much time on his back in a bassinet. On Sunday, he kept his balance in making a two-step trip from me to her. We yelled and shouted and frightened Joseph, so we calmed down and just looked at him a lot.

Brenda said, "Our son is the most gorgeous boy in the whole world."

On Sunday afternoon, two days after we adopted Joseph, there was a knock at the front door of our bungalow. A tall, elderly American man—a stranger—was standing on the porch. He introduced himself as John Westen. He said that he was an aide with the U.S. Agency for International Development (USAID) and was preparing to return to the United States. I stuck my head out the door to see if anyone else was around, possibly explaining why this man was on our porch.

Westen told me that he had heard about our success with the province chief in adopting our son and that was the reason he was here. A year ago, he had met a beautiful Thai girl in a bar and within the month they were living together in his large USAID-provided house. She had a daughter by a previous common-law arrangement with an American soldier at the air force base and asked if she could bring her daughter to live with them. Of course, said Westen. The next morning, a beautiful blond-haired child came into his life. She was the most intelligent, the most energetic, the most affectionate child he had ever known. His voice softened as he said this.

She was almost three, but the man said she acted like the lady of the house. He enjoyed his role as surrogate father. He loved coming home to that little girl more than anything else in his life.

"Her name is Mary," Westen said, "but we call her Mim."

After a fight one night, Mim's mother moved out and left the little girl behind. The mother still came by periodically, but Mim had lived in Westen's house as his daughter now for more than eight months and it was her home.

Westen said that he had expected to stay in Thailand for the foreseeable future. His transfer to the United States was sudden and unexpected. He loved the little girl and was intent in finding a loving, caring situation for her. He said he had a family in the States and could not adopt her himself. He asked if we would be interested.

"What about the mother?" Brenda asked.

Westen thought she had moved to Bangkok. She had told his housekeeper that she planned to move two months ago, the last time she came to see Mim. Westen said the mother was an exotic beauty but was very focused on her own life. She looked on Mim as competition, perhaps, or something that aged her.

The fact that an elderly gentleman was standing at our front door and trying to give away a little girl seemed bizarre, but we were excited as we put Joseph in the car and followed Westen to his house. Mim was escorted into the living room by the maid. She ran to Westen and hugged his leg.

Her incredible beauty was startling. Holding onto the man's leg, she looked at us in an appraising manner—first Brenda, then Joseph, then me. She smiled at us, and the room lit up. As we tried to talk with her, she toyed with us—running behind the furniture and peeking out, smiling. She didn't speak English and couldn't understand our poor Thai.

I loved that child. She had that about her, to make people love her on sight. She had a magnetic presence and appeared mature and intelligent for her age. When she wasn't running around, she looked boldly at us. She welcomed our attention, as if it were her due, as if she had been looked at with awe all her life. She was an extraordinary three-year-old child/woman.

The next day, I called Thai headquarters and asked Boon to meet me at an off-post restaurant after work, which he did. I told him what had happened the previous day and about our interest in adopting Mim, but first I had to find the mother. On his suggestion, we went to Westen's house. While I played with Mim, Boon talked with the house servants. They said the mother frequently made reference to a downtown bar. Possibly, someone there knew where she was.

On the way to the bar, I wondered if Mim was aware of her tenuous situation and that her future was being decided by strangers. She was so precocious that it occurred to me to ask her what she wanted. But she was only three, what did she know?

One of the bar customers told us the mother was at the restaurant next door and described what she was wearing. Boon rolled his eyes and said I lived a charmed life.

Next door, we sat down at the table where Mim's mother was eating noodles. She and Boon talked for a few minutes, and then she turned to me. ''Are you taking my baby away?'' she asked.

''Not if you don't want me to,'' I answered.

''I don't.''

I was not put off. I had Boon tell her how much love and attention we would give Mim—good schools, travel. She would have the very best. The girl seemed to soften but said as she got up to leave, ''No, no, no, a thousand no's.''

Brenda was disappointed that night when I got home, but I told her there was nothing I could do this time.

On Wednesday night, Westen reappeared at our front

door. He said he was leaving in a week and wondered what we were going to do about Mim. When I told him about talking with Mim's mother in the restaurant, he said the mother hadn't been by and he was at a loss.

"She didn't come by after Jim talked with her on Monday?" Brenda asked. "Not that night, or the next day or the next night? Knowing that you are leaving the country? That is irresponsible." She turned to me. "Do something."

The next morning on the way to work, I went by the orphanage to see the sisters and ask for their suggestions. One sister said they would discuss my situation during the day and they would pray. She told me to come by that evening.

Later that morning, Brenda came to the office and called me out to the reception area. She was standing beside a young Catholic priest, an American. He said he administered a church some distance away in the country. When he came into town this morning on routine church business, the sisters had told him about Mim. He wondered if he might do some good by talking with the mother.

I stuck my head in Jim G.'s office and told him that I had some personal business to attend to. When the priest and I arrived at the bar, Mim's mother was sitting outside. She and the priest, who spoke fluent Thai, talked for some time.

At one point, she turned to me and in English said, "What if your wife has a child? Maybe you no love Mim as much."

I said my wife cannot have children.

Finally, the priest said that, God's will be done, the mother had agreed. She would meet Brenda and me at the province chief's office the next morning at nine.

We were standing in the front of the province administration building with Boon the next morning, but nine o'clock came and went and there was no sign of the mother. At nine-thirty, a taxi pulled up and the mother and the priest got out. He said that he thought she might forget or would need moral support, so he had gone to the bar and picked her up.

Within an hour, we had completed the procedures and Mim was ours. As we left, I told the province chief that I would not be seeing him again, but we were forever grateful.

The priest wished us well but cautioned us about the mother. He said she was unpredictable—one of God's beautiful children trying to make the best for herself outside an air force base. We assured the priest that we would be the best parents we could to Mim and thanked him. We shook the woman's hand and promised her that Mim would be happy. She said she was on her way to see her daughter to say good-bye.

We decided that we could not let one of Westen's maids bring Mim over to our house because we did not want the mother to know where we lived. Boon volunteered to get her, but I said I would. It was going to be a family affair.

When I arrived at his house in the early afternoon, Westen said that Mim's mother had come by and had told him that we were adopting her daughter. She was crying, he said, and he did not know what she told Mim.

He asked how we were going to get her home. I explained why we didn't want one of the maids to come, which he understood, and that I would be taking her alone. He told the maids to get Mim's clothes and toys together, and they filled up the backseat of my car. Although Mim had been excited when I arrived, she was against having her things put in my car and then she became scared.

She was crying when Westen hugged her good-bye. As each maid said good-bye, she began to cry harder. When they tried to lead her to the car, she began screaming and grabbed at things to keep from being put inside. She was almost hysterical when I got behind the wheel and we pulled away. She pawed at the windows and screamed. In that small car, I was also traumatized and thought a thousand times that we should have done it differently.

Mim was exhausted by the time we arrived home. She fell into the arms of our maid when I opened the door. At supper that evening, however, she sat at the table with Brenda, Joseph, and me.

In time, she and Joseph settled in. They came to understand that their new situation was not altogether that bad, although it was different and they had to make some adjustments.

For as long as Mim could remember, she had been a privileged child. She knew she was beautiful; she had been told that every day of her life. Also, she had been told that she was special, an American Asian. Although she was only three, for almost eight months she had been the woman of her house—it had been her kingdom. If a maid's child was playing with a toy Mim wanted, she walked over and got it. The child knew Mim could do that, and Mim knew she could do that. She probably did it sometimes just because she could.

Joseph, on the other hand, grew up in an orphanage where the rules of the jungle prevailed. Might made right. If he was lucky enough to get a stick to play with in his bassinet and an older kid wanted it, then that was simply okay by Joe; the bigger kid got it. That made sense to him.

We bought toys for both kids at the Udorn base exchange and gave them out evenly. When Mim suddenly became interested in one of Joe's toys and walked over and ripped it out of his hands, Brenda told her to give it back to her brother. Initially, this confused both children. Joe looked just like all the other little Thai kids that Mim had always dominated. Why did she have to give in to him? As for Joseph, Mim was larger and acted like she knew what she was doing. Why did he suddenly have the right to a toy that she wanted?

Joe picked up on the nature of the new rules probably before Mim, and he began to fight loudly to keep his toys. Mim always acted as if this was unseemly behavior on his part. She thought him ill-mannered.

Within a few days, however, when I came home and unlocked the gate, Mim ran out and, hugging my leg, welcomed me home. I tossed her in the air and squeezed her.

Mom and Dad visited from the States. Brenda, in a state of bliss because of the kids, showed my parents Udorn like it was her hometown. One afternoon, I was telling Dad that we were in the process of applying for Joseph's and Mim's U.S. passports, and we had to give Joseph a middle name. I asked if he had any suggestions, and he said no one had been named after his father, whose first name was Joseph. When I asked what his middle name was, he said Elijah. Brenda said no—he was too small a boy to carry around such a heavy name.

We compromised. She could name Mim anything. I was going to name my son after my grandfather. It made my father proud.

But, that little boy from the Thai orphanage did not look like an average Joseph Elijah Parker.

Mim, on the other hand, looked just like a Miriam Kristen Parker.

7

HANG

Back in Long Tieng on 31 December, only Hog and Hardnose remained from the entire Sky contingent; everyone else had gone south for the holidays. The Thai forces previously run off the PDJ had been regrouped and refitted in the defensive positions still being reinforced on Skyline. Things were generally quiet. There had been a troublesome incident a few days before, however, when one of V. P.'s commando units discovered a five-man North Vietnamese patrol camped on top of a karst on the eastern end of the valley. In the ensuing firefight all of the North Vietnamese were killed. There was no one to interrogate about the equipment they were carrying—binoculars, firing tables, and plotting boards. They were either mapping the valley or setting up to act as forward observers to adjust North Vietnamese artillery fire.

V. P. thought they were a long-range patrol and not the tip of the artillery iceberg, as some Sky analysts thought. He was wrong. Early during the night of New Year's Eve, a tremendous round landed close to Thai headquarters in the east end of the valley. Hardnose felt the vibration rattle his bones.

The initial round was followed by another and another. Then, there was a steady bombardment, one monster round after another. Hardnose scrambled out of the headquarters bunker to another site dug into the side of the south ridge. Rounds were landing so quickly and were so deafening on impact that he had trouble talking with Hog on the radio.

In Vientiane, Digger was alerted to the bombardment and was sent up in a Twin Otter aircraft to post over the valley and maintain communication with the two Sky officers below.

The large North Vietnamese guns opened up again the next night, followed by wave after wave of North Vietnamese soldiers charging up the north slope of Skyline. Early that evening, North Vietnamese soldiers penetrated Hmong security positions around the east and west ends of the valley, and, shortly before midnight, the ammo dump exploded. U.S. Air Force planes dropped bombs on the advancing enemy in the river valley north of Skyline and tried to locate the guns in the hazy shadows of the Lao mountains south of the PDJ.

The Army of North Vietnam (NVA) pressed its ground attacks without letup for days. Finally, the NVA soldiers fell back, but the 130-mm guns continued to fire at Skyline and the Long Tieng valley.

Someone in Udorn said it was near the end of an era. Although the guns did not fire often during the day, neither Air America nor CASI aircraft could park on the Long Tieng ramp with those weapons within range. The Thais had to hold Skyline and the NVA guns had to be destroyed. The alternative was to change the location of our northern base.

Air America Volpar planes equipped with photographic equipment flew the river valley daily to look for enemy concentrations and the gun positions. The guns were firing at almost maximum range because the trajectory of the rounds was almost flat, barely skimming the positions on top of Skyline before impacting in the valley below. The Volpar crews did not locate the 130-mm guns right away, but they photographed a road being cleared by the North Vietnamese to advance their men and artillery south.

The Hmong T-28s flew bombing missions along the new road. B-52 strikes were called in. Hmong combat patrols went in. U.S. fast movers with laser-guided bombs worked the river valley.

A Volpar photo reconnaissance plane eventually caught one of the guns in the open. With its long-rifled barrel, the gun looked like an old German railroad car gun. It seemed enormous beside its smaller truck tractor and other vehicles carrying ammo. The pictures of this ponderous weapon put fear into the hearts of Sky. How could we beat something that evil looking?

Air America became selective about landing any fixed-wing aircraft, though work in the valley and on Skyline to reinforce the fighting positions cautiously continued. Aerial photography of the PDJ showed heavy tank tracks going south, first to the road leading around the first ridgeline where the Thais had initially fallen back and then toward the river valley leading down to Skyline.

For several days, there was a lull in the ground attacks, although the enemy guns continued to fire and to move south to improve their accuracy.

V. P. was unable to convince the Hmong civilians to stay in Long Tieng. They moved in droves over the southern ridgeline. Air America helicopters continued to fly in, but as time went on some of the fixed-wing pilots refused to work the area at all because of the 130-mm bombing. The Stick talked with some of the senior pilots and asked them to take reasonable risks. He was sure the Vietnamese could not adjust the fire of those guns because they did not control the high ground and had no forward observers in position. In addition, bringing out the guns in the daytime, when Air America was asked to fly in, would expose them to strikes by the T-28s or, if they were close enough, to counterfire from the 155-mm guns. The North Vietnamese guns were a psychological terror weapon and posed no real threat to aircraft on the ground, the Stick said. V. P. continued to try to talk the Hmong into staying.

More and more families moved out of the valley, however, and Air America argued daily about the danger of working the Alternate.

In Udorn, I was busy plotting maps, filing reports, and assisting Jim at briefings. Whether the combined CIA forces could hold Long Tieng was very much in question.

On 10 January, the North Vietnamese renewed their ground assaults on the Thai positions along Skyline. Hmong combat patrols on the east and west ends of the valley engaged large North Vietnamese units. For days, the North Vietnamese ground troops attacked. The intensity of the battle increased . . . fighting was under way at some point around the valley all the time. And 130-mm rounds continued to land.

On 14 January 1972, the front-page headlines on all the newspapers in Hanoi announced that NVA troops had captured Long Tieng, ''the key intelligence and the nerve center of the US 'Special War' in Lao.'' The articles concluded that the loss of Long Tieng was a strategic military and political defeat for the allied forces. Two days later, the official NVA military newspaper, *Guan Goi Nhan Dan*, carried a detail map of the battlefield and, in an accompanying article, said the CIA headquarters at Long Tieng took six years to build and was the strongest military base in Laos. This article concluded that the loss of Long Tieng was the turning point in the war and that ''confusion now exists between Laos and U.S. authorities in Vientiane.''

In the Long Tieng valley on 14 January, however, the Thai mercenaries still held Skyline and Hmong guerrillas guarded their flanks at the east and west ends of the runway. CIA case officers and Air America came to work in the valley each morning amid 130-mm bombardments. Hog, Bamboo, and Hardnose stayed each night.

*   *   *

By mid-February, the ground attacks and 130-mm gunfire at Long Tieng and Skyline were devastating the morale of the Thai and Hmong defenders. No positions were lost, but the North Vietnamese attacked every day and there were heavy casualties.

The Sky compound was abandoned, although Hardnose stayed in the Thai headquarters bunker on the east end. Hog, Bamboo, and Bag moved with General Vang Pao to a fortified position on the south ridge. Other Sky officers worked out of the valley during the day but left in Air America helicopters at dusk. Some went to Vientiane; others continued into Udorn.

Dick J. looked for an area to set up a rear headquarters to support the fighting on Skyline. He found a good airstrip near Ban Song, LS 272, at the terminus of the road leading north from Vientiane into the mountains. Proprietary interests were involved, and V. P. argued against making this airstrip a permanent Sky facility because it was out of his area of control. The government of Laos had influence there, as did the Pathet Lao, the Communist guerrillas.

With the North Vietnamese pressing their attacks on Long Tieng, however, there was no choice. Supplies could not be brought all the way by helicopter from Udorn and Vientiane. Toward the end of February, trucks began arriving overland to build up supplies at LS 272, where they would be transshipped by helicopter to the valley and positions on Skyline.

In late February, North Vietnamese forces took some of the forward positions on the north slope of Skyline. Two GMs were brought up from Savannakhet, a province in southern Laos. Led by the Indian and Super Mex, they climbed the Sam Thong road to the top of Skyline and moved down the ridge—clearing out the North Vietnamese as they went. Finished with their sweep, the GMs came down and went home.

There was a pause in the action as the North Vietnamese reassessed the battlefield, but they began large-scale attacks again in early March. Every night, Thai positions came under ground attack from North Vietnamese soldiers climbing up the north slope of Skyline. The 130-mm rounds continued to bombard Thai positions and the valley beyond.

Late one afternoon, I sat at my desk and stared at my typewriter. I had just finished reports on the previous night's action on Skyline and had dispatched them to Washington. When I started to work on the monthly "bullet report," a summary of ammunition on hand at the end of February that was a week overdue, an Air America helicopter let down on the tarmac near the Air Ops hangar. I looked out the window near my desk, one of the few in the building, and saw Hardnose sitting with his legs out the door and his feet resting on the skids. When the chopper landed, he jumped off and was quickly followed by a half-dozen Thai mercenaries—his interpreters, radio operators, and ops assistants. He carried his AR-15 rifle comfortably at his side like it was a large handgun. Turning to the helicopter pilot, he gave the signal (fingers across the throat) to cut the engine. He pointed to his watch, flashed three fingers and a circle to indicate a half hour, pointed to the building where I sat, and started walking toward it. He was wearing jungle boots and camouflage fatigues, which were dirty and torn. A 9-mm pistol and ammo pouches were on his pistol belt. A map was sticking out of a side pocket of his pants. Even from that distance, I could tell he hadn't shaved in days, and I knew he was going to smell bad.

He looked beautiful.

As he approached the front of the CIA headquarters building, he tossed his AR-15 to one of his ops assistants and waved his hand. All of the Thais squatted down to wait for him in the shade of a nearby fence.

Two minutes later, he was sitting on the edge of my desk. He smelled worse than I expected, but there was something of the outdoors to the scent—dirt and wind and sunshine and nature—in addition to the spent sweat.

His eyes were bloodshot, but his voice was firm and resonant. He said he had just come in from the valley where he had spent the night trying to break up an all-out NVA attack on Skyline. The mercenaries had been under attack every day now for two weeks, and they could not hold up much longer. His forces were starting to talk about escape routes if the North Vietnamese got another toehold on the ridgeline. The Thais knew they were expendable. Many had been on the PDJ or had friends who died there. Supplies were good, the bunkers were good, leadership was good, but Hardnose worried that some of the mercenaries might break and run if they faced two or three more nights like last night. Sky needed to do something. Vang Pao was holding out on committing his Hmong troops. Either more Thai volunteers were needed, or Lao irregular forces from the other MRs had to be called back to launch counterattacks. Something had to be done or, in couple of days, we would not have Skyline.

He left to talk with the Stick.

I sat looking at my typewriter. Goddamnit, I thought, that's it. I have to go up-country. I can't miss this next fight. I didn't sign on to do bullet reports. I wanted to be up-country. I wanted Skyline. To hell with being patient. If I waited, I might never get there.

Before leaving that night, I went into the Stick's office. He was leaning back in his chair with his feet on the desk. He was silent as he watched me walk up to his desk.

I said that I had asked him before about going up-country. He had told me to do my fucking job here and I understood and I had tried to do a good job. . . .

"But," he interrupted, "you want to go up to the valley." He reached for a stick on his desk and began slapping his leg. "You're fucking stupid, you know that? You want to get your ass shot. All the problems I've faced today, and you come in with some personal fucking problem. No one cares what you want."

I didn't take my eyes off him. I didn't want to be turned away again, but I couldn't think of anything else to say.

"Okay," he said after a pause, "I'll see what I can do. Get out of here."

Two days later, an officer who had not been in MR II long came down to Udorn to take over the MR II desk, and I was reassigned north to Long Tieng.

Before dawn the following day, I was on the tarmac in front of the CIA headquarters building in Udorn with the other Sky officers who had commuted in from MR II the previous night. We boarded a small cargo plane and arrived in the vicinity of LS 272, the new rear base, as the sun was coming up over the mountains. A low morning fog covered the area. We circled overhead for some time before the pilot could find the runway and land.

The first Sky contingent on the ground that morning, we were greeted by the local guards, stretching and yawning as they emerged from their bunkers around the airstrip. Two Quonset huts and four collapsible trailers sat along a meandering river on the north side of the runway. On the south side were Poppa Chu's mess hall, a supply area, the rigging shed, and the ammo dump.

Lao farmers were already at work in the rice fields around the runway. Monkeys and birds chattered in the surrounding mountains. There was a musty, outdoorsy smell in the air—up-country Laos. I started humming, "Nothing could be finer than to be in Carolina in the morn-n-n-n-ing."

I was just coming out of Poppa Chu's with a cup of coffee when a CASI Twin Otter pulled to a stop near one of the Quonset huts. The first off was Dick J., the base chief, followed by other Sky officers, and they all went into the hut. When I joined them, several officers were at the map board along the rear wall. Dutch was drawing new enemy designations in the river valley north of Skyline. I assumed this meant that overnight intelligence had indicated the presence of more North Vietnamese joining the attack force.

Digger was defending a proposal, developed by Vang Pao during the past few days, to move four of the Hmong GMs out of the valley to positions north and east of the river valley in order to put pressure on the North Vietnamese. He said it made sense; the four GMs weren't doing any good in the valley now except acting as a psychological blocking force to keep the Thais on Skyline.

Lumberjack, one of the new Sky officers with the Thais, said that he had a point—move the Hmong out on the wings and his troops might just break and run off the ridgeline.

Possibly, Dick said, Vang Pao had given up hope that the Thais could hold the ridge. If they came pell-mell down the valley and the North Vietnamese moved in and controlled the high ground along the ridge, the 130-mms would open up again and blow the valley apart. Which might be the reason, he suggested, that Vang Pao wanted his forces out—not to put pressure on the Vietnamese in the river valley but to get his troops out of the bull's-eye.

Bag said Hog thought V. P. wanted to get his people out of the valley because Hmong guerrillas shouldn't try to hold ground, especially in low valleys. Long Tieng and Skyline were only important because they represented a line we had drawn in the mountains. Vang Pao wanted a less rigid defense.

"Will he attack the flanks of the Vietnamese if he pulls his GMs out?" Dick asked. "Plus," he went on, "aren't the Thais going to get the feeling that they're being abandoned, that there's nothing to protect anymore?"

A couple of Air America pilots came in with coffee and sat down to listen.

"Let the Hmong go," Digger said. "The Stick said we can call in GMs from the other MRs again to help the Thais on the ridge. I say, let's go with a plan to move the Hmong forces. We have to protect them. I have always believed that the mission of the Vietnamese here is to destroy our Hmong force. Destroy them, and we're left with pretty damn few choices to defend this country. It makes sense to save the Hmong.''

Dick finally sighed and said he would go up and talk with Vang Pao later that day and then go down to see the Stick.

An Air America helicopter kicker walked in and asked one of the Sky officers working with the Thais to help him prioritize the delivery of supplies. He added that all the choppers were on the ground and the pilots were in Poppa Chu's.

The officers gradually left, leaving Dick and me alone in the Quonset hut.

He expressed some mock surprise over my interest in coming up north when I had such a cushion job in an air-conditioned office, but he said he was glad to have me on board. Some of the case officers were due for reassignment this summer, including Ringo, and he would eventually move me to a GM. In the meantime, he said he wanted me to be an outrider to the battle on Skyline.

Drawing arrows west, southwest, and south away from the PDJ on the map, Dick said, ''When we were run off of the plateau in December, Hmong families who had been farming and trading in that area moved away,'' pointing to his arrows, ''and are now scattered in the mountains. Find them for me, make contact, debrief them on Vietnamese and Pathet Lao movement in the area. Give them radios, weapons, ammunition, and training. Encourage them to move back toward the PDJ, to patrol, to find the enemy, to fight 'em.''

He pointed to several areas of known concentrations of civilians and said there were many more. Vang Pao had a loosely organized militia force, the Opération de L'Armée de Défense (ADO) headquartered southeast of Long Tieng, that provided security to Hmong villagers.

"Meet the Hmong commander of the ADO and get him involved," he said. "Help wherever you can out there to engage the Hmong citizenry in our efforts. Use fixed-wing planes—Porters and Twin Otters—we need the helicopters for Long Tieng. Most villages have airstrips, you don't need much ground to land Porters.

"Va Xiong will be your ops assistant. Plus, there are a couple more—I don't know their names—Khu Sao is one. You'll have a couple or three Hmong working for you. Hire more if you need them. Check out what you need from supply. Let me know if you want anything else. Take one of those AR-15s over there or 9-mms or whatever you're comfortable with."

He went to the door and yelled for Va Xiong. The young Hmong, who would have to stand on his tiptoes to reach five feet, came bouncing into the Quonset hut toward me with a wide smile. He stuck out his hand before we were introduced. Dick threw me a map and told me to go out and do good.

My short, friendly ops assistant and I went out to the supply area and took stock of the equipment on hand. There were crates of carbines, assault rifles, mortars, 3.5-inch rocket launchers, and tons of ammunition on pallets. In one of the shelters were radios, mostly old PRC-25s, but also a few handheld walkie-talkies. We found uniforms, panchos, and web gear in another shelter. There was no one around who appeared to be in charge. Nearby in the rigging shed, Shep was preparing supplies for delivery to the Thais. I yelled to him and asked what to do if I needed any of this stuff. He looked around curiously, as if he didn't understand my question, and shrugged. Va said Sky people just went in and got what they wanted, or they told Shep what they wanted and he got it together. There was nobody to ask. Va also looked as if he didn't quite understand what I was asking.

Not like the U.S. Army, I thought.

Va and I walked over to Papa Chu's. We laid out a map of the area around Long Tieng and began talking about what we could do. He said we would have to use a carrot-and-stick approach with the ADO. They did not have a good reputation—some young Hmong joined the militia to get out of duty in the GMs. In the field, ADO forces were not very aggressive and were often reluctant to attack the enemy. The ADOs that Va had been working with before my arrival were from villages due south of the PDJ. The villages west of the PDJ were not well identified or organized and had only a few radios and old weapons. Va knew the area well because he had grown up in the region. Pathet Lao and North Vietnamese forces operated throughout the mountains there, and we had to be careful where we landed.

We had to be careful where we flew too, he added. The previous week, Va had been in a small fixed-wing aircraft during the search for 555, an Air America C-123 that went down on a resupply mission and had not been found. The plane that Va was on came through some clouds at Site 37 near a friendly village. As he and the pilot began to search the ground for signs of the downed plane, they were caught beneath low cloud cover in a dead-end valley and started taking AK-47 fire. Rounds whizzed through the wing and came through the bottom of the fuselage. They had to bank inside of a cloud to turn around and get down-valley. Va said we had to be careful of situations like that in the entire area west of the PDJ.

We went back to the airstrip. Dutch was running Air Ops at LS 272 and assigned me a Porter for the first of my many flights to locate and organize the Hmong villagers. Porter aircraft, built in the United States under license from Pilatus Company in Switzerland, had single props, with dependable engines and long, wide wings that allowed them to glide effortlessly among the mountains. They were referred to as STOL (short takeoff and landing) planes because they could come in softly on short strips, and a pilot could stop within forty or fifty feet by reversing the engine. The planes were versatile, with a parachute drop hole in the middle of the cargo section. In MR II, a single pilot flew each plane and the copilot chair was turned around to face the cargo section in the rear. That was the seat I took as we left LS 272 and soared above the clouds.

The weather was clear over Long Tieng and to the west of the PDJ, so we took our initial reconnaissance there. Skyline ridge was clearly visible in the far distance. The reinforced bunkers on top, though low to the ground, had hard corners and stood out in contrast to the cleared, rugged terrain around them. Because of the rain, the dirt excavated in their construction had drained down both sides of the ridgeline, like teared mascara. As we flew by to the west, the battle continued to rage for the ridgeline. We could hear the radio transmissions of the Thais reporting on enemy movements and adjusted artillery fire. Air America, CASI, and Sky were busy on other frequencies as they coordinated delivery of supplies and evacuation of the wounded.

We flew farther north by the abandoned village of Sam Thong and north of that to LS 15, to which V. P. had suggested moving some of his GMs. Scattered about between these two points were small clusters of huts. Off in the distance to the east was the PDJ.

Slowly, we crisscrossed the area. Va occasionally heard a radio transmission from the huts below and identified the settlement, usually by the name of the village chief (Ni Ban). At some villages, small airstrips had been cut into the sides of mountains.

The pilot pointed out areas that Air America considered hostile. He thought some of these villagers changed their spots when the Pathet Lao moved in. The area could be friendly one day, and the next they'd shoot you out of the sky. Va was quick to say no; he'd never heard of that. He added that sometimes the Hmong would move out when they were threatened and leave the area open for Pathet Lao, but the Hmong didn't change their allegiance.

Va received a call that was louder than the rest, and the person on the ground had a different accent. He turned to me and said Father Bouchard asked for my call sign. He wanted to talk to me. I didn't know what my call sign was and I didn't know Father Bouchard, but Va handed me the radio anyway.

In a Boston accent, the caller said, "Hello, Sky. Welcome. I'm down here on a trail heading north to a little place I haven't been to in some time, and it sure is nice to look up and see that ol' A.A. on the side of that bird. Nice to see you." I asked if he needed anything.

"Oh no, no, I've got everything I want, right here. Just wanted to say hi. Hope to meet you soon. Good-bye now."

Va said Father Luke Bouchard was the best man in the world. He had lived among the Hmong since the early 1950s, spoke their language, and was an expert in treating people with leprosy and in helping women through difficult deliveries. Whenever it was felt that a pregnant woman was about to have an abnormal childbirth, Father Bouchard was called. He was known to have walked along mountain trails for days without stopping for rest to be at the bedside of some simple Hmong woman, often arriving to find that the delivery had gone without problems or that there had been problems and he was too late. Va said that he was the most loved and respected American in the mountains of Laos.

I told the pilot the good father put things a little more into perspective. I was beginning to think I was going to be the Marco Polo of the region, but I was a Johnny-come-lately, still an FNG.

Va kept up a running narrative on the background of the various settlements below, some of which were abandoned. The Hmong were slash-and-burn subsistence farmers. They moved into an area, burned acreage to plant their field rice, and homesteaded until the ground no longer nourished new growth. Then, they moved on. Slashing and burning coincided with the changing of the seasons and resulted in the smoky haze, or smoky season. The haze was the bane of Air America because it increased the dangers of flying in the mountains over contested areas. The enemy welcomed it, however, because the smoky season meant more dependable cover for their activities on the ground than even the rainy season.

Returning to LS 272, I asked Va about himself. He said his father was a well-known regional chief (Ni Khong) appointed by Vang Pao to coordinate the activities of the Ni Bans southwest of Long Tieng. Va would have had a chance to follow as a headman in due course, but he had elected to attend school in Vientiane, the political capital of the country, where he studied French and English and was graduated with honors. Rather than pursue employment in the capital, he returned to the mountains to help his people. He was referred to Hog by another Hmong who lived near Long Tieng and accepted Hog's offer of employment. The Hmong considered it a high honor to work for Sky. Because of Va's job, his father's prestige increased among his followers.

For the next few days, I left Udorn at first light and did not return until 2100 or 2200. If the Air America shuttle van was not around when we landed, I had to walk to the edge of the air base to get a taxi and I did not get home until about 2300. Almost every plane flying south at night carried body bags that contained Thai mercenaries killed during the previous twenty-four hours. This gruesome cargo was a grim reminder of the ultimate cost of war.

Va and I continued our reconnaissance of the countryside with a variety of Air America Porter pilots and tried to fix the friendly and hostile areas. Because we found the villages south of the PDJ more settled and less responsive, we concentrated our efforts to the west of the PDJ, where most of the new settlements were.

The battle for Skyline continued. Documents were found on some dead North Vietnamese soldiers that encouraged them to fight diligently: Long Tieng was to be captured this season by the North Vietnamese "at all costs."

Vang Pao prevailed in the debate over deployment of his forces and moved four GMs out of the valley. Suddenly, my areas were overrun with Hmong soldiers.

We were flying south of the PDJ one afternoon when Hog called and asked if we would go to LS 15 and pick up a Hmong commander needed for a planning session in Long Tieng. Although fighting continued along Skyline ridge, Porters landed regularly and parked in the protective shadows of rock karsts around Air Ops. Larger resupply planes, the C-130s and the C-123s, did not come in, however, because of the occasional 130-mm gunfire.

When we landed in Long Tieng with the commander, I commandeered a Jeep for the ride to Hog's bunker on top of the south ridge. Surprisingly, I passed huts occupied by Hmong families. When the GMs pulled out, some villagers had returned to look after family homes, but the place was still mostly a ghost town. Thai artillery fired irregularly as I drove up the hill. When I got closer to Hog's bunker, I noticed more bomb craters, testimony that the North Vietnamese had attempted to hit this prominent position with their 130-mm guns.

Inside, the bunker was similar to Redcoat's at Bouam Long—dirty and cluttered with weapons, smoke canisters, C-rations, bunks, maps, and radios. I laid out my map and pointed out to Hog the various concentrations of Hmong civilians in the area west of the PDJ. Va stood behind me. Hog, making comments about a few Ni Bans he knew, said that Va's father was a Romeo in the area and had a slew of wives, some younger than Va.

Suddenly, we heard the heavy whine of a large incoming shell, followed immediately by a tremendous explosion. Dust drifted down from the top of the bunker. I looked out of the front ports of the bunker and saw a dust cloud rising off to the side like the mushroom of a small atomic bomb. The round had landed on the eastern end of the runway, away from where our Porter was parked behind a karst.

Bamboo came in from another earthen room off the main area of the bunker. "Damned nuisance," he said. While Hog was on one radio talking with a Thai ops assistant on Skyline about counter-battery fire, Bamboo picked up the binoculars and looked at the site where the round landed. He went to another radio and asked someone to check on casualties. Bag was up in a helicopter and called in the coordinates where one of the pilots spotted what might have been a muzzle flash from the North Vietnamese 130-mm gun that had fired the round.

Hog turned to me when he had finished and asked, "What's your call sign?"

"I haven't got one yet," I said.

Hog continued to look at me. "Well?"

"Well, what?"

"Give me one. Who do you want to be?"

I had thought about my call sign, of course, but I had assumed Hog or Dick would assign something. Like the supply at LS 272, I expected things to be issued. The only name that came to mind was Cottonpicker, my boyhood hunting partner, but here with these people it suddenly sounded too silly. Shouldn't have been—I was looking at an individual called Hog and over there was Bamboo and Bag was just on the air. What was wrong with Cottonpicker?

"I'm just a small-town boy from North Carolina. Never wanted to be much," I said with a heavy southern accent. I was looking for an opening to suggest Cottonpicker.

Bamboo bayed, "Mule. He's a mule. The Mule."

"Mule it is," said Hog turning back to the radio.

Later in the Porter after leaving the valley, I had the opportunity to use my call sign and I blushed, hesitant, and had to repeat it several times before I made myself understood. It was more than a radio call sign. I had been Red Cap Twigs Alfa November Six with my Army platoon in Vietnam—that was a call sign. Here, my call sign was my name. In MR II, I stopped being Jim or Parker or the FNG. I was Mule—to Air America, to the Hmong, to other Sky officers. Getting my Long Tieng name was proof of residence. It was like getting my badge when I first joined the Agency in Langley and, later, my in-house alias.

Mule.

Within the week, I flew with Va to LS 353 to meet the ADO commander, Col. Youa Va Ly. He was a venerable old Hmong who started out working for the French with Vang Pao. He was known as a brave man who had taken to drink, a failing that affected his judgment and made him dangerous. He had also become ruthless, which made him a liability. Sky did not condone unnecessary force. Consequently, he was assigned to the ADO, rather than to a line GM.

Among the many stories Va told me about the man was an incident many years ago when he landed at Long Tieng, then a rear base. The colonel became excited when he saw a Hmong workman, on a bulldozer, clearing an area beside the runway. He jumped off the plane, walked up to the dozer, pulled out his .45 caliber pistol, and shot the driver dead. Unfortunately, on instructions from someone else, the bulldozer driver had been clearing an area that was part of the colonel's family burial plot.

The colonel was sober the day we arrived, but his face showed the ravages of a life in the mountains. His voice was raspy; his hands shook. We sat in his straw-thatched house most of the day and talked about the Hmong civilians around the PDJ. We decided that I would give him a radio that would net with Va at LS 272. He would contact the villages south of the PDJ every day and call in a situation report to Va at dawn. I was interested in any sightings or any contact with the enemy—Pathet Lao or North Vietnamese. In order to accomplish a similar mission in the area west of the PDJ, Colonel Ly agreed to provide ADO soldiers who would travel north out of the far western end of Long Tieng valley, away from the fighting at Skyline, to contact the closest village to the north. This patrol would ensure that the landing strip near the village was clear of mines and the area was secure enough for a Porter to land so that I could visit it. We would then contact neighboring settlements by sending out men from that first village and continue until we netted all the villages west of the PDJ.

As it turned out, Va found the ADO soldiers that we needed for the assignment in Long Tieng, and we didn't have to rely on the colonel's men. Two days later, we dispatched them with radios, new weapons, maps, marking panels, and smoke canisters to contact Moung Phun, a village about ten miles north of Long Tieng. Once they arrived and determined the area to be safe, they were to call us and lay out panels that I provided to form two letters, LL. These panels were the safety signal. I explained to them that if they were captured by less than friendly villagers who wanted to do us harm and who would be beside them when they made radio contact with us, the fact that they did not lay out the panels would tell us it was not safe to come in. This was our secret—they were to lay out the LL signal only if the area was absolutely safe.

I had just landed at Long Tieng, after my first check on the ADO patrol's progress, when Father Bouchard came across the ramp and shook my hand. He said I was a person he wanted to know because I was out there everywhere and so was he. Sometimes, I might be able to pick him up if I was going his way and he could get there faster. This might do some people some real good. He looked willowy and frail, not like a mountain-climbing saint.

"Oh, it's a wonderful place here," he added, "and the Hmong, they're good people, hardy and strong." He wished me well and went past Air Ops into a Hmong hut.

The ADO patrol made it to Moung Phun without problems and radioed back that it was safe for us to fly in. That day, I happened to draw a helicopter because all the Porters were needed to make drops for the Hmong GMs. Frenchy Smith was the pilot.

I should be so lucky to get Frenchy Smith, the original Mr. Smart Ass.

When I walked up to his chopper that morning and briefed him on the mission, he said, "Fuck you, Mule. I ain't going into no site that ain't secure."

I told him it was.

"How the hell do you know?" he asked.

"My patrol said it was."

"Patrol worked for you a long time, has it, that you bet your life on what it says? Maybe I think more about my life than you do yours. Maybe I've been up here longer than you have, and I know the questions to ask."

"Let's go up to the site," I said. "If you're not sure it's safe, don't go in. I don't want you to do anything you don't want to do."

He agreed, and we flew up to Moung Phun. As I was looking for the LL panels, our secret code that the area was absolutely safe, I saw something like TI near the edge of the village. I had told Frenchy about the safety signal, something I seriously regretted now that we were overhead. Va talked to the patrol over the radio; they put out IE and then II. While they were doing this I looked at the airstrip, because the patrol expected us to come in by fixed-wing. Two rows of villagers were walking down the strip shoulder to shoulder. Frenchy said, "Polish mine detectors." Va said they were having trouble with the panel markers because they couldn't spell LL. Super, I thought. Nothing like my first field operation getting off to a good start. Va said the settlement was, in fact, safe and secure. He'd bet his life on it.

Frenchy, living up to his reputation of being testy but effective, was slowly spiraling down, as the team continued to make two-letter combinations below. We noticed

Hmong standing on top of all the karsts and mountain peaks in the area, like Indians in a grade B cowboy movie, and we landed near what had become TL.

As I started to take off the customer headset, Frenchy said, "Don't worry, partner, nothing ever happens here exactly the way it's planned. You just gotta hang in, as they say, and keep on planning. You are lucky, ain't you?"

"I got a lucky dog," I responded.

"That's good enough," he said, turning and smiling. He promised to be back to pick us up by midafternoon. I took off the headset, and Frenchy lifted off. After his noisy helicopter was out of hearing, I noticed how quiet it was here on the edge of this native village and how alone I was among all these Hmong.

Va was talking with the patrol members, who were proud of the job they had done and unconcerned that they couldn't spell LL. It wasn't their fault—that letter wasn't in their alphabet.

Va knew the Ni Ban and introduced us. We were led to the largest thatched hut in the village where the Ni Ban lived with his several wives and dozen or so children. The Hmong are polygamous, brought on at times out of necessity—if a head of family dies, his widow and children are usually taken in by a brother. It was a common show of prominence, however, for the leaders or chief merchants of a village to take several wives, and they often married young girls of fourteen and fifteen.

The chief's wooden hut had a large center room lit by the front opening, with a cooking room and several lean-to sleeping areas off to the sides. There was a poignant, arresting smell of cooking and heating fires. Although the hut was dark and drab, it was warm and had a sense of community. The Ni Ban had prepared a feast, by his standards, and the food was laid out on a bamboo table in the center room. Although I had never seen some of the dishes before, I was game. After I had managed a portion of blood pudding, the main dish in the meal—the head of a chicken—was placed on my plate. I looked down at it with a blank expression. Va, sitting beside me, said the guest of honor got the chicken head. I smiled weakly, looked around the table, and then ate some of the meat on the neck. I didn't try the head.

After the meal, we talked about the local situation. The Ni Ban said that there were no friendly Hmong to the east, but settlements to the north supported Vang Pao. The closest friendly settlement was another ten miles north at the base of Red Mountain.

The Ni Ban said he did not have a radio and his weapons were a collection of old assorted French, Chinese, and American rifles, although his people hunted with the traditional Hmong muzzle-loaded muskets. He had limited ammunition. The settlement at the base of Red Mountain also had no radio and few weapons. I told him I would supply him with new equipment if he would send some of his people to the next settlement to give them a radio and help arrange for our visit there. I also wanted him to send in regular radio reports to Va at LS 272.

He agreed and, through Va, we went over the information I wanted him to provide. I said we were going to win the war; he said no, there was always war. In other conversation, as we waited for Frenchy to return, the Ni Ban asked me about rumors they had heard that some Americans had flown to the moon.

The battle for Skyline raged as the days progressed. I continued to pursue my relatively calm civic affairs work. When I flew near the valley, I could see dust clouds from incoming rounds that hit around the Thai positions and hear cryptic radio conversations: "Incoming." "Fire counter-battery to point XL." "We have wounded. We need Air America medivac or they die for sure." "We are out of grenades, we fight them with our hands. OK, no sweat." "Ten, twenty bad guys moving up that draw between CA and CW helipads, fire artillery, fire artillery."

True to V. P.'s promise, his Hmong were able to put some pressure on the rear positions of the Pathet Lao and the North Vietnamese who were moving on Skyline. U.S. Air Force bombers and fighters also inflicted some damage when the weather permitted, but the fight came down to the North Vietnamese crawling up the north slope of Skyline and the Thais holding their positions on the high ground. The 130-mm gunfire continued to pound the ridgeline and the valley beyond.

In March, North Vietnamese tanks began maneuvering up the Sam Thong road toward Skyline. Two tanks were destroyed near the western end of the ridgeline by the Thais' antitank mines and rockets, and the rest fell back.

At night, Sky officers alternated duty in a Volpar that circled over the valley to augment the U.S. Air Force radio platform. The Stick wanted Sky people coordinating communications to the Thai and Hmong positions. He also wanted a controlled, direct link to Hog and the other Sky officers in the bunker on the south ridge and to the Thai headquarters bunker. Whether the Thais could hold Skyline was still in question.

All officers not on duty in the Volpar or in the valley had to go through Vientiane in late March to brief Ambassador G. McMurtrie Godley, nicknamed the Field Marshal. Although he did not advise us about how to do our jobs, he expressed continuing concerns that we must not lose Skyline. He saw it as the dam holding back the North Vietnamese in the mountains that prevented them from marching south to the Lao capital.

In early April, with the rainy season just days off, the North Vietnamese got another toehold on Skyline and captured one of the most forward of the Thai positions.

Less than two days later, elements of two GMs arrived in the valley, one from MR I and the other from MR III. They were a combination of ethnic Lao hill tribesmen and overland Chinese, both well trained and responsive. Brought into the valley by troop carrier aircraft, they walked up the winding road to the top of Skyline. By midday, they began moving slowly down the ridgeline, amid the Thai positions, toward the one captured by the Vietnamese. It was a welcome relief column. The two Sky advisers, Tahn and the Sword, stayed in Hog's bunker and maintained contact with their lead elements. As dusk fell, they moved close to the captured Thai position, but they had encountered clusters of Vietnamese all along the ridgeline. Every yard had been contested.

That evening, the Sword joined the rest of us for our briefing session with the ambassador. Tahn stayed with Hog.

Until now, our briefings had been short, lean, and heavy on nouns and verbs. We did not dissemble; we answered Godley's questions completely, but we were brief.

The Sword did not pick up on this tone. He was dramatic. He and his GM had saved Skyline. According to him, the whole of the war in Indochina had turned on the arrival of his people to the ridgeline. He briefed as if he was auditioning for the lead in a war movie. He spoke louder than the rest, used more hand gestures, paused more for effect, and implied in his closing statement that the next day his GM would rouse the Vietnamese from the Thai position and pursue them down the north slope of Skyline and up the river valley to the PDJ.

The ambassador looked around at the rest of us as if to ask why we couldn't have done this. There was some small sense of guilt among us in MR II because, in fact, we couldn't do it; we had to call on forces in the other MRs. But we knew the sacrifices and casualties our Hmong GMs had incurred in fighting the enemy every day for years. They would still be needed in the area after the battle for Skyline was won or lost. The GMs from the other MRs were fresh and, at this time, unchallenged in their home areas. Bringing them in was part of the chess game aspect of the war in Laos. The North Vietnamese would move, and we would countermove. Or we would move, and the North Vietnamese would countermove. We built bunkers on the PDJ to withstand the NVA units traditionally committed to our theater, and then they brought in more troops and tanks and 130-mm guns to gain the advantage. They sent enough troops and ammunition down the river valley from the PDJ to Skyline to take the ridgeline defended by the soldiers we traditionally kept in MR II, and then we brought in the soldiers from the other GMs to give us the advantage. Move, countermove.

The Sword's GM was pinned down the next day and could not maneuver. He did not go down for the briefing. Tahn did and explained to the ambassador that the GMs were pinned down and could not move. Concise, good briefing—the ambassador was disappointed.

The following day, the two GMs retook the Thai position, with the loss of several men, and the Sword briefed that night with a flourish. He explained how his men maneuvered under murderous fire to the door of the position and there, after throwing in grenade after grenade, they charged the door and beat the remaining North Vietnamese inside in hand-to-hand combat.

Better than TV, Digger said on the way out. He hadn't realized before the entertainment value of our work.

Within the week, Skyline ridge was completely under friendly control again and the Thais could move freely from position to position. The enemy's 130-mm guns and other howitzers, however, continued to fire on the various positions and into the valley. To preempt any further North Vietnamese efforts to make an end-around play against Skyline, two additional GMs were brought in from Savannakhet.

Electric left, and a new case officer arrived to work with the Thais. The first day, he wanted to go up to his unit. He went down to the helipad in front of Hog's position and waited for a helicopter.

Frenchy flew in. The young case officer went up to

Air America helicopter delivering Hmong to a forward position. (Courtesy Dick J.)

Hmong soldiers in movement inside a fixed-wing Air America airplane. (Courtesy Dick J.)

A North Vietnamese prisoner under the watchful eye of a Hmong guard. (Courtesy Dick J.)

GM 22 position near the PDJ. At that time, the Hmong were bait as they waited for the NVA to attack.

T-28 that crashed into the Air Ops building. Mule and Digger pulled the pilot from the cockpit. (Courtesy Digger)

A T-28, loaded with bombs, taking off from the Long Tieng airstrip. (Courtesy Dick J.)

A Porter, flown by Matt Daddio, after it hit a mine on the Red Mountain airstrip. (Courtesy of Civil Air Transport/Air America Archives, University of Texas, Dallas)

Fire along the Long Tieng airstrip that started from an incoming NVA 130-mm artillery round. Earlier that day, an NVA artillery round had landed in the same general spot and killed eighteen Thai mercenaries waiting for a helicopter lift to fighting positions on Skyline ridge. (Courtesy Hardnose)

GM 23 soldier, approximately fourteen years old. He was certainly assigned duty at night to squat in holes on the forward slope of defensive positions and roll grenades down toward the advancing enemy. (Courtesy Digger)

View of the Long Tieng airfield, looking east. The ramp is in the left foreground. The Sky compound is on the right around the tall karst.

A North Vietnamese soldier killed in the Long Tieng valley. (Courtesy Dick J.)

Young Hmong soldier, wounded at a forward position, being loaded onto an Air America helicopter. (Courtesy Civil Air Transport/Air America Archives. University of Texas, Dallas)

Greek (seated) and Ringo (standing) on the south slope of the Long Tieng valley as the North Vietnamese attack Skyline. Greek is coordinating Air America helicopter resupply to the fighting positions of the Thai mercenaries. (Courtesy Digger)

Mule coming into the Sky compound from the field with a captured SKS carbine.

the helicopter and yelled over the noise that he wanted to go up to the CD pad.

Frenchy said, "So does the Queen Mother. Why you want to go to CD?"

The case officer said loudly that that's where his men were. Frenchy asked if anyone had told the FNG that CD was taking a lot of fire, mortar and howitzer.

"Yes," he said loudly, "I've been told."

"And you still want to visit your men?" Frenchy asked.

"Yes, it's my job," he said, standing taller.

"Well," said Frenchy, who, for some reason, could be understood over the noise of the helicopter without yelling, "I have to go into another area near CD so I'll drop you off, but I will tell you, son, that I will be skids down for only three seconds on that pad. You get off then. It'll be your only chance. I'll be back in for three seconds later on in the day to pick you up. That's it, and it's a better deal than any of the other pilots will give you. What's your call sign anyway, FNG?"

"No Man," yelled the young officer.

On the way up to the pad, Frenchy called Hog and asked who named this dude Norman. Hog said it was not Norman. It was No Man, and he didn't know who named him.

"No Man, yes ma'am, this guy's sitting in the back of my helicopter like a school kid waiting for the bell to go home. He thinks three seconds is not long. Three seconds is a long, long time."

Frenchy gained altitude behind the karst at the eastern end of the runway. When he got above CD, he came out of a turn and, making a sudden dash into the pad, flared out some fifty meters away to arrest his air speed. The kicker in the back opened the door to the helicopter so that he could stick his head out and help the pilot land.

No Man, feeling the helicopter come almost to a halt and seeing the kicker open the door, thought the helicopter was on the ground or almost, and he went charging out the door. He wanted to establish a reputation from the first day of being someone who didn't cause problems, who would use only, say, one second of a three-second skids down window to do something.

The helicopter, fifty feet from the pad and closing, was fifty feet off the side of the mountain. No Man ran out into the air, fell to the side of Skyline, and rolled halfway down the south slope.

Frenchy said, "Where'd that sumbitch go?"

In Udorn, Brenda was enjoying her role as mother. She waited for me each night to tell me incredible stories about Mim and Joe—how they were relating, learning English, and laughing and crying.

She was worried that Mim's mother might suddenly appear and, claiming a mother's natural right, take Mim away. Brenda said she would die if anything happened to her new daughter. Because of her concerns and because the sixteen- and eighteen-hour work days were wearing me down, I asked Dick about moving my family to Vientiane. He agreed and received approvals from Udorn. Brenda was left to her own devices, however, to travel to Vientiane, find a house, negotiate a lease, and move the car, dog, kids, and household effects across the Mekong River into Laos.

She flew up on 50-Kip and taxied around Vientiane looking for houses for rent. She soon found quarters within our budget and arranged with the Udorn office to have the family moved north. Labor was cheap in Thailand, but it was even cheaper in Laos. She hired two maids and a gardener for under fifty dollars a month for the group, and they moved into the servant quarters in the back. With the guards who were provided by the embassy, it was like coming home to a department store at night; there were so many people and so much going on. Maids, guards, gardeners, the dog, wife, children. It was a happy place.

Brenda was brought into the tight sorority of Vientiane

wives whose husbands worked up-country. Her days were filled with mothering the kids, shopping, running the house, playing bridge, and socializing with the other wives. It was an unusually robust, intriguing life for her. She always seemed so happy as she stood on the porch with the kids when I came home at night.

The U.S. Air Force bore down on the North Vietnamese as they pulled back from Skyline and licked their wounds. After being rousted from the Thai position, they eventually retreated up the river valley to the PDJ. Their offensive for this season was over.

We had lost ground, but overall we were not disappointed with the way the battle had gone. The North Vietnamese had taken the PDJ, but they had not taken Skyline. Our forces were intact. We had done our job by tying up two divisions of NVA mainline forces.

The focus of the American involvement in Indochina continued to be South Vietnam. Ours was a sideshow, out of the public eye and generally ignored by the media in gauging the progress of the war. The men who worked up-country Laos did not consider their contributions in terms of the developing overall U.S. strategy in the region. Most had served with the U.S. military in Vietnam, where their work had been roundly criticized at home and perceived to be a slowly losing effort. Laos was more rewarding for us. As the North Vietnamese pulled back, the few of us who worked the area took personal pride in the Thai mercenaries coming out of their Skyline bunkers and firing their guns in the air because they had held—the North Vietnamese had not taken Skyline. It was an insulated, contained, personal victory. We had won our battle this season.

8

VILLAGE MILITIA

In late March 1972, young men from Moung Phun, the village that Va and I had first visited, made contact with a temporary settlement located at the base of Red Mountain and gave the Ni Ban there one of our new radios. When we next flew up, Va and I had extended radio conversations with the Ni Ban. Matt Daddio, an Air America Porter pilot, flew for us almost every day. Jovial and even-tempered, he seemed to have a special rapport with his flying machine. Occasionally, he feathered the prop, and the plane soared as the wind took us along its course. When we talked with people on the ground, Daddio slowly banked the plane in an easy circle. He appeared not to move at all, as he held the stick against his leg. To him, flying was a natural act.

The Ni Ban of the temporary settlement said there was no place near his lowland village to build an airstrip. He suggested an abandoned landing strip, LS 90, on top of Red Mountain. He could send men to the top to secure the high ground, but he had only a collection of old rifles and needed more weapons, mortars, and grenades.

Va knew that the home area of this Ni Ban was on the other side of Red Mountain in a valley now controlled by a joint Pathet Lao and North Vietnamese unit. It was a reasonable proposition to supply him with the weapons he requested so that he could secure the mountaintop in a gradual move back to the eastern valley. When we told him this, he said, "Give us weapons, and we'll go home."

Back at LS 272, I collected carbines and assault rifles, plus some claymore mines, radios, and batteries, and asked Shep to rig them for a drop from the Porter. Later that day, Daddio flew us over the settlement with two loads to drop. The first load, in the drop bay in the back of the Porter, had a parachute on top and a static line running to the side of the plane. The other load was behind it at the rear of the bay area.

As we made a run over the small field where the Ni Ban wanted the supplies dropped, Daddio noticed unusual wind currents coming up from the draws. He said he would have to make a steep dip near the field so that the supplies would land on target and not be carried by the currents into the nearby mountainside or down into the deep ravines. Coming around after making the trial run, he reached behind his seat and grabbed the handle to release the bomb doors beneath the drop bay. He lined up with the field, figured for the wind, dipped the plane's nose, and dove toward the field. He pulled the handle as he bottomed out of his dive and brought the plane back up. The load dropped out of the bomb bay, and the static line caught, pulling open the parachute. As Daddio began to come around for his second drop, we watched the load drift down almost into the hands of the Hmongs below.

Because the second load was mostly heavy ammunition, I had volunteered to manhandle it into the drop bay. I was in the back, and Va was sitting in the reversed seat beside Daddio. I pulled the static line in from the first bundle and, as Daddio closed the bay doors, quickly began to maneuver the next bundle into position. Daddio continued to come around and said that he would be on target within a few minutes.

The bundle was heavier than I thought. I had problems moving it in the cramped compartment, and it got stuck at the edge of the bay. I pushed and shoved and kicked, groaned and cussed, but the bundle would not move into the bay. Daddio said he was going to be on target in one minute. I stood over the bundle, grabbed the sides, lifted up, and moved it forward, edging it into the bay. When I stepped down into the bay to lift it up again, something gave a little bit under my feet. I reached for the load and pulled it forward with two hands as I stepped up. The edge of the bundle tipped forward and then down, striking the bottom of the bay. Suddenly, the doors fell open and the bundle was gone, free-falling to the side of the mountain below, with the static line acting as a streamer.

My knees were shaking as I straddled the open bay and watched the ground rushing by below me. Va reached out and grabbed my pistol belt, and Daddio closed the bay doors.

This was not my first near encounter with death. I had been only inches away from it on a number of occasions in Vietnam—often unscathed when other men died around me. But why this wasn't my time to go, I didn't know. I had been standing in the bay pushing up on the bundle and down on the doors. They should have burst through.

All I could think of was a well-known story that had come out of Pakxe, Laos, in MR IV. A road-watch team had moved in too close to the Ho Chi Minh trail and was discovered by North Vietnamese trail guards. The Sky officer, in a fixed-wing plane, received a situation report not long after the patrol started maneuvering to get away from the North Vietnamese. The patrol leader said that it appeared to him that they were cut off to the west and he was forced to head back east to find some place to hide and wait out his pursuers. He said he was going off the air to save his batteries, and then he disappeared.

The Sky officer flew the area every day for the next two weeks—looking for the patrol and calling it on the radio—without luck. Weeks later, he was back in the area on other business and picked up a very faint signal from the road-watch team. The signal led him to the Ho Chi

Minh trail and then east of the trail into Vietnam. On the side of a bomb crater, he saw a panel laid out by the team leader. Over the faint radio signal, the leader said most of his men had been killed but he and a couple more were still alive. They badly needed food, medicine, batteries, and ammo.

At Pakxe, while the Sky officer was having the supplies rigged, the village chief from the area where the road-watch team had been recruited happened by. The chief was ecstatic that the team had been found and asked to go on the flight so that he could say a few words to the men. Flying high over the bomb crater, the pilot said that he would make a low run from south to north. With one pass, they might get away without being hit; twice over the same area so near the trail would certainly result in being shot, as well as giving away the position of the team. Two bundles had to be kicked out during the one pass.

The village chief was in the back to help the Air America kicker get the two bundles out the door. Approaching the bomb crater, they kicked out the first bundle. Unfortunately, as they were rushing to get the second bundle out the door, the village chief was caught in some of the straps and jerked out the door. He fell to his death before the parachute bundle reached the ground.

There was nothing they could do in the plane but gain altitude and move off to the west. After a short pause, the patrol leader, booming loud with his new batteries, came on the air. He said he was thankful for the food, medicine, and ammo, but, he asked, "Why did you send the village chief?"

When I sat down in the back of the Porter after Daddio had closed the bay doors, I was thankful that I had not put these people in the same quandary. "Why did you send the Sky man?" they might have asked.

We supplied the Ni Ban later that day with a new load of ammunition and figured that it would take a full week for his people to secure the top of the mountain. Va suggested that, while we were waiting, we pick up a Jeep he had found near LS 353 and drive it to LS 272. Va lived a couple of miles from LS 272 with Bea, his wife of less than a year, and he had to walk to the airfield every night and every morning. We had almost all the supplies needed to do our jobs and always received any additional items requested, but I had been reluctant to ask Dick about a Jeep for Va because of our plans to move back into the Long Tieng valley. This seemed like a good opportunity for him.

I told Va to take off a couple of days and get the Jeep. I'd send him to LS 353 on a Porter. He thought things would go better if I came along. He was unfamiliar with the territory between 353 and 272, although he knew it to be secure, and he was worried that he might run into someone along the way who would want the Jeep. If a Sky man was along, there'd be no problem. It would take only one day.

"One day? We can get a jeep from 353 to 272 in one day?" I asked. "Over that big mountain in between? And it's secure?"

"Yep," he said. He continued to look at me without blinking, but I sensed he wasn't being completely honest about something.

Two days later when I flew in from Vientiane, Va was waiting with a mechanic, plus three other large Hmongs, some rope, and gas. We took a Porter into LS 353 and walked to a hut on the edge of the village, where Va had found the stripped-down Jeep. The mechanic got it running, and we headed out of town. Then, the road stopped.

"No road, Va?" I asked.

"No road," he responded.

"We have to climb over a very large mountain in one day. And there is no road? You said we could do this in one day. And there's no road. We can't do this."

"Can do," Va said, looking straight ahead as the Jeep began to negotiate down the footpath into the valley be-

yond 353. It was a wide trail, but it was crowded with
people and we had to go slowly, sometimes straddling
the trail, sometimes on one side or the other. There were
no other vehicle tracks.

"Va, has anyone else ever driven a Jeep down this
trail that you know of?"

"No," he said, still looking straight ahead.

"Have you ever heard of a horse-drawn wagon going
down this trail?"

"No," he said.

We finally reached a village in a high valley. People
stared as we drove through it toward a river on the other
side. Some children were chasing one another around a
thatched hut. When they saw the six of us moving
through the center of their village in that slow-moving
Jeep, they stopped dead in their tracks. The Jeep could
have been a UFO. They simply couldn't believe their
eyes. It wasn't seeing an American that amazed them so
much—it was the Jeep. The Hmong, descendants of Chinese who had drifted south over the mountains, had no
experience with Western technology. They stood in awe
when planes flew overhead. Some who lived south of the
PDJ near villages with airstrips had flown in the planes,
but first-time flyers were always deathly afraid and always airsick. The majority of the Hmong, however, knew
nothing about world events, modern medicine, electricity,
or the internal combustion engine. This Jeep rolling
through their village was as strange to them as it might
have been to their Chinese ancestors in 500 B.C.

When we got to the river, we found people using a
swinging bridge and a log footwalk to cross. Neither, I
suggested to Va, was appropriate for a Jeep. A mountain
loomed large and forbidding on the other side.

I was on the point of saying that this was far enough
when the driver swung the wheel of the Jeep to one side
and took us on a four-wheel slide to the bottom of the
riverbank. We forged the river and headed up the footpath on the other side.

Soon, the trail became so narrow and the falloff to the side so severe that I said I was walking and the Jeep could follow along behind. I took off walking ahead, but the grade was so steep that I tired after only a few minutes. We were going too slow anyway, so I got back into the Jeep. The driver gunned the engine when he put it into gear—so as not to roll back down the trail—and almost sent us over the side.

I got out again and took one of the ropes and tied it to the back so that the Jeep could pull me along.

We climbed the mountain, and we climbed and we climbed. My hands were sore from holding onto the rope, but the top of the mountain was finally in sight. As we crested it, I saw that it was just a ridge and the mountain still loomed in front of us. The air was thin, and I was having trouble breathing. My hands were getting worse, too, so I got back in the Jeep.

At the next high ground, we found the mountain still going up, higher and higher. Before we reached the top, I had been fooled four more times.

Looking down the other side, I gasped. It went straight down. I was afraid that the Jeep would start tumbling end over end. The brakes couldn't possibly hold it. As I stood beside the Jeep, absolutely convinced that we could not travel down the trail before us, the Hmong got out and tied the rope to a nearby tree. The driver inched the Jeep slowly over the edge, and the Hmong began letting out the rope. This is how we made most of the trip to the bottom of the mountain, in increments along the length of the rope, as the driver guided the Jeep down the steep decline. The only one in the Jeep, he looked like a cartoon character waiting for the rope to snap and send him hurtling down the trail into the center of the earth.

We were near the bottom of the mountain when we saw a trailside stand ahead. An enterprising young Hmong girl was selling sundries. Like others on the trail, she was shocked speechless as we came slowly down the footpath. Possibly for a dozen generations, Hmong and

Lao had used that same trail to climb the mountain. They sometimes used small horses as pack animals, but I am sure there had never been a Jeep on the trail. Maybe, when Father Bouchard had walked this way for the first time, people had gawked at him like they looked at us, I don't know, but that girl had never seen a Jeep before.

We pulled up beside her stand, a small rough-hewn wooden table in front of a thatched shelter. Va asked her the price of a Pepsi. Six Pepsis sat on a bamboo shelf behind her, probably her prize merchandise. The mountain people used Pepsis for special occasions, much like Americans use champagne. She didn't answer but continued to look at each one of us and then back to the Jeep. When Va suggested 200 kip, she looked at him but said nothing. He counted out 1,200 kip and laid the money on the counter. We picked up the Pepsis and drove on down the trail, the girl still staring at us.

We were in the river valley on the other side of the mountain by late afternoon. It was apparent that we would not get back to LS 272 by nightfall if we continued down the footpath leading through the small settlements. According to my map, a creek meandered in the direction we were heading and emptied into the Nam Nung River, the last obstacle we had to face. I suggested we go down to the creek.

The Hmong phrase for "follow the river" sounds like "today" in English. While the mechanic charged along close to the side of the creek and sprayed water all over us, we kept up the chant, "Today, today, today."

Amid the chants, I said to myself, "Let me get back to LS 272 today, today, so Dick or Hog won't kill me tomorrow, tomorrow."

At the Nam Nung River, we loaded the Jeep on a raft ferry, gained the road on the other side, and sped down it toward LS 272. We arrived at dusk, just as the last of the Twin Otters was getting ready to take off for Vientiane.

Va picked me up the next morning in our Jeep, which we named "Today."

Within a few days, the Red Mountain Ni Ban had secured the high ground around site 90 and pushed off a small group of Pathet Lao to the east. I located a mobile Thai training team in Long Tieng to teach the Red Mountain Hmong how to use rocket launchers and mortars, and it accompanied us the first time we landed at the airstrip on top of the mountain.

The Ni Ban received us warmly. Although he didn't have much to offer in the way of a welcoming party ("baci"), we had a meal of rice and canned meat. Later, over hot beer, we tied strings on each other's wrists in the Hmong tradition to bring luck. Va and I left the Thai team there and returned to LS 272.

Two weeks later, on 5 April, we flew back in. For graduation, the Thai training team had the Hmong demonstrate their new mortar rocket launcher skills by hitting a rock formation that I picked at random on the east side of the mountain. We then worked out a plan with the Ni Ban to send some of his men on a reconnaissance into the valley toward the east.

Daddio was scheduled to pick us up in the Porter later that afternoon. He had told me before that he didn't like the site—it was not the highest point of the mountain, and rock formations on either side looked down on the dirt airfield and made it vulnerable. The PDJ was not too far in the distance, and there were no friendly forces between it and us.

To allay Daddio's concerns, the Ni Ban stationed men on top of each tall rock formation so that Daddio could see them as he circled before landing. When he landed, he motioned for all of us to get on quickly. The plane was rolling into the wind for takeoff as the last man crawled aboard.

At LS 272, Va and I went to the supply area and began collecting ammunition and web gear to outfit the Red

Mountain men for their reconnaissance. The material filled Daddio's Porter. There was room for only one of us to go. I nodded to Va because no one at the mountaintop spoke English.

On the flight up to the mountain, Daddio asked Va to open the side door to the plane as soon as they landed and to start kicking off the supplies when they came to a stop. Daddio said he didn't want to be on the ground for more than a minute. Although Va and I had just been there for several hours and felt it was completely safe, Va agreed without arguing.

As the Porter touched down, Va opened the sliding door on the side. At the end of the runway, the plane spun around and Va began to heave the supplies out the door. Within the minute—some of the Hmong were still running down to the strip to help—Va had the plane empty and Daddio gunned the engine to take off. Va moved back to the reverse seat next to Daddio.

As the plane gathered speed down the runway, the left wheel struck a mine. The explosion blew off the tire and one of the wing struts. The plane careened to the left toward a ravine.

Va forced open the forward door. He didn't know what had happened, but he was instantly aware that he would die if he stayed on the plane. It was reeling madly to the left, with the left wing almost touching the ground. He got a foot out the door and dove.

Daddio got his door open under the dipping wing and tumbled out, missing the rear stabilizer by inches as he bounced and rolled along the ground. Within seconds the plane hit the ravine and crashed behind him.

Thinking that they were under ground attack, Daddio got to his feet. He saw Va lying very still next to the runway and yelled. Va rolled over and sat up. He had broken ribs and shrapnel in his back and was in a daze. Daddio yelled again. He ran to the small ops assistant, picked him up, and ran off into the bush. He was joined by some of the Hmong from the position, and they climbed to the top of the small rise where Daddio slumped down, exhausted. Below, Daddio could see that the mine crater had slashed the airstrip from one side to the other.

Va gradually gathered his senses and sent the Hmong down to get their radio so Daddio could call a Mayday. Air America, hearing the distress signal, scrambled everyone for the rescue mission that brought Va and Daddio back to LS 272. Daddio was taken directly to Vientiane. Va, though more seriously hurt, was admitted to a local Hmong hospital.

Daddio would not be back for a year. He had to undergo a series of operations to repair broken bones and other damage to his body. Smiling when he came back, he called the incident an occupational hazard.

Va lay in the open air ward of the local hospital for days. The shrapnel was so near his spinal cord that the doctors were reluctant to operate for fear of causing permanent paralysis. His wife camped in a chair beside his bed, and his father moved into a nearby village.

I drove Today over every morning. When it became apparent that Va needed an operation requiring better facilities and possibly a more experienced team, I took a morning off in Vientiane and found a hospital where he could be treated. That evening, I returned to the LS 272 hospital to pick him up. Bea said she was going with him.

We loaded Va in a Jeep ambulance for the ride to the airstrip. His father, clutching a bag of Va's clothing, Bea, and I followed in Today. Va was propped up on a stretcher so that he could see us out of the back of the ambulance. It was the dry season, and the ambulance kicked up a rooster tail of dust. I could either lay way back out of the dust or stay in close, but I chose the latter. It wasn't a long drive over the ridgeline to the airfield, and I squinted into the dust at the ambulance and Va looking back at us. We were going around a curve when

Va suddenly became excited. His eyes got big, and he began waving frantically at me.

For what? I thought. What could he possibly be that excited about? And he was getting more excited, trying to sit up on the stretcher and waving. This is crazy, I thought, squinting ahead. What's going on?

His father, sitting in the backseat, put his hand on my shoulder and pointed behind us. Looking around, I noticed that Bea was no longer sitting in the passenger seat. She had fallen out of the Jeep and was tumbling over the side of the bank behind us, out of sight.

She rolled halfway down the slope. By the time we returned, she was climbing back up and dusting herself off.

Unfortunately, Va didn't know that Bea wasn't hurt because the ambulance drove on. People at the airfield were surprised at the tearful reunion when we drove up.

Va said his wife didn't have much experience riding in Jeeps.

9

BARBECUED PIGEONS

I continued to work the ADO and the villagers north of Long Tieng with Khu Sao, another ops assistant, until May when Ringo left for the States. I was assigned his Hmong unit, GM 22. Nhia was my new ops assistant. A bright, personable young Hmong, with a swagger to his walk, Nhia was one of the most popular men working for Sky. He claimed he had learned everything he knew from Ringo.

The GM was camped south of the PDJ, dug in across a no-man's valley from a ridgeline controlled by the Pathet Lao. The North Vietnamese were not in sight. The Pathet Lao and the Hmong GM across the way often exchanged greetings.

One morning in late July, a flood destroyed the LS 272 rear base. Most of the buildings were washed away. Vehicles, heavy equipment, and pallets of heavy ammo were strewn down the valley, some hundreds of meters from the creek, now quiet and peaceful again. Someday people are going to come across howitzer ammo deep in some clumps of trees and try to figure out how it got there.

The LS 272 flood hastened our move back into Long Tieng. Skyline was completely secure. The main North Vietnamese and Pathet Lao units had been pushed back to the PDJ, and Hmong patrolled the river valley. Hog and Bamboo came down off the south ridge, and we

reoccupied the Sky compound. This ended my nightly
returns home to Vientiane—I went on a schedule of ten
days up-country and four days with the family.

During the summer, there were other personnel
changes in the Sky ranks. Dick, the chief of unit, and
Bag left. Shep, the rigger, was scheduled to leave in the
fall. This was Shep's second tour in MR II. He was our
special person, and we loved him. He worked hard every
day, out on the ramp before the sun came up, rarely talking, always working, rigging things exactly right, and
then checking and rechecking. He absolutely refused to
have anything go out from his rigging shed that wasn't
perfect—the right supplies, rigged with the right parachutes, on the right planes in the right order. It was an
uplifting experience to work with Shep because he was
so conscientious. Like Hog and Bag, he had come from
the hills of Montana and was, for the most part, a silent
frontiersman.

He could get drunk on three beers. We marveled at
this. We watched him come into the mess hall at night
and silently, slowly sip his first beer. With the second
beer, he drank a little faster and might quietly agree with
something someone said. Then, maybe he disagreed with
something someone said and then he might tell someone,
"Goddamnit to hell, you're just full of goddamned shit,"
as he crumpled up the beer can, opened another, and
drank almost half the can in one gulp.

If I smiled at him, he'd say, "What da' fuck is funny,
Mule? I don't see nothing funny except maybe this whole
friggin' group is funny. Full of 'girl singers.' "

"Girl singers" was a Hog phrase; it took me awhile
to get its exact meaning. It meant a man who did a lot
of posturing and acted romantic, with half-crossed eyes,
like a male crooner singing love songs. One had to use
it a lot before it made sense—most politicians were girl
singers.

Once, when we still lived in Udorn, Shep and I went

out for a beer. Brenda went over to Shep's house to play bridge with his wife, Jan.

Jan had a glass eye. Big and blocky, she appeared intimidating at first meeting, but she was actually kind and gentle—a good wife to Shep and one of Brenda's best friends.

That night, the air conditioner in Jan's living room wasn't working, and the only cool place to play cards was on the landing to the stairs going to the second floor. Jan set up the card table on the landing, and no one wanted to argue with her, even though she was kind and gentle.

After more than three beers, Shep was drunk and wanted to go home. I reminded him that the girls were playing cards at his house and suggested that he could just sit with me and maybe drink coffee. I didn't think Jan would want him to come home right yet.

"Nope," he said, "I want to go home and go to sleep, goddamnit."

When I took him home, Shep went inside. I didn't follow—I thought Jan might be angry with me for taking her husband out and getting him drunk or, worse, for bringing him home. I heard the rest of the story later.

As he began to climb the stairs, Shep looked at the girls playing cards on the landing and just couldn't figure it out. He weaved back and forth, with a confused, curious expression on his face.

Jan spoke sternly, "Shep don't you come up the stairs, you drunk son-of-a-bitch, there's no room for you to get by. Go sleep in one of the empty servants' rooms or on the couch. You hear me, Shep? Don't you come up these stairs."

Shep shook his head in confusion. All he wanted to do was to go to sleep in his own bed, so he started up the stairs. Jan stood up.

"Shep, if you come up here I will hit you," she said.

Shep was halfway up the bottom flight of stairs by that time. He jumped up, grabbed the banister to the next flight, and climbed over, just missing the girls. He crawled up the remaining stairs and went into his room.

"Don't you come out of the bedroom, you son-of-a-bitch," Jan said. "You go to bed and sleep or die, but don't you come back out of that bedroom. We're playing bridge."

Shep was back in ten minutes. All he had on was a sarong around his waist. He wanted to go downstairs for some reason, but he knew he had a problem when Jan stood up. Suddenly, he jumped over the top banister, with the idea of dropping to the lower flight of stairs, only he didn't clear the banister. He straddled it in midjump to keep from falling. As he started to slide down, his sarong hiked up.

Just then, Jan yelled, "Shep, you son-of-a-bitch."

Brenda jerked around to see Shep sliding down the banister to the landing. The sarong was up to his armpits.

Like the rest of us, General Vang Pao liked Shep and admired his work ethic. He planned a large farewell party ("baci"). All of Sky was invited, including Hugh T., the CIA station chief in Vientiane, and his very cultured wife Deborah, plus all of V. P.'s officers. The war stopped for Shep's baci.

Shep did not like crowds and did not like to be called on to speak in front of them. He did not like being the guest of honor and the center of attention. And, he certainly did not want to go to his baci.

Jan told him, "Don't you drink too many beers and embarrass me, you son-of-a-bitch. It'll just be a couple or three hours. Just go, drink Coke, smile. You don't have to say anything. Just don't drink any beer and get drunk and embarrass me."

Shep had trouble dealing with all of those people in V. P.'s house. Not long after he arrived, he went upstairs and had several beers.

After most of the guests had arrived, V. P. called everyone to the table. He sat at the head; Hugh T. sat on his left. Hugh's wife, a polished lady who was comfortable in diplomatic reception rooms, sat on V. P's right. There was an empty seat for Shep and one for Jan. Other guests were mixed, boy/girl, boy/girl.

When everyone sat down, Shep was conspicuous by his absence. V. P. looked around. "Where's Shep?" he asked.

Jan knew, but she was very happy that he was upstairs out of sight and did not answer. A Hmong waiter told V. P. that Shep was upstairs, and V. P. told the waiter to get him. This baci was for Shep—he mustn't miss his own baci.

A couple of Hmong got Shep under each arm and dragged him downstairs toward the table. Shep's head was on his chest, and his feet bounced on the stairs behind. When someone at the table called to him, he lifted up his head and stared. Jan turned around and glared with her good eye. Her husband was drunk, embarrassing her, and she was obviously angry.

Shep looked at the people sitting around the table like he was a condemned man looking at the electric chair. His eyes got bigger, but he managed to get his feet under him and walked stiffly to the table. One of the Hmongs pulled out the chair and Shep sat down—two feet from the table. He didn't move closer.

V. P. looked one way and then another around Deborah as he tried to say something to the guest of honor. He motioned to the waiters to move Shep's chair closer to the table. Now sitting between his angry wife and Hugh's very proper wife, Shep was most uncomfortable. And drunk.

He listened to V. P. for a few minutes, but then his eyes began to droop and he began to weave from side to side. He touched Jan. As she elbowed him away, he leaned in the opposite direction and touched Deborah. She quickly took in a breath; Shep recoiled and leaned back toward Jan. This started a game of horizontal yo-yo—back and forth.

Finally, he lost his balance and fell off the chair and under the table.

And he immediately tried to stand up, spilling everyone's water.

He knelt down and started to climb up a female leg. He thought it was his wife's, but it was Deborah's leg. Halfway up, using her leg for a banister, an errant hand hit her right side near her breast. She involuntarily gasped, not being accustomed to this type of behavior at dinner parties. Alerted by the sound, Shep looked up and realized he had his hands on Deborah, who was looking at him strangely. He stood straight up at attention. This resulted in his pushing back the dinner table a couple of feet. He just stood there looking down at Deborah.

Jan pulled him into his chair again as everyone rearranged themselves at the table and the waiters helped clear the spilt water.

All the Sky people, including Hugh, and V. P. thought it was a hoot. Jan did not. And Deborah did not.

Shep did not. He sat frozen in his chair.

Then the first dish, barbecued pigeon, was served. The pigeons, smothered in barbecue sauce, had been prepared with their tail feathers still intact, sticking up, poised. Everyone picked up their utensils to clear away the barbecue sauce and get at the meat, except Shep, who sat motionless and looked at his pigeon. Apparently feeling that he could not handle his knife and fork, he reached out with one hand, grabbed the whole pigeon, and put it in his mouth.

The barbecue sauce dripped down his chin and into his lap. He sat there chewing, his eyes half closed, with the feathers, halfway in and out of his mouth, bouncing up and down. People up and down the table snickered. Jan elbowed him. He looked at her and stopped chewing.

When Deborah noticed that Shep was the center of attention, she said in her cultured voice, "Shep, Shep, what are you doing?"

Turning in her direction, he paused before saying slowly, "Eating pi . . . geon."

And as he said, "Pi . . . geon," he spit all over her.

T. J. arrived for an extended overlap with Shep; Clean, with a shaven head, replaced Bag. No one was scheduled to replace Digger, who was leaving in the fall. It was 1972, and the war in Indochina was looking for a place to end.

Zack temporarily replaced Dick J. as the chief of unit. Although probably rewarding for him, Dick's tour had been difficult. He had been placed in an awkward position, particularly in his dealings with General Vang Pao. He was between Hog at Long Tieng, who was revered by V. P., and the Stick at Udorn, who had seniority and influence. Not everything Dick tried to accomplish got off the ground, but he was very popular in his own right with the entire Sky group. His policies were cost-effective, and he demanded accountability from the people who worked for him. He was an intelligent Agency professional. On the other hand, Zack, an ex-marine who had fought in the Second World War and Korea and had also served with the Agency in Vietnam and previously in south Laos, did not compete with Hog and the Stick or become contentious with V. P. He was unassuming in manner and had a personality that clicked with Sky, Air America, CASI, and the Hmong from his first day. He was an excellent complement to Hog in the valley. Nothing really mattered to Hog except doing the job—he was there for no man. Zack was different. He was tough but considerate and accommodating in a way we rarely saw up-country.

In mid-August 1972, shortly after we reoccupied the Sky compound, the Hmong T-28s began to return to the valley. When the North Vietnamese had been pushing on Skyline, with 130-mm rounds landing every day, the T-28s moved to Vientiane. They were Vang Pao's air force: less than a dozen old T-28s, prop-driven trainers from the Second World War that had been outfitted with 50-caliber guns and bombs latched under their stocky wings. They were clunky but durable. The Hmong pilots, who flew almost every day in support of ground operations, were heroes to the Hmong tribe. They affected the swashbuckling manner of men who had often challenged and beaten death and would do it again. The senior pilot, Vang Sue, who was in his late twenties, once told an Agency visitor from Washington that he would fly until he died, a phrase that was used often to describe the dedication and daring of the Hmong T-28 pilots.

Veteran pilots brought in the old squadron from Vientiane. Later, four newly commissioned Hmong pilots were to bring in recently overhauled planes. This would be their first landing at Long Tieng. Nhia and I had just come down to Air Ops from our office in the Sky compound when the flight of four planes came over the south ridge. As they flew along Skyline, each pilot, one after the other, made a slow pass over the valley, went back over Skyline, and then began banking slowly around to the south to land.

The Hmong from the valley had come out to welcome their new heroes. Nhia and I were standing at the very end of the runway in front of a huge karst as the young pilots made their flybys.

The first plane touched down and pulled off to the ramp near us. The pilot landed short, near the far end of the runway, and threw back the canopy to wave at the Hmong who had run down to the airstrip.

The next plane landed a little farther down the runway—they were coming in quickly now—and that pilot threw back his canopy and waved to the crowd as he turned off onto the ramp.

The third plane landed at about the same place as the one before. The pilot triumphantly shook his fist in the air as he pulled onto the ramp.

The last plane had trouble getting down. It finally touched down near the end, not far from Nhia and me, and it was moving fast. There was immediately some question in my mind about whether the pilot had time to slow before he had to turn off on the ramp. As I turned to Nhia to say that I thought he was maybe going too fast to make the turn, I saw Nhia running in the opposite direction. If the pilot didn't make the ramp, he would run into the karst. Suddenly, I realized that I was alone in front of the karst. The T-28 was coming straight for me. I couldn't decide which way to run.

Looking straight at the plane, I saw the wheels squall as the pilot tried to make the turn onto the ramp. He was going too fast, and his turn was too wide. I figured he wasn't going to hit the karst or me, but he was headed dead-on toward the concrete Air Ops building.

The canopy was thrown back. As the plane rushed by me, no more than twenty feet away, I could see that the pilot had his hands down. He was struggling, as if he were caught. For an instant, we made eye contact. Although alert, he seemed confused but not overwhelmed. He was quickly past me, his scarf fluttering madly in the wind.

The plane slammed into the bombproof side of the building next to Air Ops—from more than forty miles an hour to a dead stop, from a festive atmosphere to a tragedy.

A rocket went spiraling up from the wreckage, and a parachute was blown up, weakly, and landed over the fuselage. Dust and smoke drifted up, and then there was quiet.

I ran toward the plane half buried in the rubble of the building. Digger joined me within moments. Gasoline was draining from the back of the plane—we heard clicks and whines. If the gasoline ignited, the plane would explode and the pilot would be cremated.

Digger and I climbed up, thinking we only had a few seconds to get the pilot out. The canopy had been slammed shut from the force of the impact, and I shoved it back. Straddling the cockpit, I grabbed the pilot's shoulders and tried to pull him out. He wouldn't budge. The crackling and popping from the engine continued, and I smelled the gasoline. Time was important, and I couldn't lift this guy out of his seat. I told myself to calm down and leaned forward to see what was holding him down, but nothing was caught. He was a mess, with blood coming from a dozen cuts.

Digger was standing on the wing. As I pulled up on the pilot's shoulders again, he tapped me on the knee and said calmly, "His seat belt. He's still strapped in."

Digger released the seat belt. I pulled him out and handed him down to some Hmong who had run up to help.

Almost every bone in his body was broken. He died on the medevac going down to Udorn—brave soldier, Hmong hero. As he passed me, he apparently had been trying to eject. To do this, the pilot activates a simple mechanism by pulling up on a handle between his feet. It didn't fire in this case because he had the canopy back. The rocket, which should have blown him out away from the plane, went off when the canopy slammed forward.

The ramp area had never been a safe place. Previously, another T-28 with a young pilot landed long, had trouble making the turn onto the ramp, and slammed into the side of a C-123 boarding Thai mercenaries. The pilot of the T-28 was not killed, but the prop of his fighter impaled one of the soldiers inside the C-123.

One day, I had gone into Air Ops to ask the Greek about using a Porter that had just arrived on the ramp and was unloading civilian passengers. A Hmong woman came off the plane and ran straight into the propeller, which chewed her into small pieces.

Another time, H. Ownby, a U.S. Air Force Raven pilot who arrived in the valley during the summer of 1972, was bouncing along the taxiway in his O-1 Birddog spotter plane from the T-28 area when six or seven of his eight rockets accidentally fired. One of the rockets hit a

T-28 parked in front of Air Ops; two hit the Air Ops building, near where Greek was sitting; and several slammed into the karst at the end of the runway, near the top where the Hmong manned a .50-caliber machine-gun position. The Hmong, thinking they were under attack, started shooting the machine gun in a wide, sweeping arc across the valley, which prompted other sympathetic firing.

Sitting in his plane, Ownby wondered what was going on.

Greek was going crazy inside Air Ops. Stumbling out a side entrance and seeing Ownby in the O-1, Greek yelled, "Why is everyone trying to kill me? Why me, God? Why me?"

After Va was discharged from the hospital, he returned to the valley, and soon left for the States to live with my parents. He planned to finish high school and go on to college. I promised to look after Bea and their unborn child.

At Long Tieng, plans were to train up the GMs and, by early fall, get them reoutfitted and ready for a push to recapture the PDJ. Digger and I took our GMs to a training facility out of MR II that was run by Harry M. and Tony Poe (Poe was short for some unpronounceable Polish name). Like Hog, we had heard about Tony Poe throughout our training in the States. A big, brawling ex-marine paratrooper, he had a BA in English literature from Santa Clara University and had been a scratch golfer with the country club set of northern California before joining the Agency. He had worked for the Stick in the mountains of Laos for most of his Agency career.

Tony had become an alcoholic. He was sober when he arrived at the training facility in the morning, but by noon he was tapping into Mekong, the local liquor. By mid-afternoon each day, he had finished off a bottle and was loudly drunk.

The locals loved him. He was married to a Hmong

princess. Although he didn't speak the language very well, he was an adopted member of the Hmong tribe— a Sky man and a Hmong. He had lost the middle two fingers on his left hand in a booby-trapped grenade accident. He waved that hand around, yelling at the instructors, and everybody smiled and got on with their jobs.

Tony had given his life to the Lao program, and it had consumed him. The Stick had him in a job where he could not hurt anyone and where the Hmong's love for him was a contributing, positive factor. V. P. had no problems about sending his people out of the mountains to Tony's place for training. If it were anyone else, the mountain leader would have been concerned about his soldiers being subverted and used against him, but Tony was Sky and part Hmong.

Tony and his Hmong wife had several children. His youngest daughter, possibly eleven, came by to take him home in the late afternoons. Yelling and screaming at people by this time, he calmed down when his daughter arrived and went quietly with her when she said it was time to go home. The big, hulking, bald-headed, drunk brawler meekly followed the small girl out to a Jeep. She sat in the front beside the driver, and Tony slumped down and fell asleep in the rear.

While the GMs were in training, Brenda, the kids, and I went to Sydney, Australia. We visited the Opera House and the zoo and went shopping. To our amazement, we discovered that July is not hot in Australia. It was the dead of winter—in July. How crazy, we said. No wonder they talk funny. It was a grand experience, seeing Australia through the eyes of our kids, who months before had not known there was a world beyond Udorn.

Tony was sober and entertaining at the graduation of the GMs. V. P. attended. He and Tony laughed and drank from a bottle of Mekong.

When I told the old war-horse good-bye, Tony yelled at me and said it would be my fault if we didn't recapture the PDJ. My GMs had been trained to a razor's edge, and they were ready to go.

10

RETURN TO
THE PDJ

Digger and I brought our GMs back to Long Tieng in early September 1972 and joined Tahn, who was returning with his forces from MR I, and the Bear, who was coming in with his GM from MR III to help in the offensive drive. Kayak and Clean, with two GMs apiece, and Bamboo and his commandos were already on the scene in defensive positions around the valley.

Bamboo's forces secured a narrow hilltop in the northwest section of the PDJ for Digger's people. Kayak's two GMs were moved to the south, and my GM was moved to the north. Once Digger's GM was in position on the hilltop, Kayak's forces and mine began moving out to retake the PDJ. Kayak's forces had the first contact, and Tahn's GM was moved in near the clash site as reinforcement. Tahn stayed in the position the first night and was killed when it was overrun by North Vietnamese.

The area along the edge of the plateau and in the river valley, near where Tahn was killed, was bombed constantly throughout the following week by all the planes the U.S. Air Force radio platform could get. The Ravens, in their small O-1 observation planes, directed and spotted for most of the fighters.

The Ravens were a breed apart in MR II. To the people

who worked up-country Laos, the Ravens were always respectfully described the same way: "They got balls." They were there day after day in those tiny unprotected planes—leading the T-28s into dead-end valleys; looking for enemy positions; spotting for sleek, fast U.S. Air Force attack planes. The Ravens reminded me of Civil War flagbearers, who ran onto the field of battle, with their flags streaming, headlong into the fire of the enemy. They were utterly fearless. Because they were assigned to MR II for only short periods of time, six months or so, we rarely got to know them all very well. We never doubted, however, that they were all of the same breed, confident and courageous with nerves of steel.

Something about their eyes stopped people cold when they first saw the Ravens. They told people to be careful—the Ravens were different from everyone else. They looked preppy, but they didn't bluff. They weren't angry, but they were here to hunt and kill the North Vietnamese. That was their job. They killed people. Everyone knew that the Ravens were fit, alert, ready, and lethal. Their eyes told us—unblinking eyes, the whites whiter than anyone else's.

Sky officers were often confused about why these promising young men were so willing to get in harm's way, so willing to die, but we all considered them one of the most dependable and courageous elements in the Lao program—the American equal to the Hmong T-28 pilots.

My GM eventually gained the western edge of the PDJ with only light resistance, and some patrols ventured out onto the Plaine itself. They ran afoul of mines, probably left behind by the Thais the previous year, and pulled back.

We established positions on the high ground, along the end of a ridgeline overlooking the western area of the plateau. Vang Pao did not like the Hmong taking hard positions, and there was continuing discussion about the deployment of our forces. We were at the edge of the PDJ, what next? Were we actually going to occupy the PDJ? Were we going to try and hold ground? If we didn't seek a hard defense position, where were we going to draw the line this year?

Again, the final answers came down to Skyline. We could not prepare better positions. Nothing tactical could be gained by reestablishing ourselves on the PDJ. In fact, we could deny the PDJ to the North Vietnamese if we maintained our soft positions in a crescent around the southern and western sides of the plateau. Also, by sitting on our positions overlooking the PDJ, we would probably draw out the North Vietnamese, and we would have the high ground.

We waited beside the PDJ for the North Vietnamese reaction. We planned for the Hmong to make tactical retreats, and we would hit the North Vietnamese with our artillery, the U.S. Air Force, and Hmong T-28s.

The North Vietnamese probably knew we were not back at the PDJ to stay. We didn't have the Thais, the "hill sitters," and we weren't hardening our positions. But, we could sense that the North Vietnamese wanted to attack. It was their nature, and we also believed that one of their principal missions was to destroy the Hmong, and we were dangling the bait.

I postponed trips south to Vientiane as we waited for the North Vietnamese to attack. Most mornings, Nhia and I met at the ramp at first light and took an Air America helicopter out to the GM. Although we were usually aware of activity the previous night, Nhia received a situation report from each site as we approached. We didn't land at positions that had been recently probed unless they had critically wounded soldiers, and we rarely visited some small forward positions because of exposed landing pads. I did get to all the sites while we were waiting for the attack and tried to improve their defensibility. When the headstrong Hmong thought they were prepared, I had problems getting them to make improvements. One of my concerns, a carryover of my American sensitivities, was that the commanders of most of the exposed positions had little spider holes, dug in the forward slopes, that were manned at night by the smallest soldiers with boxes of grenades. When a position was probed, the youngster there pulled the pins on grenade after grenade and tossed them out to roll down the hill toward the attackers. These young soldiers tended to be the first and the most badly wounded. I was always disconcerted when I saw young boys put into body bags in the early mornings or watched them, so terribly hurt but never crying, as they were put on board Air America helicopters.

I spent most of my time at the GM commander's position. A strong believer in putting patrols out in front, I worked on getting the Hmong out on patrol and coordinated with the manuevering soldiers as they tried to determine the present and past positions of the North Vietnamese. The Hmong would not patrol in front unless I forced them. I actually had little leverage, so it often became a battle of wits.

Ravens were usually overhead; we worked together in targeting U.S. warplanes on suspected enemy locations. Locations that couldn't be hit during the day were passed to Dutch for nighttime B-52 strikes. Hmong T-28s, also on station throughout the day, dived low at suspected enemy positions across the western edge of the PDJ.

We were never attacked by ground forces during the day while I was out with the GM, although we occasionally received mortar fire. These events were startling when the rounds burst nearby, but they helped us to direct air attacks in the area. Being bait was not relaxing— the NVA would have sacrificed hundreds of its soldiers to capture a CIA officer—but I did not have reservations about being left on hilltop positions around the PDJ every morning. If things got too hot, I knew I could depend on Air America to get me out. The pilots worked the area with daring and cool precision. Despite occasional testy confrontations around the ramp between individual pilots and Sky officers, the pilots never refused me any task in the field.

Early one morning on the way to the western PDJ, Nhia got a radio call from a patrol saying that one of its members, who had been wounded in a confrontation with a North Vietnamese patrol the previous night, was dying. The patrol leader said there was not enough time to get him back to one of the GM positions. Flying high and to the east, we asked him to mark his position with a smoke grenade. Off to our front on the sheer side of a ridgeline next to the PDJ, a smoke column began to rise in the early morning haze. B. K. Johnson, one of the more flamboyant pilots, was flying a Twin Pack and had come up behind us to work resupply that day. As we were talking with nearby units of the GM to determine that no North Vietnamese controlled any of the commanding hilltops, B. K. volunteered to go in for the wounded man. He descended into the ravine, hovered to get around several tall trees obstructing his descent, and picked up the soldier. After making his way up through the trees, he pulled off at an angle for Long Tieng. He and his crew would get only a hundred dollars or so for the hazardous mission, the young Hmong soldier probably did not live, and no one would have questioned a decision not to attempt the rescue. This unheralded event, however, clearly demonstrated the true character, day in and day out, of the Air America pilots. Because I knew Air America would come to get me, no matter what the situation, I never hesitated about going out to the edge of the PDJ.

The North Vietnamese finally attacked in force. They hit both GMs, Digger's and mine, in the north one morning as dawn was breaking and when the whole area was socked in with unseasonable weather. They came from the area north of the PDJ, where they had built bivouac areas in the sides of mountains. Hundreds of North Vietnamese sappers and ground soldiers moved from their hiding places, across the PDJ, and up the hill toward the

Hmong. In their final assault, they were blowing whistles and beating drums.

My GM held through the first assault and then pulled back to the next ridgeline. Thai mercenaries fired artillery rounds at the Vietnamese until the guns were too hot to handle. The Ravens brought as much air power to bear as they could. B-52s bombed the Vietnamese concentrations and suspected supply routes. The Vietnamese tried to stay as close to the Hmong as they could to avoid the bombardment, but the Hmong pulled back as far as LS 15. Digger's forces also pulled back and were eventually brought back to Long Tieng.

Within a few days, the two Hmong GMs on the south were also hit. They scattered to rally points before pulling back.

A month after retreating to LS 15, my GM began moving back to the PDJ. The main Vietnamese attack force had withdrawn across the Plaine, although the GM encountered mines and pockets of small North Vietnamese ambush groups left behind.

Sitting on the ramp one afternoon and waiting for a Porter to come in so that I could fly over the lead elements of my GM, I watched H. Ownby, the Raven, land for refueling. He was heading out for an aerial reconnaissance of the PDJ and asked if I would like to go along.

"Thanks but no thanks," I said. "Ravens work a little closer to the edge than I normally do."

"OK," he said.

But I was thinking that I had never been in an O-1 before and hadn't flown over the PDJ in almost a year.

"It's just a milk run," Ownby said and turned toward his plane.

"I've changed my mind. I'll go." I picked up my survival gear and AK-47.

We went up. And I almost died of fright.

We soared over the PDJ—north where both Ownby and I knew there were surface-to-air missiles, over North

Vietnamese troop concentration areas, and near peaks where the Pathet Lao might have antiaircraft weapons—in that tiny plane, without parachutes.

I well knew the nature of the North Vietnamese on the ground below us. What chance would we have if the engine on this little plane quit? If one stray bullet came up and knocked out Ownby, how the hell would I get back? I couldn't fly a plane. And if we did get hit, landed, and were captured, what chance in hell would a CIA guy have with the North Vietnamese?

Whether it was my fear of the North Vietnamese getting their hands on me or my feet-on-the-ground infantry orientation, I felt vulnerable and exposed. We were high, but the enemy on the ground could still see us; they could still hear us. I knew that thousands of North Vietnamese were watching us from below and following us with their guns.

H. Ownby chatted merrily away as we continued to soar above the PDJ. I was so frightened that I felt pressure on my chest, and I had trouble talking.

I was grateful when we finally got back to Long Tieng and I could hardly resist opening the door before we came to a stop. As I climbed out of the plane, I kept telling myself to move slowly, carefully, don't shake. Hog was coming out of Air Ops. He cocked his head to one side as if to ask what I was doing. Sky people in MR II were not hot dogs.

Later, I told Hog that he did not have to worry about my flying with the Ravens ever again. Maybe there was nothing wrong with it, maybe he didn't care, but he should know that I would never again fly in one of those little planes over all of those enemy troops. H. Ownby and all the other Ravens were crazy.

In all of my experiences, I had never been as scared. On the ground under fire in Vietnam and out with the GM, my fear made me more alert, quicker—I used it. Up in that plane with H. Ownby, with no place to go, I had felt just plain, raw, unusable fear. All of my developed senses to avoid unnecessary exposure to the enemy had screamed at me: ''What are you doing, you idiot?''

My GM eventually reached the ridgeline overlooking the western PDJ and reoccupied its previous positions. Again, our plans were to use the Hmong to entice the North Vietnamese out into the open so that we could pound them with artillery and aircraft.

At one site, the body of a young Hmong killed the previous month was recovered. Rather than bury him there, the GM commander wanted the body sent back to his relatives for the traditional Hmong wake, a ceremony that releases the man's spirit and allows for a dignified death and eternal peace. On the way out to the position that day, the commander and I talked about the difficulties in getting in a helicopter to that particular position. We decided that the soldiers had to bring the body down to a landing site on the edge of the PDJ. The commander called ahead and gave the instructions. After landing on the edge of the PDJ near the helipad where the body was to be taken, the commander, Nhia, and I, with a couple of Hmong soldiers, walked up the trail toward the position and met the detail bringing the body down.

The body had been rotting for a month. It smelled vicious, incredibly noxious. Even breathing in through my mouth, my eyes teared and the rancid odor seeped up my nose and exploded. It was battlefield refuse I had never known in Vietnam.

A small banana republic in Latin America was known to use an interrogation/torture technique, in which the interrogators tied the prisoner to a table with his head hanging over the edge. His mouth was covered with tape and Coke poured up his nostrils. As the prisoner tried to breathe, the Coke drained down his nose into the sinus passages. It was like a bullet shot right between the eyes. Whether the carbonation caused it or what, the pain was worse than a nerve being hit with a dentist's drill. It was the most pain a man could endure without passing out—

like a bomb going off in the skull, behind and between the eyes. Once during a prison riot in that Latin American country, the prisoners saw the guards bring in a single case of Coke and they stopped rioting.

The smell from that body was a comparable assault on the senses—it had to be the worst smell in the whole world.

The detail bringing the body down had to pause every so often and move away from it to catch their breath. Nhia, who was in front of our group, lost his breakfast when they got close.

It was apparent that the body would have to be slung under a helicopter to get it out of the area. I told Nhia to go up to the position with the commander, while I went down to the edge of the PDJ to coordinate the evacuation with Air America by radio.

I walked ahead of the detail as it continued its cock-eyed cadence: take a few breaths off the trail . . . in . . . pick up the litter . . . move down the trail . . . lower the litter . . . off the trail for more breaths.

Arriving back at the PDJ, I looked around in the sky for an Air America chopper. Frenchy Smith was flying in supplies.

Ol' Frenchy. Ol' give-Sky-a-ration-of-shit Frenchy Smith.

I called him on my radio and told him that I had a KIA (killed in action) and asked if he'd drop by my position after he delivered his supplies and take it back.

Frenchy asked if I was sure the person was dead and not just trying to get out and go to the mall downtown Saturday night to rock and roll.

"No," I said, "this one's dead."

The detail arrived behind me and I almost choked. But then I had a thought. With the swirling winds of the helicopter, even though the smell was godawful, Frenchy wouldn't be able to smell this fellow if we put him inside. He would be up in the air before realizing how special this particular body was.

Frenchy asked me to throw smoke as he came back from dropping off his supplies so that he could see exactly where I was. He didn't want to land in the wrong spot on the PDJ.

Frenchy bayed like a mule over the radio as he came in for a landing.

The Hmong picked up the body—the nearby grass had begun to wilt—and we ran out to the chopper. Frenchy kept up full power without settling completely on the ground, and the wind turbulence was strong. The kicker threw open the sliding door, we put the body inside, and Frenchy lifted off as the kicker closed the door.

After I breathed in some fresh air, I started laughing because I knew in that closed helicopter, about right now, Frenchy was smelling that body.

The helicopter stopped in midair. Stopped. It had its nose down and was gaining altitude, and it stopped.

Over the radio, I heard, "Holy God Almighty, God . . . God . . . God . . . damn."

Other Air America pilots in the area heard the same thing and tried to break in on Frenchy to find out if he was in trouble, if a Mayday was imminent.

"What is that smell? What . . . God . . . God . . . God."

The copilot apparently took the controls because Frenchy continued to yell on the radio. The helicopter turned around and came back over the helipad.

Everyone on board had their heads sticking out the side. The kicker disappeared inside briefly, and the body came flying out to land, with a thud, near me.

I was doubled over with laughter. Never before had I seen a helicopter flown by men with their heads sticking out the windows.

Frenchy finally came on the air and told everyone to leave Mule on the PDJ. "Mule is not a nice person," he said.

I was on a schedule of ten days up-country and four days down in Vientiane with the family. It was, in real terms, ten days, nine nights up and four days, five nights down, a good distribution of time.

Homecomings were joyous. I came in on a resupply fixed-wing aircraft or on a helicopter heading down for maintenance and took a taxi near Poppa Chu's to the front gate of the house. It was usually early evening, and music from Walt Disney movies and other musicals were on the tape recorder. On the nights I came home, it was always turned up loud. The house was lit up; Brenda and the kids often turned on every light. I tried to bring things for the kids. Once, I brought them a little pig, but he ran away the second day. That's what the guard said, although he looked unusually well fed at the time. I had brought them rabbits, a dog, and an ocelot before Brenda asked me not to bring anything else that was alive. So I stuck with Hmŏng toys and such items as web gear, lenses from old binoculars, and an interesting old pump that looked like a goose.

The kids usually got me off to the side the night I came in and each told me their versions of things that had happened while I was away. Their English improved each time I came home, and they picked up a new slang term every week.

Brenda made Mim's and Joseph's costumes for the embassy Halloween party. Dressed as a clown, Joe was a jack-in-the-box. We cut a round hole in the bottom of a cardboard box and cut the top on three sides so that it opened like a door. Joe got inside from the bottom, sang out in his tiny little voice, "Jack-in-the-box, still as a fox," and then jumped up, throwing open the top. He squatted back down to lift up the box from the bottom and walked around before squatting down again. "Jack-in-the-box, still as a fox."

Mim was dressed as a sunflower. A circle of cardboard petals, each covered with a gauzy yellow fabric, framed her gorgeous little face with its big, toothless smile. Her body was draped in a tube of green fabric. She was the most beautiful flower. How I loved that child.

Joe was my buddy, a clown who loved to laugh. But Mim was my sweetheart, as daughters can be to their fathers. I hurt when she hurt and felt sad when she was tired and crying. She always knew that I would be a sympathetic listener, and she always got her way with me.

A part of my homecoming from Long Tieng was to sit down on a couch in the living room and let Mim take off my boots. I usually came directly from the field, and my pants, often blood-smeared and torn, were rolled up at the bottom. Mim never asked why I was so dirty or what I did that produced such evidence of pain and suffering. She knelt down, pushed up my pants, and unlaced my boots from top to bottom. She struggled the first few times—pulling and tugging to get the old army boots over my ankles after undoing the laces, but she got the hang of it soon and knew where to grab them at the heel to get the best leverage. Lifting one of my feet off the floor and straddling my leg with her back to me, she reached down, grabbed the heel, and pulled up, grunting and straining, until the boot eased off. When she had them both off, she ran and put them in the bedroom closet. She then ran back to where I was sitting and snuggled up beside me. She basked in the glow of what she had done, sitting there with her dad who was home for a weekend from the fighting.

The kids knew how to operate the tape deck and loved to play movie sound tracks. Mim's favorite was *Sound of Music*. A ritual developed with the song "Do, Re, Mi." After the shoes were off, often when the excitement was waning from the actual coming-in-the-door welcome, she put on the tape and cued it to "Do, Re, Mi." Racing back to my side, she looked up, right at my lips, as I sang with the tape, "Do, a deer, a teenage deer, Re, a drop of . . ."

"Nooooo," Mim said and reached up to put her hand over my mouth, "It's Do, a deer, a *female* deer, not a *teenage* deer, Daddy."

I was so proud of my family. The three of them were my greatest joy.

The situation up-country was demanding and dangerous. There was so much giving, warmth, and happiness at home. I had the best of two worlds, so unusually balanced. What other combatant in the twentieth century could have had this? I always said to myself during my home visits, "I am so lucky."

Most of the Sky men I worked with were bachelors. They had very different experiences when they came down to Vientiane. They lived in what was called the "R&R" house and spent their nights carousing the local bars: Lulu's, the White Rose, the Lucky Bar, and the Tropicana. Lewd, lusty, fleshy drinking places—holdovers from the anything-goes days of the French foreign legions. Set in the tranquil, tropical setting of Vientiane, hard along the Mekong River, the bachelor nightlife scene was a bawdy "Xanadu." There were no rules or restrictions in these bars, and the Sky bachelors had fascinating, almost unbelievable stories to tell when we returned up-country.

11

WHEN A
RAVEN FALLS

Early one morning after a four-day home visit, Brenda
and the kids drove me to Poppa Chu's restaurant near
the airport ops center. I waited there, drinking coffee and
reading, until midday before a helicopter coming up from
Udorn picked me up. Izzy Freedman, our former neighbor, was copilot. The area to the north had been covered
by haze for days, but the skies had finally opened up and
Izzy's helicopter was among a flock heading up to the
valley.

Sitting in the middle of the row of rear seats and wearing the extra headphone—the customer set—I chatted on
the intercom with the crew. I could hear the other pilots
on the command air frequency talking among themselves
and occasionally caught glimpses of other helicopters flying ahead of us.

"OK, so I'm telling my broker, I know you can buy
titanium mine stock." Pilot B. K. Johnson was talking.
The airways on the common frequency were always busy
with small talk. The pilots never stayed on the air long,
however, saying only a phrase or two and then pausing
to see if anyone was trying to break in. There would be
a quiet but distinctive break in the squelch as someone
came on and went off the air. Conversations were casual,

145

about everyday things, although there was generally no profanity.

"Some of my friends have bought it." Pause. "My broker said titanium is manufactured." Pause. "It's man-made, how can it be mined? he asked." Pause.

"I said I have dumb friends." Pause.

"And poor," someone added.

"Titanium is not manufactured," someone else injected, "it's a natural element."

"Oh yeah," B. K. said, "wanta buy some stock?"

"Oooh," came over the air from one of the pilots, obviously in pain.

"My boss has a problem," someone said.

"Ooooh, I gotta go to the john." It was Bill Hutchinson, one of the most senior helicopter pilots flying for Air America. He was leading the pack up north in a Twin Pack.

"Well, with one of those super-duper recharged machines you fly," Izzy said before pausing, "you oughta just wander on back through the lounge to the rest area."

"Oooooohhh, I'm in pain. I almost wish we'd crash so I'd get some relief. How do you make this thing go faster? Oh God, it's a 105."

Because profanity wasn't generally allowed over the open frequencies, some of the Air America pilots had developed the falcon codes—common, earthy, profane expressions designated by numbers—and a laminated list was often taped to the instrument panel near the radios. A 105 was "It's so fucking bad I can't believe it!"

Other listings included:

104	"What the fuck, over?"
108	"Fuck you very much."
109	"Beautiful, just fucking beautiful."
112	"Let me talk to that sumbitch."
118	"What are you trying to do, kill some fucking body?"
169	"Fuck it, just fuck it."

272   "One good deal after another."
274   "I'd rather have a sister in a whorehouse than
            a brother in a Twin Pack."

"Oooooohhh, 105, good God Almighty," Hutchinson said.

"There are some people you just can't carry on a trip, you know what I mean," from some unidentified pilot. "Gotta go potty all the time. Reminds me of my first wife." Pause. "No, maybe it was wife number two. Wasn't married to wife one long enough to take a good trip."

"Ooooooohhh." Pause.

"Mayday, Mayday, Mayday, I'm hit." It was a faint but clear signal.

"Give us your location," said Hutchinson, suddenly serious and speaking in a calm, even voice.

"I'm over the PDJ." It was John Carroll, a Raven who had recently arrived in MR II. A 1962 graduate of the Air Force Academy, Carroll had been a test pilot at Edwards Air Force Base and had qualified for the astronaut program. According to the other Ravens, he was certainly scheduled for space flight after he had his "ticket punched" with a tour in Southeast Asia. He had been socked in at LS 20A during the past few days and was up on the afternoon schedule to scout the PDJ.

"How high are you, how bad you hit?" The senior pilot again. Standard operating procedure (SOP) was that the senior man was in charge during an emergency and everyone else stayed off the working frequency. Air America handled emergencies weekly—mechanical failures, shot-up planes, downed pilots—and the response among this group of veterans was practiced and sure. In front of me, the pilot reached over and got a map. He told Izzy over the intercom to turn to a new heading. Izzy was giving the helicopter maximum power, almost redlining the engine.

"I'm at 5,000 feet and dropping. I got a round in the

engine and it's losing compression. Still going but losing compression. It's throwing out oil!'' The pilot's voice was loud, stressed.

Elevation of the PDJ was 3,500 feet. At 5,000 feet, the plane had either dropped dramatically since it was hit or had been flying very low. Carroll, in fact, had been reconning the southern PDJ and had taken a hit from a 12.7-mm antiaircraft round.

''You're going to be OK, don't worry. If your engine is still going, you're OK.'' The senior pilot's voice was reassuring.

''It's sputtering. Shit. Throwing out a lot of oil. I can barely see in front,'' Carroll yelled in panic.

''You're flying, and we're going balls out to get to you. Don't worry, you're going to be OK,'' Hutchinson told him.

''The engine quit! Froze. Prop is not moving.'' Carroll was still yelling.

''What's your altitude?''

''Four thousand five.''

''What's your location?''

''Southern PDJ.''

''We've got two choices. You can try and glide into Sam Thong or circle around and land on the PDJ. We'll be in and pick you up. You're OK. What do you think? What's best?''

''Those ridgelines between me and Sam Thong are too high. I'm going back and land on the PDJ,'' Carroll replied.

A new voice came into play. Another Raven, Steve Neal, began talking to Carroll. Their conversation was technical, but it appeared to soothe Carroll somewhat. He sounded less frantic after Mike Jarina, flying an Air America helicopter out of LS 05, came on to tell Hutchinson that he was close by and would go in for the rescue.

''OK, there, Mr. Raven, we're not far from you,'' Jarina said. ''How long can you glide and circle?''

"Not long. Shit, it's quiet up here. All I hear is my heart."

"You're OK, OK. There are several runways on the southern plains. You know 'em?"

"Yeah."

"You want to make for one in particular or land on a road or what? You tell us."

"I want to come in on the first piece of flat ground I see."

"OK, listen to me." It was Neal, the other Raven. "Your rescue radio isn't damaged, is it?"

"No, it's OK."

"You land, you get out of the plane, and you get away from it," Neal said. "Unless you land right on top of some bad boys, we've got time. We're closing in on your position. We'll be there. Throw smoke when you see us coming in."

Before the bad weather, our intelligence had indicated only advance elements of North Vietnamese along the southern PDJ; most of their forces were north of the Plaine. If there hadn't been any significant movement, the Raven could land safely. Four Hmong GMs were still loosely positioned on the south and west of the PDJ. They had not reported any significant contact recently. These were all reasons to believe that Carroll could get down safely and be picked up.

The U.S. Air Force radio platform came on to report that fast movers were being diverted from southern Laos but were several minutes out. The Udorn air rescue squadron had scrambled and was en route.

Air America, however, had responsibility for the pickup. Jarina's helicopter was the closest to the southern PDJ, by several minutes over the helicopters coming from the south. Jarina was going in first. He and his co-pilot, George Taylor, knew they would not have any fighter support, but they reasoned that time was essential. To wait for U.S. Air Force fighter aircraft or a backup chopper, although both would be on the scene in minutes, meant wasted time that might otherwise make the difference in getting the Raven out.

"OK there, Raven, my friend, how's it going?" Jarina, taking over control of the rescue, also had a reassuring voice in talking with Carroll, who had heard the preparations to make the pickup.

"OK, I'm at 4,000 feet on the west side," Carroll screamed. "I think I can pick up one of your choppers coming up from the south. I'm going in!"

"I see him, eleven o'clock, low," someone said.

"OK, big fellow, we've got you," Jarina said. "We'll be right down. Get out and away from your plane. Get on your radio. Get smoke. Good luck."

"Roger! I'm going in, going in some bushes. Going in now!"

Then there was quiet. All the choppers were at full power. Our helicopter was vibrating terribly. The southern PDJ was in the distance up front. I saw what might have been Jarina's helicopter ahead, close to the first ridgeline and dropping.

"I'm on the ground. I'm OK. I'm getting out and going on my handheld."

"Goddamnit, we're five minutes out. Five minutes. Get away from the plane. Get away from your plane! Hide! Get away," Jarina yelled.

"I'm out, under the wing. How do you read me, how do you read?"

"We've got you ten bye," Jarina said. "You're sounding good. Get away from the plane."

"There must be fifty of 'em coming this way. They see me. . . ." Carroll was yelling frantically when Jarina's transmission ended.

"Don't fire your gun. Run. Run. Anyone see him?"

"They're shooting at . . ." The Raven screamed.

"Where is he?" another voice asked.

"I've got the plane. I see it. Oh, shit. Fuck," Jarina hollered. "There are gooks all over the place." Jarina was still coming in. Taylor saw six or eight people running around near the downed O-1. Descending to a hover fifty feet away from the plane, Jarina hoped the pilot would break from some of the nearby bushes and run to the chopper.

"Come on, come on, come on, come on!" Taylor was yelling over the open mike.

Suddenly, Jarina and Taylor felt the helicopter shudder from the force of the intense ground fire. They could hear the impact of some of the rounds off their engine.

"We're taking a lot of small-arms fire. I'm breaking away to the east," Jarina said.

Izzy yelled to Taylor, "Shoot your gun."

"Shit, I'll need my bullets if I'm shot down," he answered.

The console dials in the helicopter were going crazy. Some of the rounds had hit the fuel line, and gas began pouring from the fuel tank. Immediately, the low fuel warning light came on. Jarina struggled to bring the crippled helicopter up and began to head south. The flight mechanic, Tod Yourglich, began firing his M-16 at people running toward the helicopter as it lifted away.

Three helicopters, including Frenchy Smith's, just coming on the scene, dropped off their rush toward the downed Raven and escorted Jarina and Taylor back to LS 05, where they abandoned the badly shot-up helicopter.

Ted Cash and his copilot, Roy Heibel, continued toward the downed O-1. Neal was directing the first flight of fast movers into the area around the crash site. Hutchinson and Cash talked briefly about making the next charge in to get the pilot. After the fast movers made their second pass, Cash led several helicopters as they swooped down toward the ground.

Cash and Heibel, the first in, hovered near the O-1's wing. The ping of small-arms fire into and around the helicopter made every fraction of a second perilous.

"There he is, under the wing," Cash yelled.

"Shit. He's blown away. Ah, shit, shit, shit. We're

taking rounds broadside,'' Heibel shouted. Most of the other helicopters were also being shot up as they tried to land. They began to pull back.

"I see him. They've gotten him. He's dead. We've got to pull out," Cash said.

There was quiet. Izzy pulled off on the power, and the vibration of the helicopter slowed down.

The pilot of another helicopter asked if there was any chance the Raven was still alive. Cash said no; everyone on his helicopter had seen the pilot, under the wing of his plane, with parts of his body shot away. One minute, he had been alive—talking, trying to make the best of the situation, trying to stay alive. The next minute, he was dead.

Everyone in the air was tired as the adrenaline began to fade. The choppers gained altitude. There was concern about Cash because of the rounds he had taken, but apparently nothing significant had been hit and he was airworthy.

Because we were at the rear of the group, we were the first to come around and land at Long Tieng. I got off the helicopter as Zack came riding up in a Jeep. I was explaining what had happened when Cash and Hutchinson landed their helicopters. Soon, Frenchy flew in with Jarina, Taylor, and Yourglich on board. Cash bounced out and began examining the bullet holes in the side of his chopper. Hutchinson had a harder time getting out of his Twin Pack. Burdened by his painful, long overdue call of nature, he finally, slowly got to the ground. Bent over and walking mainly from the knees down, taking very short steps, he began to cross the ramp. Halfway across, he stopped and stood there for a long time, looking straight ahead, before walking on, more upright, soiled and sad.

The North Vietnamese had indeed taken advantage of the haze to begin moving en masse across the PDJ toward the south. The Raven had landed in their midst.

The U.S. Air Force fast movers, coming from the south to support the rescue, worked the area. B-52 strikes were called in. Aircraft returning from North Vietnam were asked to drop leftover ordnance in the southern PDJ. The area was bombed for days, and North Vietnamese casualties were high. They paid dearly for the death of John Carroll. Special intelligence indicated that he had shot at the North Vietnamese soldiers as they approached, and they had returned the fire. If he had not fired, the North Vietnamese could have waited and perhaps destroyed all of the Air America choppers as they came in, one after the other, to attempt the pickup.

In giving his life, Carroll probably saved ours

Although hundreds of North Vietnamese were killed or wounded during the bombing, they continued their move south. By the first of November, they were attacking Skyline again.

12

CHANGES IN
THE VALLEY

Redcoat left Bouam Long in October, and Digger replaced him. The deuce-and-a-half truck had been moved out of the Sky bunker by then.

Earlier, Redcoat had requested a large truck to move ammunition and other materiel around the high mountain compound. There were no roads in or around Bouam Long, but Redcoat thought that various chores near the airstrip could be made easier if Yer Pao Sher had a truck.

"OK," T. J. said, "a plane large enough to carry a deuce-and-a-half truck can't land at Bouam Long, of course, but we can drop one in. The army does it all the time; 82d Airborne paratroopers jump in an area, and right behind them come the trucks. All we need here is just a big parachute."

So they rigged a truck for drop, loaded it on a C-130, and took it up to Bouam Long. Unfortunately, the lines got tangled when they pushed it out the back door of the plane and it did a nosedive into the Sky bunker. Redcoat, luckily, was not inside—the engine and cab ended up in the radio and cooking area. It looked like Air America had bombed the bunker with a truck.

For months thereafter, when Air America pilots went up to Bouam Long, they said among themselves: "Don't land near the bunker. That's where Redcoat parks his truck.''

Zack continued to be acting base chief until Dick J.'s replacement arrived. A seasoned bureaucrat, the new man had no conspicuous talent for the job and no rapport with the gruff Air America contingent or the lethal, risk-taking Ravens. He acted as if he were above, certainly separate, from Vang Pao, and he did not seek Vang Pao's confidence. He also did not inspire respect among his Sky officers. The consensus was that he played to Washington, where he had contacts and experience. He studied cables that came in and often unilaterally composed responses—he saw no need to get others involved, and he never participated in the give-and-take around the map board or in the bar.

Zack, never openly critical, was protective of the man and forced compliance with an increasing list of administrative chores levied on the field officers by the new chief. One of the most restrictive and unpopular new items was an organized daily staff meeting at 1800. We had to start coming in from the field around midafternoon. Air America did not run fixed schedules, and, when there was contact with the enemy or troop movements or problems with resupply, logical priorities committed Air America to duties other than ferrying case officers to staff meetings. The new man understood this to a certain extent, but he was always visibly upset when we came in late.

Then there was the chair, and it signaled the beginning of the end. A large easy chair, of the living room variety, appeared one day in the briefing room, off the ops assistants' quarters. It was front and center of the map board. When Hardnose came in and saw the chair, he sat down in it. The idea of a ''chief's chair'' was so pretentious, so unlike anything ever done in the valley that Hardnose honestly believed it was just another chair, albeit a very nice one. The chief came in, looked down at Hardnose without smiling, and cleared his throat. Hardnose said, "Oh," and he immediately got up, as he realized that the new man must be completely out of touch with the Long Tieng situation. The next night, another case officer was in the chair when the chief came in. He glared, cleared his throat, and took the seat without comment when the case officer got up.

The new chief did not operate in a vacuum, as insulated as Long Tieng was. The Stick, Hugh T., and people in other MRs soon learned of the chair and how it implicated the man as an officious misfit. His days in the valley were brought to a conclusion by a most unlikely person. Mark Samuel Pearcy was the Long Tieng representative of the U.S. Army's Attache (ARMA) office in the U.S. Embassy in Laos. A teenage military dependent from Vientiane, Mark had been hired to run the ammo dump off the ramp. He didn't look threatening. He had enormous feet and walked around like he was wearing frog feet or clown shoes. His hair was long, and he kept pushing it off his face. He was the youngest, least imposing member of the round-eyed force at Long Tieng, but he was quiet and competent, worked hard at the ammo dump, and always kept things in order.

A few weeks after the chair appeared, a problem centered around fuses for T-28 bombs. The ammo dump had the right ordnance but was short on the correct fuses. This became a long, involved subject of discussion at a staff meeting. At its conclusion, the new chief issued complex and confusing instructions on how fuses were to be ordered and stored. The next night, Dutch, who was master of ceremonies at these briefings, went around the room to ask everybody if they had anything to contribute. At his turn, Mark said he didn't have anything to add.

The new chief spun around in his chair and said, "Well, just how many fuses do you have?" Mark told him in a youthful but calm voice.

The next night, as Dutch went around the room asking for contributions, Mark again said he didn't have anything to add. The new chief stood up slowly and demanded, "How many fuses?" Without listening to the response from Mark, he said, "Every night, when it comes to you, you are to give a report on your fuses."

The next night when Dutch was making his rounds, the new chief was sitting rigid in his chair, looking straight ahead, waiting. Dutch came to Mark. Just as Mark started to say he didn't have anything to add, the new chief jumped straight up and out of his chair. "You're out of here," he shouted, "you're out of the valley. I guarantee it. You're gone."

Mark didn't go anywhere. ARMA brass in Vientiane made the point to Hugh T., to the Stick, and eventually to the new chief that ARMA was not answerable to the CIA base chief at Long Tieng, and its guy would stay. Hugh T. said OK.

Not long afterward, the new chief left short of his tour. Riding in a Jeep toward the ramp, he passed Mark walking up the street, those big feet plopping along.

We quickly got back to a more natural routine with Zack as the base chief. The chair disappeared.

One afternoon, we received a message that a group of U.S. Air Force officers from the 7/13 AF out of Udorn would arrive in Long Tieng to brief on the employment of F-111s in our area.

Gen. John W. Vogt, commander of the Seventh Air Force, had visited earlier with Vang Pao and spent most of the day with the Hmong T-28 pilots. Vogt conveyed a sense of command, a reflection of his senior military rank and position, and he was not easily impressed. After a day out in the Long Tieng elements, however, and talking with the tough hill tribesmen who flew the T-28s day after day into withering North Vietnamese fire (Vang Sue, the senior pilot, had more than five thousand combat missions), Vogt was indeed awed, according to people who knew him. The unpretentiousness of the Hmong pilots and how they mixed with the villagers and GM guerrillas in the valley made a strong impression on Vogt. There was no politics involved, no sterile high-tech environment where the converted T-28 trainers from the Second World War were parked. It was honest warring, primitive, a throwback to combat flying during the First World War. The Hmong flyers strapped as many bombs and bullets as they could get on their planes and went out and found North Vietnamese to attack—flight after flight, hour after hour, day after day. At that time, the U.S. Air Force was sending thirty to fifty sorties of fighter aircraft daily to MR II. Most were fast movers, F-4s, A-6s, and A-7s, not often used in close support of maneuvering ground troops. The major part of our close fire support was left to the T-28s.

When he left the valley that day, Vogt said the Seventh Air Force could help more and offered the possibility that F-111s from the 474th Tactical Fighter Wing might be assigned exclusively to MR II, probably for close support. The team coming up from Udorn indicated that Vogt was true to his word and that F-111s were in our future.

When the team members arrived on an Air America cargo plane, they were easily identifiable for several reasons. We didn't have that many strangers in the valley, plus they walked more upright than other Americans in the area, their haircuts were shorter, and they wore odd-looking low-cut shoes, like those used for indoor work.

Curious about this new high-tech addition to our fighting force, Kayak and I followed the team up to the Sky compound. As we walked in, the air force people were finding places to sit among the boxes, weapons, and typewriters that littered the main room in the headquarters bunker. Hog was standing off to the side. Bamboo, tall and scruffy, and Clean, shaven-headed and bulky, were sitting near Zack's desk. When Dutch and Hardnose walked in, Zack told the air force officers that they had the floor.

The officers tried to act relaxed, but they were rigid

and obviously uncomfortable. One of the older men, wearing prescription aviation glasses, began by saying the F-111s (he called them "F One Elevens") had been deployed to South Vietnam for some time, although the media rap on them, which we might have heard, was that they ran into mountains. This was overstated. They were, in fact, quite effective precision bombers that were able to deliver bombs in close support to ground troops. The planes were the first equipped with on-board, computer-aided gyrocompasses and capable of offset guidance from ground beacons; their pilots knew where they were every instance. They could deliver their five-hundred-pound bombs on target in all weather; each plane carried twenty-four bombs. If it was known where enemy troops were marshaling for an attack, F-111s could get there and kill them.

"So we're getting F-111s?" Hog asked.

"Roger that," said the air force officer.

"Now you know we didn't ask for F-111s," Clean said.

"Roger that," the air force spokesman said. "It's been coordinated at very senior levels. The U.S. Air Force presence in South Vietnam is being reduced, and the Joint Chiefs of Staff want to continue the deployment of these state-of-the-art aircraft. With the Vietnamese just starting their offensive here, your T-28s need them. The 474th Tactical Fighter Wing out of Takhli in Thailand is being dedicated for your use in MR II."

I appreciated what the air force people were saying and was impressed with the F-111's capabilities, but I sensed something about the presentation that meant more work for Sky. The F-111s were going to take care and feeding, and our war was not going to be as private as it had been. The Joint Chiefs of Staff were not often mentioned in our ops work.

"The 7 AF targeting facility in Saigon has large hold-ings of potential targets in your area for the planes. But we would like your contribution to this database," the air force officer continued. "As you know, because of the rules of engagement, we are not allowed to have forward observers on the ground in Laos. So we cannot assign U.S. Air Force personnel here—on the ground—to coordinate on the targeting. Raven support is not appropriate. Your Hmong have to be used, and we suggest a two-phase program to get this started. First, we get a number of coordinates from you of possible enemy positions, staging areas, road junctions, enemy gun emplacements, etc., to augment our target database."

Dutch said, "We can provide those. It's something we have plenty of here, targets."

"Second, we train your Hmong radio operators here in the valley and when our F-111s come into the area going to one of the preset targets from the database and you have new targets, say a position is under attack and you need supporting fire, then your Hmong talker calls up a divert and we scrub the first run and hit the new target. That's the way it will work."

After they finished talking, Zack, looking at Hog, said, "I see no problems in getting you coordinates and training the Hmong if the Stick has agreed. Do you, Hog?"

"The Hmong will run the radios?" Hog asked.

"Roger."

Hog looked at Zack and shrugged an OK. Later, Hog said the air force wasn't seeking our permission. They were giving us a done deal, telling us what they were going to do.

Over the next few days, Dutch worked on little else except collecting targets for the F-111s.

In the valley, Glassman, the senior Sky ops assistant, had been placed in charge of what would be the F-111 radio station, which was named Red Dog Control. He and the other talkers were trained by the air force team on authenticating targeting information and on communication procedures.

Sky never developed rapport with the targeting officers; they talked a different talk, walked a different walk.

At night in the inner sanctum of the headquarters bunker, Clean was the one most against their unsolicited help. He said he believed the F-111s flew into the sides of mountains. They had ground-hugging radar, but he understood that it didn't work altogether that well. The planes flew most often, according to Clean, on automatic pilot with its altitude set by computer and radar, but they flew too fast, too low, and when they approached mountains the plane couldn't pull up in time. Even if this wasn't often the case, it meant these bombers made mistakes sometimes and weren't always as on target as they'd like.

"Say we've got some action going near Skyline and the Vietnamese are marshaling for an attack, can we afford to give the F-111s targets fifty meters, four hundred meters, or what from our troops? Is their accuracy range within a thousand meters? Maybe they bomb our own people some of the time." Clean pursed his lips. He had, in fact, been bombed once in the valley by U.S. Air Force planes.

The things that Kayak was concerned about were the imprecise geological mapping of the area and the haphazard way the field commanders often gave coordinates of enemy locations. Plus, the F-111s flew on a flat plain. Our ground here was very up and down. A few lateral feet in the air could mean hundreds of feet up and down the sides of mountains, not to discount the wind drafts that bounced planes around. Wouldn't the wind drafts affect the fall of a bomb? Kayak asked.

I said that in Vietnam, while I was there, the air force used forward air controllers (FACs) when they supported ground troops. Too much chance of error otherwise. Man was being replaced here by technology. I liked a man sighting for those bombers. Did they use the the F-111s in Vietnam in support of ground operations involving American troops? I wondered.

"And the F-111s carried a lot of stuff, five-hundred-pound bombs—twenty-four apiece. Not a single bomb had any eyes or consciousness after it was released," I went on. "Plus, like Kayak said, this is rugged territory here, sheer drops of five hundred to a thousand meters and overhangings, and there were many mistakes in the mapping. Lot of loose variables. Plus we're doing OK without them. We got the Ravens eyeballing in other fast movers. Seems to me we got enough."

Zack called us little old ladies. He said we were afraid of new technology. We couldn't identify with anything that didn't have bodily functions. This F-111 can kill 130-mm guns. And if it has had problems in the past, well so what, the F-4 has had its problems—wasn't always on target—and with the crazy, unpredictable commitments we got sometimes from the ABCCC, the Air Force radio and command aircraft that overflew our area twenty-four hours a day—we didn't always get the F-4 support we wanted.

"The F-111s will work for us," Zack said. "Directly. We won't have to clear through ABCCC. Give them a chance. You don't have any choice anyway 'cause the deal has already been made. They are coming."

The attacks on Skyline continued to be low-intensity probes. There was no indication that the battle for Skyline would be raged with the same ferocity as during the previous year. One reason might have been the peace talks that had been initiated in Vientiane. Possibly, the Pathet Lao and North Vietnamese were coordinating their field activity with an overall eye toward the negotiations. Perhaps they were not as able to launch strong attacks because of the casualties they had taken after the Ravens went in or, another possibility, North Vietnamese forces could have been pulled out of Laos for deployment in South Vietnam. Ours was still a sideshow.

While the occasional skirmishes continued along Skyline, our main concern was that the 130-mms would begin bombing the valley any time. We knew some still operated in the area.

In early December, the first enemy round of the season landed in the valley, but it was not a 130-mm round. It came from an assault rifle. We were expecting a big crashing boom from a 130-mm and got a zing. A North Vietnamese or a Pathet Lao soldier, making his way through the Thai positions on top of the ridgeline and hiding in the rocky south side, began to fire at random targets.

"Damned nuisance," Bamboo said.

The following day, another sniper opened up from a second position. Our routine in the valley wasn't affected much by these enemy sharpshooters, but we tended not to lounge on the ramp the same way we had done in the past. At times, I had the feeling that someone up there on the ridgeline was looking at me as I walked near the Sky compound.

The snipers quickly became just a part of our lives. After the first day or so, whenever we heard the zing of a round going by and pinging off a rock, we dived for cover. Smoking cigarettes or reading books, we waited until someone fired from the valley floor or from the ridgeline into the general direction of the sniper. After another pause, we put out our cigarettes and put away our books, got up, and continued on the way. There was no rush of adrenaline, no fear. Zing, and we'd duck. Ten minutes later, we were back to normal routine.

But Bamboo was right—they were a damned nuisance.

I inherited Digger's GM when he was reassigned to Bouam Long. Most of his unit was in position east of the Long Tieng valley, though one element was detached to join my old unit, GM 22, which had pulled back from the PDJ and was dug in around LS 15. This augmented GM force patrolled east and southeast and occasionally engaged Pathet Lao and North Vietnamese. We were unsure how many North Vietnamese were in the river valley north of Skyline or exactly what their plans were for the coming offensive. Our plans generally were to hold Skyline by using the Hmong on the flanks as ground maneuver elements and reserves. A 105-mm howitzer was moved out to LS 15, and the Hmong in my GM began to fire their own close support—mostly by dead reckoning. Thai mercenaries came out and helped set up a fire direction center and patiently taught the Hmong the concept of indirect fire. When the Thais left, the Hmong took their own bearings and used sticks and knotted string to align the gun when they fired. They were more or less accurate, although they continued to adjust their sticks for months. They also had a random way of selecting fuses, but we were self-contained. We had maneuver elements and artillery, and the Ravens were usually around. From LS 15 down to the river valley was a tiny theater of war within the little Lao theater of war. The U.S. Army might be pulling out of South Vietnam, but we were still fighting and holding on.

In late November, we received the air force radios for our Hmong to communicate with the F-111s when they arrived.

I roomed with Kayak in the barracks building. With Shep gone, Kayak was always the last one off the ramp at night. He came into the mess hall, with his toothbrush in his shirt pocket, and ate. Later, he often sat by himself and read a book, although he talked with Father Bouchard when he visited.

Air America pilots and flight mechanics were often involved in animated conversations among themselves or with Sky officers during the evening meal. If they were flying the next day, the pilots weren't allowed to drink. Most of them spent an hour or so in the mess hall after the meal, drank coffee, and talked, or sometimes read a magazine or newspaper. Occasionally, they took food out to the bear, but generally, after leaving the mess hall, they went to their temporary trailers, relocated from LS 272, and read before going to sleep. They had to be up before dawn in the morning.

Each night, the four or five pilots who had finished their up-country flying and were catching rides back to Udorn the following morning could drink if they wished, and they were usually the only customers in the bar area in the early morning.

Sky officers ate at irregular times. Some, such as Hog, Bamboo, and Zack primarily, ate at Van Pao's residence. The officers working with the Thais ate in a mess hall at their end of the valley. The Sky officers working with the Hmong often just came in, took some food out of the cooking pots on the stove, put it on bread, and walked over to the headquarters bunker. Some Air America pilots also went to the headquarters building at night. This was the quiet inner sanctum of the valley, although it was busy and active around dusk. Dutch, aided by Wimpy, Scott, and the Big O, collected information for nightly situation reports, for B-52 targeting, and for the F-111s when they eventually arrived. We usually stood around a map board and talked about developments during the day—sniper locations, intelligence reports on enemy troop movements, patrol reports. Everyone made contributions; Sky people, especially among themselves, were not shy. Conversations shifted quickly from subject to subject. Topics ranged from a serious discussion on something like the downing of a T-28 to someone suggesting that Digger had been left so long at Bouam Long that he had molded in his hole. We missed the rational contributions that Digger had made to our evening meetings. He would be leaving in December, to be replaced at Bouam Long by Kayak.

When business was finished, the conversation degenerated into locker room banter with Clean usually acting as the master of ceremony. Hog enjoyed this give-and-take with the Sky contingent in the headquarters bunker and often later in the bar, but he did not participate when any outsiders were around. When prompted, Hog could be brutal in his comments to Bamboo and Clean. He called Bamboo "the flying zero" for a while because

Bamboo appeared to have grounded himself in the valley, rarely ever going anywhere. Hog also came up with phrases that became part of our language, such as the "dreaded" Lumberjack had "darkened his door" the other day "for a pair of seconds" to "hunker down" and talk about the Thais. "Not a pretty sight."

One of Hog's Hmong ops assistants—not his best English speaker—once described a field situation as "highly dangeral." This became a Hog term to describe anything with a high risk factor. Someone might tell Hog that Frenchy Smith would be flying him out to the PDJ and Hog would say, in jest, "That makes it highly dangeral."

His comments stood out because of his usual laconic nature. Sometimes, I found myself saying to Zack, "Oh, I've got to go darken the dreaded Hog's door." Or out at LS 15, I'd call in and say, "I'm going to hunker down here for the rest of the day and keep my distance from all you girl singers back there doing indoor work."

"Indoor work" was anything a bureaucrat did and not necessarily to be taken seriously.

After our map sessions in the bunker, I usually wandered back to the bar. It was not ornate—twenty feet square, a door in the back to the dining area, the front door with a screen and a spring that slammed it shut. The room was lit by a bare 100-watt light bulb in the ceiling. There was a plywood bar against a side wall, with liquor bottles lining a warehouse shelf behind it. Beer was in a refrigerator nearby. A dart board collected dust on the back wall; a poker table with kitchen chairs was off to the side. There were no pictures on the walls. No bartender. We put money in a cash box when we got drinks, although Clean was usually behind the bar and fixed the drinks, or not, depending on his mood.

The place always seemed crowded, maybe because everyone tended to talk loud. War stories predominated— there were many old warriors around. Clean, as an eighteen-year-old paratrooper, had jumped into Normandy with the 101st Airborne Division. Since then, he had been around every conflict involving the country and the Agency. The Air America pilots were equally seasoned and had their share of distinctive personalities. Greenway, a Bell helicopter pilot, had been a B-52 pilot in the air force. He said once that his squadron was visited by a shrink and each pilot was given a psychological readiness test. One of the questions was, if they were flying for the Strategic Air Command and received orders to fly over the United States and drop their bombs on their hometowns, would they comply? Everyone in the squadron said they would not. Except Greenway—he said he would. "You either obeyed orders, or you didn't," he commented.

Air America folklore was a popular topic, and the same stories changed with each telling. There was an incident some years before when an Air America test pilot fell asleep while ferrying a plane from Udorn to Savannakhet. He overflew Savannakhet and North Vietnam above the DMZ. He woke up over the South China Sea. Depending on who told the story, he had North Vietnamese rockets fired at him as he flew along, asleep; he had U.S. fighters chasing him; he flew back into Hue and filled up before trying to land at Savannakhet as if nothing had happened; or he flew back into Udorn via South Vietnam, landed, went home, packed his bags, and left. The story was always funny—like a situation comedy with new episodes.

If there was a quorum for a poker game, I played. Zack was the only other Sky officer who participated. Most of the players were Air America pilots. I was a constant winner. Brenda and I went three months that fall without cashing a check by living off my poker winnings.

The Air America pilots played poker like there was no tomorrow. Their salaries weren't enormous, but they were well paid. Helicopter pilots averaged perhaps $4,000 a month, including overtime and hazardous duty pay. They wore a lot of gold and usually carried large amounts of money wherever they went because they believed they might need gold and money to ransom themselves to safety if they were shot down. In poker, they went against long odds and won some big pots but lost many more.

"Part of their nature," Hog said. "They like long odds. More action, more adventure in it. No excitement in betting on a sure hand."

Kayak, the loner, usually slipped away from the headquarters bunker when business was over and went to our room. He had no interest in small talk. He took a bath before going to bed, naked, and read late into the night.

I usually went to my room before midnight. Kayak, awake, reading, stayed in one position on his bed for only five minutes at a time and then flipped into a new position as he hit the pillow with his fist to get it readjusted.

He also ate crackers, constantly, like a rat—gnawing away, taking small bites, for hours on end.

The incredibly dull books he read tended to be heavy, and he manhandled them from his chest to his pillow, where they made a whoosh sound as they hit the bed clothing. The area around his bed was littered with big books. I never did know where he got them.

I often thought the Sky case officers at Long Tieng were uniquely suited to the job: by experience, temperament, and personality. All were men of accomplishment, self-starters, with years of combat experience. Some were suspicious about Stateside society and uncomfortable with the social revolution of the sixties. Certain Sky behavior could have been looked on as antisocial. Were we this way before we arrived, or did we develop suspicious attitudes because it was part of the culture? Why did we love this godforsaken place, the stone-age Hmong, and the rowdy Thai mercenaries? We were a closed society of little more than a dozen men by the end of 1972, and there were no other officers in the pipeline to replace us. We were a dying breed and clannish. We were all so different, yet we had become so similar.

Why, though, didn't Kayak wear any clothes to bed? I asked around one time—everybody but Kayak slept in their shorts.

Lying there across the room, reading those dull books, eating crackers like a rat, hitting that pillow every five minutes, naked—he was on the other end of the spectrum from the girl singers of the world.

I just wished he'd wear shorts. And why did he walk around with a toothbrush in his mouth during the day? Why was he so restless, always anxious to get out there in the thick of the action?

The Air America pilots, who did not understand this man, said he had a death wish. I lived with him, but I didn't understand him either.

And who gave him all those crackers?

13

THE CHRISTMAS SEASON IN LAOS

Shortly before Christmas, the North Vietnamese produced a new weapon. Their sniper fire had not been particularly accurate. They did not have long-barrel sniper rifles and used their AK-47s and carbines at maximum range.

Early one morning near the Thai positions at the east end of the runway, we heard a zing and a ping from a sniper bullet, and everyone casually ducked. After another ping, we continued to hunker down, scratching and yawning. Then, zoom-kaboom—a DK-82 round came in screaming and exploded.

The pinging was from the spotter rifle mounted on a Soviet DK-82 rocket launcher. The Soviet gun had two triggers, one for the small-caliber rifle mounted on the tube of the DK-82. The gunner identified his target and fired a round or two with his rifle until he had the target spotted. Then, he pulled the trigger of the larger gun and fired the rocket.

Thereafter, the zinging from Skyline got more respect. When we heard a zing, we said, ''Holy shit,'' and ran like sumbitches.

The Christmas gifts we had ordered from the States for the kids started to arrive—dozens of them. This would be their first Christmas with us. Mim and Joseph had some problems understanding the concept of Santa Claus and gift giving, but they knew that other kids did not question it. Our two finally decided that this Santa Claus thing sounded very good for children. Christmas was about as much excitement as they could stand. I thought Mim would burst, she was so excited.

Brenda wanted a sewing machine. I had to go to Udorn in mid-December to pick up some radios for my GMs and photo interpretation (PI) work from overhead photography for Zack. While there, I bought a Singer sewing machine in a nice wooden cabinet at the base exchange. It had all the whistles and buttons and could do anything, maybe even microsurgery, said the clerk. Brenda was going to like it—state of the art, top of the line. I took it back to Long Tieng with me. Within the week, I would be heading down to Vientiane for the holidays.

The day after I arrived back in the valley, two new DK-82s started firing from the south slope of Skyline and there were several new snipers. Getting these pests became job one. Possibly, some slipped away over the ridgeline at night, but most stayed in place and hid among the rocks when combined Thai and Hmong forces swept the area. Watching through binoculars as the men scoured the south slope of Skyline for the snipers reminded me of bird hunting as a kid, only the game here was deadly and shot back.

I was supposed to leave on 22 December. All that day, I was busy working with Nhia to insure that our GMs were well supplied and would not go wanting while I was away. I had a variety of distractions, and the day had not been particularly successful. In late afternoon, the two new DK-82s, which had gone undetected during that day's sweep of the ridge, began firing at the ramp. Most of the Air America fixed-wing planes took off, which meant that I would have to go down to Vientiane on a helicopter with a large sewing machine in a box.

Nhia helped me carry the sewing machine down to the

ramp. One of the DK-82s, which was still working the area, aimed at the ammo dump in an effort to ignite some of the rounds. Several DK-82 rounds landed as we came around the last karst and trotted behind the bombproof Air Ops building. I was the only Sky man trying to get out at the time, and I joined a group of Thai, Lao, and Hmong.

I told Nhia to go on home and I would manhandle the box by myself. He wished me a Merry Christmas and left. There weren't many helicopters still in the area, and those that were around didn't want to come in on the ramp, which was hot from the DK-82 fire.

One helicopter finally came in. The pilot said over the Air Ops radio that he was leaving after the first eight paxs got on board or in three seconds, whichever came first. As I trotted out in front of Air Ops, a dozen or more people joined me. Suddenly, it did not seem appropriate to displace anyone with my box. I went around to the pilot's side of the helicopter when it landed and asked him if he could take this box in addition to eight paxs. He motioned that he didn't understand me, and then the helicopter took off, leaving me on the edge of the ramp with this large box.

Most of the other people who did not get on were hurrying back to the side of Air Ops. When I reached down to pick up the box, I heard a zing. The bullet hit behind me, near where the helicopter had landed.

"Holy shit," I said, running as fast as I could with the box.

Another helicopter came in and landed in another part of the ramp that was partially hidden by a karst. I ran out and asked the copilot if he could take my box and me in addition to the paxs. He said sure, but by that time the helicopter had been filled with passengers and there was no place even for me, much less the box. The helicopter took off.

I was the only one left in that particular part of the ramp. When I reached down to pick up the box, I heard another zing—between me and Air Ops. So I ran the other way and hid behind the karst.

When the next helicopter came in, I ran out, threw the box on, and jumped in behind it. Screw being polite.

That night, we went to the small embassy commissary and bought a large tree from New Zealand. We tied it to the top of the car, drove it home, and decorated it. The kids had trouble understanding the role of the imported tree and the snowlike decorations, but they were very excited. On Christmas Eve, we attended church programs and read ''The Night Before Christmas'' to Joseph and Mim when we put them to bed. They listened to every word.

We were up on Christmas morning before the kids, laid out the Santa Claus gifts, and set up lights and a movie camera around the tree. Then we sat down and waited for them to wake up, but they didn't. Why weren't they so excited that they would wake up at the crack of dawn?

Finally, Brenda went in and called them. Waking up gradually, they suddenly realized it was Christmas and were wide awake. Joe started running down the hall, with Mim right behind him. They turned the corner to the living room, and then I turned on the lights.

They froze, blinded. They couldn't see. I had too many lights. Both kids squinted because the lights hurt their eyes. They tried to make out their toys, but my million megawatts still blinded them. It was hard for them to be spontaneous at their first Christmas when they couldn't see what was going on, but they didn't know any better. They thought everybody's Christmas was the same—toys hidden behind blinding lights.

Returning to Long Tieng before New Year's, I was greeted by most of the bachelors who were leaving for their holiday break.

In Air Ops, I heard that one of the Ravens, Skip Jackson, had been killed over Christmas. He had been spotting an enemy position in the southern PDJ when one of the planes he was directing came out of the sun, and they clipped wings. Skip's little plane immediately spiraled to the ground. He had been a very bright person, kind of bookish bright like a lawyer, but he didn't look bookish; he had the physique of an athlete—small waist and broad shoulders. He had been the wing boxing champion at the Air Force Academy, had lettered in football, and had earned his master's after serving for a year as an assistant football coach at the academy. As a "fast burner" in the air force, what a life he was going to have. His death erased all the joy of Christmas.

Because the Ravens couldn't get Skip's body out, they later directed a fast mover to destroy his O-1 on the ground, so that the flames would consume their comrade inside. Like sailors burying their dead at sea, the Ravens looked after their own.

The snipers were still firing at us from the south slope of Skyline, but the Thais had some success in ferreting out the DK-82s so they weren't bothering us as much as they had been.

A group of technicians arrived to solve the problems we were having with our generators. Since we had moved back into the valley, the generators had been burning up after only a few days of operation. When we got in a new generator—heavy, expensive equipment—it was installed by techs from Udorn. They hung around for a day or two, and the generator worked fine. A couple days after they left, it inevitably burned up. We had gone through this several times, and we couldn't figure it out.

The techs went out on the porch of the mess hall the first night they were there and immediately saw the problem. Half the houses in the valley were lit. The generators were only large enough to power the Sky compound, Vang Pao's compound, the Thai area, and a few other select sites—not every household in the Hmong nation.

The next day, the techs found the switching station for the Long Tieng Outlaw Municipal Utilities Service. In the rear supply area of V. P.'s compound, they discovered a single outlet with twenty-five multiple plugs, stuck together, coming out of it. About fifty extension cords ran from the plugs out a window and into a lean-to, the outlaw switching station. At the end of each extension cord in the shed were more multiple plugs and more extension cords. We never did find out who was responsible.

Hog said, "Can't blame the Hmong for trying to capture a little bit of the only electricity they ever seen. It's amazing 'Merican magic, you know. Electricity is 'Merican. Makes the Hmong feel like your regular Seattle homeowners when they can go in their huts and switch on the lights."

About this time in Vientiane, the wife of an Air America official was terrorizing the commissary. An ethnic Lao, she had married an American several years previously. Her husband had died mysteriously. Next, she was married to an Air America pilot, but there was something he had found unsettling about her and they divorced. After looking around, she finally married her third American husband, who worked in Air America flight operations. She was known as a hard, opportunistic woman, and the other wives looked on her as a predator and local homewrecker. Possibly because she was unpopular with the Air America wives, the Lao woman did not give a tinker's damn about protocol or accepted norms of behavior in the American community.

Cosmetics at the commissary were a case in point. They were purchased in bulk at the Udorn base exchange and sold at a small glass counter in a corner of the commissary. The woman who ran this concession looked on her job as community service. She knew basically what products the women liked and placed her bulk orders in Udorn accordingly. When the Lao woman appeared on the scene, she went up to the counter and bought everything—every tube of lipstick, every compact, every rouge. These items soon appeared on the black market downtown. When the cosmetic section restocked, the Lao woman reappeared and again bought everything. A limit was then put on the amount of cosmetics that a woman could buy at any one time, but the Lao woman came in every day and bought her limit until she had bought out the counter again. In the eyes of the American women, she was a Lao she-devil.

Then, her American husband was found strangled to death. During the subsequent investigation, the usually inept Lao police discovered that the woman had a Lao boyfriend who had a shaky story about where he was the night of the murder. He later confessed that the woman had put him up to the killing and had, in fact, grabbed her husband's gonads, crushing them in both her hands, while the boyfriend strangled him.

Brenda boiled in indignation over the evils of that woman. She could hardly talk about anything else when I came in from up-country.

The woman was tried by the Lao courts, convicted of murder in the second degree, and sentenced to life in a Lao prison.

Brenda continued to bristle over the incident for a few weeks after the Lao woman went to jail, and then it was forgotten.

There was continuing interest in the number of North Vietnamese coming down to the PDJ to join in the attack on Skyline, as well as interest in those who might be leaving because of the peace talks. In an effort to monitor this probable ebb and flow of Vietnamese soldiers, Zack increased efforts to send out road watch patrols. Some teams were sent south from Bouam Long. He told me to send some around the northern edge of the PDJ to the area near the abandoned village of Ban Ban, where the road from North Vietnam entered the PDJ.

I told the commanders of my GMs that we had to get together four road watch teams of ten men each and dispatch them to the northeast. I would provide per diem, or bonus pay, plus new equipment, radios with signal scramblers, weapons, binoculars, and training. They had to provide only the men.

The commanders produced forty more or less healthy men for the job, although none showed any enthusiasm for the task. Road watch work was not part of their culture. The Hmong were pretty much here-and-now people, very basic in their approach to life. Analyzing enemy movements was a difficult concept for them. I was not sure that, even under orders, they would make a maximum effort to get through the North Vietnamese bivouac area north of the PDJ and move on to Ban Ban. Sky units in the southern MRs had found that road watch teams sometimes just moved over a few ridgelines and made up reports to send back.

Running road watch teams successfully always had been a challenge to Sky. Years before, Clean had the responsibility of sending out teams to monitor the traffic on Route 6. To enhance security, he sent out the teams with homing pigeons. There would be no radios for the enemy to vector, no batteries, no need for a rear radio headquarters. Each report would be sent back in a tiny pouch attached to the leg of a pigeon. The pigeon would fly back to its roost on the karst behind Air Ops in Long Tieng. This signal system was in harmony with the environment, Clean said. He provided small portable cages, made out of bamboo slivers and nylon thread, that could be attached to a pack harness. Clean also tested the birds. He carried them several miles south of Long Tieng, released them, and watched them fly in circles above him before setting out for Long Tieng. They always arrived at their cages before he did.

Clean started out with a large group of birds but soon developed what he called the first team, his favorites, and selected these for the first patrol. He was justly proud of his silent and sure messengers and helped the bird-carrying Hmong patrol member on with his special pack. The patrol pushed off for its road watch work.

The patrol ate those pigeons.

Ate every one.

To check the location of my teams once they were dispatched, I ordered some beacons. I could fly in a Porter over the general area where the patrol might be and, by triangulating, get a true fix on their position. Nhia and I trained the men near the old hospital in Long Tieng. Some were good; some were not. Three of the patrol leaders knew what they were supposed to do, but one was in a daze.

I did the beacon training myself. To mask the real purpose of the beacons and to simplify the training, I told the patrol leaders that these beacons were the most sophisticated thing of this type available. They were made by the same U.S. company that built the spaceship that went to the moon. The beacon would be their most important piece of equipment because, with it, they would stay plugged into all of the U.S. Air Force. Its inter-workings were so complicated that I did not understand it. All they had to know was that they turned it on at midday and let it run for one hour. It would be picked up by satellites, and they would be in contact with the overall Allied fighting machine. They would not be alone out there. Turn on this beacon, and the force was with them.

My plan was to stagger the patrols going out so that I would have one on the way out, one in position, one returning, and one in reserve. I sent out the first patrol, the one I thought was the best, at the end of January. A few days later at midday, I went up in a Porter with Nhia to the area where the patrol should have been. I had a simple hand-held antenna that I could turn in the direction of the beacon signal.

There was no beacon signal. Nhia got on the radio to

the patrol and said the U.S. Air Force was very mad at
them. They had to turn on the beacon.

The signal came up, and I took a reading. We flew to
another location, and I took a second reading, then another location and a third reading. Where the readings
intersected was the patrol's location—on a hilltop near
the jump-off point. The patrol was not making its way
north around the PDJ.

We brought the commander up later, and he yelled at
them. They started moving that afternoon, and from future beacon readings we tracked their progress north.

The following day, I was lounging on the ramp, lying on
top of some canvas, and taking the early-morning sun as
I waited for Greek to get me a helicopter.

Nhia came up and asked to review our schedule for
the following day. "We get a helicopter and go up north
of the PDJ and spot our patrol," I said, "and then we
go on up to Bouam Long so we don't give away the
patrol's location. We come back and drop your scuzzy
little butt off here, and I'm going down to Vientiane and
spend some much-deserved time with my family."

I closed my eyes again and got some more sun. Nhia
did not move.

"Why?" I asked, with my eyes closed.

"No reason," said Nhia.

After a pause, he asked, "Do you know who is flying
for us tomorrow?"

I turned to look at my ops assistant, as clever and de-
liberate as any man I had ever known. He did not ask
senseless questions.

"Why?" I asked.

"No reason," he said.

"This is a very good conversation we have going
here," I said, with one eye open. "Izzy is flying I think.
What's up?"

"Nothing."

I closed my eyes again, and Nhia continued, "Only

you know we fly over my home village. Well, not right over, but it's off to the west some, and you said once that my brother could live with you down in Vientiane and possibly go to school there, that you have plenty of room in the servants' quarters behind your house. If we can pick him up tomorrow and if you still think he can stay at your house in Vientiane, then he can fly right on down with you. Izzy wouldn't mind stopping for you in my village.''

Nhia stood there unashamed, looking me in the eye. I had, in fact, once mentioned that we had room behind our house if his brother wanted to live there while going to school. I had assumed his brother lived around Long Tieng, however, or would meet me in the valley.

''Where's your village, Nhia?'' I asked. He produced a map and pointed to an area west of Bouam Long.

I said, ''I don't know anything about this area, and Air America doesn't like to fly below high points and ridgelines they don't know for sure are controlled by friendlies. Your village here looks like it's halfway down the mountain in a part of Laos I've never been in before. Father Bouchard is probably the only round eye to have ever seen this area.''

''It's safe,'' Nhia said. ''And Izzy will fly in for you.''

''How old is your brother?''

''Twelve.''

''OK, if we have time and if the pilot will fly in, then we'll pick up your brother.''

The next day coming back from Bouam Long, Izzy and I were chatting on the intercom when Nhia punched me on the leg. He had his map stretched out on his lap. He pointed to Bouam Long, to Long Tieng, to where he thought we were, and then to his home village. He smiled.

I told Izzy that Nhia had a pax he wanted us to pick up.

''Who? Where?'' Izzy asked.

"His brother at about," and I gave him four-digit co-ordinates.

"You are full of crap. No way are we going in there. No way. Tell Nhia no way. No, put the headset on him, I'll tell him."

So I passed the customer headset to Nhia, and I looked out the side of the helicopter.

Nhia listened for a few minutes, talked a little, and then listened and talked a little more. He handed the headset back to me. Izzy said we were going in to pick up Nhia's brother, and I asked what Nhia had said to change his mind.

"I don't know," Izzy said. "Maybe it was Hmong hocus pocus. Nhia said it was safe and this was about the only chance in the boy's life to get out and it's only ten minutes out of our way. I don't know. Nhia's never ever lied to anyone I've ever known. Have you heard of him lying?"

"No." Nhia was a man of his word. He was calculating but absolutely truthful. If he said it was safe, one hundred percent safe, even though this was not that far from North Vietnam, then I'd believe him. So apparently did my friend Izzy.

We diverted our course and flew more to the west and then north. Soon, Nhia began pointing out mountains and rivers he knew. He directed us up a long valley and started to give me instructions. I gave my headset to Nhia, and he directed Izzy around a peak and then over a ridgeline. Ahead, we saw a large mountain village, and down the mountain slightly was an area that had been cleared and some letters staked to the ground. A helipad. The villagers were standing on the mountain between the village and the pad. One individual was standing below the rest near the panel markings. From a distance, it looked like he was lecturing the crowd that was spread out above him. As we came in closer, however, I could see that he was a young boy looking in our direction and holding a cloth bag by the straps in front of him. The bag hung to his knees.

When Izzy landed, Nhia jumped out and the boy came running through the turbulence of the helicopter and climbed on. Nhia waved to the villagers, got back on the helicopter, tapped Izzy on the shoulder, and helped the boy buckle his safety belt.

I could feel the energy and excitement in the cleanly scrubbed, neatly dressed youngster sitting beside me. He ignored me as his eyes roamed over the cockpit dash, up to the top of the helicopter, out the sides, at the headsets, the automatic rifles, my boots. I put the headset on him, and he listened while he looked straight ahead.

We landed in Long Tieng about nightfall. While Izzy refueled, Nhia and I walked off to the side of the ramp, the boy trailing behind. Nhia said his brother's name was Pao Vang. He had never flown in a helicopter before, seen television, ridden in a car or Jeep, talked on a telephone, slept on a mattress, used an indoor toilet, or eaten with a knife and fork.

"But he is a smart kid," Nhia said, "and he will learn fast and he will help around the house."

"OK, Pao Vang," I said turning to the boy, "you are our boarder. I'll get you back up here educated and toilet trained." Pao, who did not speak a word of English, looked at me with a blank expression.

"By the by, Nhia," I continued, "how did your brother know exactly when we were coming?"

"He's been waiting for days," Nhia said.

Behind us, Izzy was cranking up. Pao Vang and I got back on the helicopter, and we took off. Nhia, holding my AK-47, watched us leave.

I liked flying at night. Izzy and I continued talking. We passed high over the mountains, then the dam—the Vientiane reservoir—and finally over the rice fields of the Mekong River valley. In the distance, I could see the dim lights of the city.

Beside me, Pao Vang was looking around. He did not

miss any movement, any flash of light, any sound. His head was in constant motion.

Landing at Poppa Chu's, Pao Vang and I went out back and got a taxi. In the back seat beside me, Pao Vang continued to swivel his head toward everything that moved. He was suddenly afraid when he saw traffic coming in our direction. When we stopped at one of the few stop signs in town, he couldn't understand and knitted his brow. He looked in the different shops as we passed, sometimes turning to look out the rear window.

We got out of the taxi near the front gate, and I rang the bell. As the guard let us in, Brenda and the kids came running out. They all stopped when they saw Pao Vang.

Brenda said she told me not to bring back any live thing. I said this boy was Nhia's brother, and he was going to live with us while he learned English.

In the house, he almost tiptoed, not wanting to scratch the floor. He looked at the lights, at the windows, at the couches and chairs. Mim talked to him in Thai, but he didn't understand. The maid came in and spoke to him in Lao. He didn't answer right away, and we thought he hadn't understood. He kept looking around. Very quietly, he then said something to the maid. She smiled and said he was thirsty. She led him out to the kitchen, but in a few minutes he was back looking around. Joe walked up and hit him in the knee with his fist. Pao Vang smiled, and the two began to wrestle.

Brenda and I had been amazed at our kids' discovery of household items that we took for granted. We were equally amazed at Pao Vang as he came across the everyday things around us, one by one: the air conditioner, the refrigerator, the telephone. How can sound go so far in "no time?" he asked the maid.

Pao Vang had an incredible curiosity. Within the four days of my home visit, he knew where everything was.

Once, for instance, I came in and asked, "Pao Vang, where are the scissors?" as I made a scissors gesture with two fingers. He led me to Brenda's and my bedroom and over to the dresser, down two drawers to a small bag in the back under Brenda's underwear. That wasn't the pair I was looking for, so he took me outside and showed me hedge clippers and pliers. When I shook my head, we went back inside and he handed me staplers and Mim's hair clasp. If I had not stopped him, he would have shown me everything in our house that might have resembled something like two fingers scissoring together.

Brenda had given me a Leica camera for my thirtieth birthday. As I took photos around town, I threw the exposed film cartridges into a bowl in my study. When a dozen or so cartridges collected, I took them to a local developer.

After Pao Vang had been at our house for three or four months, I told him I would take him back to Long Tieng for a visit the next time I came home. Soon afterward, I noticed that the number of film cartridges in the bowl had increased. There were four or five cartridges when I looked one time, and the next day there were eight or nine.

When I had the film developed, I discovered that the extra cartridges belonged to Pao Vang. He had learned how to use the camera by watching me, although I could not fathom how he figured out the F stops, shutter speed, and focus. The photos were for his return trip up-country. He had held the camera out at arm's length to take several close-ups of himself. By using mirrors, he had pictured himself lounging around the various rooms. He had photos of the telephone lines coming into the house, the toilets, the kitchen and the opened refrigerator, and the television set from all angles.

Back up-country, my first road watch patrol ran into North Vietnamese north of the PDJ and turned back. The second patrol also encountered North Vietnamese, and they scattered, individually returning to LS 15. The third patrol was led by the Hmong who was painfully slow in understanding what I wanted. I had no hopes of his mission being successful. His men seemed to gaze around most of the time. Nobody talked much in his group. If I told them, "Go over there and wait," they went over there and fell asleep.

When they were dispatched, they moved north through the area controlled by the North Vietnamese and eventually to a hill overlooking Ban Ban. They set up an observation post and clearly reported activities on the road below them, exactly like I had asked them. Their beacon was on at precisely 1200 and went off precisely at 1300. Their information was invaluable.

They eventually ran out of supplies and had to return overland to LS 15. On the way, they were caught in a B-52 strike.

It was difficult to blame anyone else. It was my patrol. I had coordinated its route. I was around when Dutch made up the Arclight strike. I had to take responsibility. Hog and Zack made no comments to me about the incident, although Hog's hard look clearly indicated his reproach when I told him. It was the most severe reprimand I was ever to receive from Hog.

I knew the B-52 bombardment hit exactly on top of the patrol. I had taken a reading of its position not long before the afternoon bombing.

Maybe all the patrol members were not killled, I told Zack. Some could have made it through the bombing. I asked Air Ops for a twin-engine Cessna so that I could go up and post over the area as I tried to make contact with the remnants of my patrol. I sat beside the pilot, and Nhia was in the back with the radios. We were silent as we flew north—fearing the worst.

When we got over the area north of the PDJ, we were very high and began flying in a wide circle. Nhia called for the patrol.

The patrol leader came on immediately. All was well. They had no casualties.

"What about the bombing the previous day? Weren't there a lot of bombs going off?" I asked.

"Yes, thank you."

"Thank you?"

"Yes, there were enemy all around, and the bombs made them go away and hide. The air force did a very good job. Bombs landed very close, but we weren't hurt. We all gathered close together, and we turned on the beacon and put it over our heads. Good beacon. It worked perfectly. We are OK. Thank you."

Thank *you*, Lord.

14

F-111S AND
HMONG TALKERS

The day the first F-111 came over the Mekong River from Thailand and entered MR II, Glassman was manning the radio.

"Red Dog Control, this is Show Boat 42," the pilot said.

"Roger, Show Boat 42, this is Red Dog Control." Glassman turned and smiled at the Sky officers who had gathered to watch this inaugural contact.

"Do you have a divert?" asked the pilot, in accordance with the communication SOP. He was asking if Glassman had a new target for him or was he free to hit the target provided to him before the mission by the 7 AF targeting staff in Saigon.

"No divert," Glassman said. The F-111 pilot's "Roger" indicated that he was continuing to his primary target.

Within fifteen minutes, we heard, "Red Dog, this is Show Boat 42. I am RTB [return to base]. Good afternoon."

There was a lull in action for the first few days after the F-111s came on the scene, and there were no diverts. The conversations between the F-111 pilots and the Hmong radio operators remained cryptic and correct, although a noticeable warmness seeped into the communications. It was the pilots' first opportunity to deal with the Hmong, and it must have personalized their work to put them into contact with the ground fighting force—mountain men, guerrillas—working with the CIA.

For the Hmong in Red Dog Control, it was a recurring highlight of their lives to communicate directly, in English, with Americans flying up in the heavens. American space explorations had captured the imagination of the Hmong at Long Tieng. For those assigned to communicate with the F-111s in Red Dog Control, it was as if they, in their small way, played a part in the space game as they talked to "almost" astronauts. They looked forward to their short conversations with the pilots almost every waking minute. It amazed me how proud these Hmong could be over so simple an act, and they communicated that enthusiasm in their transmissions. The pilots knew that someone on the ground really appreciated them.

The protracted, celebrated peace talks in Paris produced a cease-fire in Vietnam on 28 January 1973. On 21 February, peace agreements were signed in Laos. This peace lasted two days. U.S. Air Force bombing was renewed on 23 February when the North Vietnamese showed no intention of quitting the fight in Laos. For us, the two-day peace was something that went bump in the night. We saw the Lao peace accords as an incidental consequence of the talks on ending the war in South Vietnam but not relevant or enforceable in up-country Laos. Also, in the absence of media coverage, no one in the United States particularly cared.

Shortly before the cease-fire, the Bear from Savannakhet and I were talking with Greek in Air Ops one afternoon. It was the rainy season. The weather was bad, and Air America was having trouble getting around. The skies over the valley had just opened up, and Bear was going up with me to recon the area to the north.

From the U.S. Air Force guard frequency on one of Greek's radios, we heard "Mayday, Mayday." A frightened pilot gave four-digit coordinates for his location and said he was bailing out.

A Twin Pack had just shut down on the ramp, and the pilots were walking across to Air Ops. Bear and I were out the door and running in their direction by the time the air force pilot had finished his Mayday signal. Catching the Air America pilot by his arm, I said, "MAYDAY." He and the copilot turned and caught up with Bear and me as we reached his helicopter. He was cranked and rolling within seconds. We got up in the air, and the pilot called around to get fixes on other helicopters working the area. There were none anywhere close to the downed air force pilot, who was somewhere east of us.

We were monitoring the guard frequency, and the air force pilot came on. Using his hand-held survival radio, he told us that he was on the ground. He had heard people in the distance and was running to the top of a nearby peak to hide.

Once activated, the survival radio emitted a beacon signal. The Air America pilot slowly turned the helicopter from northeast to east to southeast. He had a directional antenna in the nose, and we headed where the beacon signal was the strongest. The closer we got, the stronger the signal and the easier to home.

The U.S. Air Force radio platform was active on other frequencies. It was heading all planes in the theater toward the downed pilot, who had been heading back to Thailand from a rescue mission over North Vietnam. The planes with him were low on fuel and had to continue going south. Other planes were in the air, however, and were going all out to assist in the rescue.

We were the closest, and the platform told us to go in. The Bear and I chambered rounds in our rifles. The memory of the unsuccessful attempted rescue of the Raven on the PDJ and Skip's death were still very clear in my mind.

The downed pilot came back up. He was on guard and, in a low whisper, said people were on the trail below him—dozens of men. He had a pistol, and he was going to try to hold them off until we got to him. The Air America pilot told him we were probably close. He asked if the pilot could hear the helicopter.

"Yes, yes," he said, no longer whispering, "I hear you."

Unknown to the pilot, he had landed near a friendly settlement, one I had visited often. The people he heard were friendly Hmong villagers, who were probably excited about some man dropping out of the clouds in a parachute.

"I see you, I see you. Come on this way at your two o'clock. I'm at the top of the hill. I'll stand beside the big rock. Do you see the big rock? Be careful, the people are on the other side of the hill."

The Air America pilot said, "Roger, you're going to be OK. I see the rock. Wave your panel. OK, good work, my friend, I see you."

As we approached, Bear and I unloaded our rifles. I could see the villagers crowded near the base of the hill. Some were pointing to the top where the pilot was hiding behind a large boulder. They had stretched out his parachute and were examining it. Some men had righted the ejection seat, which I suspected would be in the headman's hut that evening.

When we got over the rock, the flight mechanic dropped a line from the helicopter. It had a large metal ball on the bottom that acted like a sinker. The pilot got on the ball and was hauled back up to the helicopter, which had turned and was heading back to Long Tieng.

Bear and I helped to get the pilot inside. He was very grateful, a happy individual. He said he became disoriented after going through a rain cloud, developed vertigo, and had possibly turned upside down. He had ejected because he was afraid he was going to run into a mountain.

He did not listen when we said that the village was friendly. To him, he had punched out over Laos, not far from China and North Vietnam, and had been rescued. He probably didn't think there were any friendly Orientals in the country.

This was reinforced when the air force rescue team arrived in the valley later to pick him up. Jets made passes over the valley as if to tell everyone to keep their heads down. Two Jolly Green Giant rescue helicopters landed in the middle of the runway, their gunners standing by their positions with their fingers on the triggers. Hmong hid along the runway. They were afraid even to look at the U.S. Air Force helicopters, on the chance that they would be shot.

Hell, this was our home, our workplace. The American helicopter crews acted like they had landed in the middle of the valley of the shadow of death, for Christ sake. We were going to invite them in for a cup of coffee, but they weren't smiling and didn't leave their guns in the helicopters. Not very friendly guests. One of the officers from the Sky administrative staff took the pilot down to one of the Jolly Green Giants by himself. No case officer wanted to go out in front of those guns. Those people were dangerous.

When the Jolly Greens took off, the jets made one last pass before they disappeared.

Boy, oh boy, we said that night at the bar, that U.S. Air Force is tough—comes from being so far up in the air away from things on the ground. They don't know the good guys from the bad. We told the Ravens that we wondered what they had been telling their air force brothers to make them so hostile.

Jerry Conners, the Air America base manager at LS 20A, was married to one of the most beautiful women in the world, a Thai lady named Prou. She and Brenda struck up a friendship in Vientiane, and Jerry and I got along famously up-country. Jerry played poker, and I liked my poker-playing friends. He and I eventually arranged our Vientiane time together so that he and Prou and Brenda and I could spend time together. On one trip down to Vientiane, Jerry said that, although he had lived in Laos for several years, he had just heard about a golf course some five miles out of town toward Nong Khai. It was a local operation, but a golf course was a golf course, and he asked if I wanted to join him in a round of golf. I said sure; I had a set of clubs at the house. We made arrangements for him to pick me up the following morning. This is just like they do it back home, we agreed. Get some time off. Go play golf.

The next morning, Brenda left early with the kids to attend a function at the American school. I waited for Jerry to drive up.

He arrived late in the back of a samlor, a three-wheel bicycle with a hooded rear seat, the local taxi. He had forgotten to tell his beautiful wife that he needed the car and she had taken off somewhere, so it was samlors or nothing. His clubs were on the seat beside him and he had another samlor waiting to take me and my clubs.

"Five miles in a samlor?" I asked.

"Sure," he said. "It's level, and we ain't peddling."

This was not quite the way we would have gone to the golf course back home, but it would do. The golf course was not like anything back home, though, not close. But it would do.

It was an open rice field. The only way we knew it was the golf course was because the samlor drivers said so, and there were, in fact, sticks scattered randomly around in the ground, with rags tied to their tops. A thatched roof hut was off to the side near a shade tree, the pro shop, we assumed, but no one was around. We walked out to the closest stick and found that, sure enough, it was sitting in a hole the size of a beer can. We were on the golf course.

We hired our samlor drivers to be our caddies and helped them on with the golf bags. After selecting a tee area and a hole to shoot to, we teed off.

With only thirteen sticks in the field, we had to plot our own course. We used some of the holes several times, but with different approaches. Because it was a make-your-own course, we made our own rules. If a drive landed nearer a flag that was not the one we were playing to, we could play to that flag with a one-stroke penalty. Also, if we caught the caddy of the other player moving the other player's ball, we got a one-stroke bonus and the right to hit the other player's ball away from the flag. The other player would have to play it from where it landed. For the first violation, we could hit the other's ball with a nine iron. For the fifth violation, we got to hit it with a driver.

We also made up our own pars. One hole was a par eight, and we had several par sevens. One was a hundred-yard par seven, and we both bogeyed it. Jerry did because I caught his caddy walking toward the flag with the ball between his toes, and I gave it a penalty hit across the field with my four iron. And I bogeyed it because, when I got to the flag, we found it was just a stick stuck in a grassy part of the field. There was no beer can-size hole. So Jerry pulled the stick out, which left a small hole in the ground, and I had to putt until I got my ball to rest on top of that tiny hole.

We finally finished our round of golf and returned home in the samlors, peddled by our caddies. It was almost like playing golf back home, only different. I played par golf that day, the only time in my life.

In the days to come, the Hmong talkers up-country began giving diverts to the F-111s when they arrived in our MR. Working up the divert information for passage was complicated, but the talkers did their job well, checking and rechecking their calculations. Passing on the divert information also gave them more opportunity to talk with the pilots, which further enhanced their bonds.

We received mixed reports from the field on the accuracy of the F-111 bombings. Then, one of our photo interpreters in Udorn noticed from some overhead photography that an area supposedly hit the previous day by an F-111 showed no signs of any bombing. We requested that all F-111 missions be held up until we could determine the problem and whether it was a one-time miss or if it happened more often. We heard from one of the Ravens that the F-111 targeting people went crazy when we challenged them on the accuracy of their planes. They sent up a high-level delegation to check our computations, test our talkers, and generally get us back in line as happy customers.

These people seemed uncomfortable in dealing with non-U.S. Air Force people, especially those who did not look particularly military, and they did not have a friendly attitude. Greek, for one, thought they were brassy. He stayed close, smiling when they made eye contact, intent on challenging any unsubstantiated knock on the way we did things in MR II.

At the request of the air force delegation, Greek ordered two Air America helicopters for an aerial reconnaissance. It would conclude with the helicopters hovering two kilometers off to the side of Sam Thong within sight of a suspected 130-mm position up the river valley north of Skyline. The coordinates for the position would be passed as a divert to the next F-111. Greek and Hardnose accompanied the targeting officers. Hog and Clean went up on Skyline in a Jeep to watch the bombing run from ground level.

Everyone was in place before the next F-111 arrived. They heard Glassman divert it to the suspected 130-mm position. Per the communication SOP, there would be no radio contact with the plane from the time it received the divert information until it had released its ordnance and turned for home. So Greek, Hardnose, and the rest of the team in the helicopters and Hog and Clean on Skyline kept their eyes on the target, and waited and waited. Finally, Red Dog Control reported that the pilot had signed off and gone south. He had dropped his bombs.

"Not on any target we can see," Clean said.

Greek could hardly contain himself in the helicopter as the air force people squirmed and talked among themselves. They left the valley without comment, intent on getting back to Udorn and Takhli so they could staff out the problem.

The F-111s continued to fly in our area, but we made sure that their targets were farther and farther from friendly positions. One day, when Lumberjack was on duty in the Thai headquarters area on the east end of the valley, a 130-mm round landed nearby. Lumberjack thought it was one of the more common DK-82 rounds and began calling around to people on Skyline and up in the air, trying to get counter-battery fire. Another 130-mm round came roaring over Skyline and hit near the first.

"Holy shit," Lumberjack yelled, "Somebody get that sumbitch."

An F-111 happened to be en route at the time. The pilot was diverted to the nearest suspected 130-mm position and was asked to drop all twenty-four of his five-hundred-pounders.

Another 130-mm round landed close to Lumberjack. He was now becoming convinced that the fire was not coming from a DK-82 because the ground shook when the round landed. It also left a huge crater in the ground.

More rounds landed as another F-111 reported in. Red Dog Control told the pilot to drop twelve of his five-hundred-pounders at another suspected 130-mm site and then come around and drop the remaining twelve bombs on the same site.

The F-111 pilot said, "Roger, Red Dog Control."

There was silence on the air until Lumberjack began yelling that another big round had just landed.

Then there was quiet.

"Tonto," a Thai radio operator in a forward position on Skyline, who had been in the middle of the efforts to fix the muzzle blast of the 130-mm gun, suddenly came on the air and began yelling, "You got it, you got it, you got it. I can see it. You blew it out of its hole."

The F-111 had hit the 130-mm gun dead-on. This was confirmed later by aerial reconnaissance. The gun, lying on its side, had been reduced to rubble.

Lumberjack joined Zack in praise of the F-111s thereafter, and Hog, Clean, Kayak, Greek, and I had less to say.

Yer Pao Sher, commander of Bouam Long north of the PDJ, which had been the recipient of many F-111 sorties while we decided on their dependability, reported that the F-111s had changed things where he lived. They delivered. Vang Pao, he said, could keep all his GMs, his 105-mm and 155-mm howitzers, all his mines and rockets—just give Bouam Long the F-111s.

15

HMONG
NEW YEAR

The Hmong New Year, like Tet in Vietnam and the Chinese New Year, came in February. Because of the peace talks or the F-111s or for whatever reason, our forces were not under attack this February, as they had been in years past. Vang Pao wanted the troops in the field to celebrate the New Year in traditional fashion. This had something to do with killing a water buffalo and dressing it for a New Year's Day feast. It was an important part of the tradition for the buffalo to be sacrificed where the Hmong lived—an integral part of the Hmong belief in the trees and the mountains around them. Where the buffalo was killed was significant in bridging the distance between the Hmong people and their environment.

Hog was the first to learn that V. P. wanted live water buffalo delivered to all forward Hmong positions. It was one of those cross-cultural propositions that sounds simple in each language but had different meanings. Sky and Air America had plenty of planes and helicopters, and V. P. was sure there was some way to get the live animals out to the Hmong sites. It was important to him and to the Hmong, but it did not appear important to us. We saw no value in heli-lifting live buffalos. Nice buffalo steaks in cardboard boxes we could do.

I went with Hog to argue with V. P. on the matter. Maybe, I suggested, we could rotate some of the men from the different sites back to a special area in the valley where they could kill the buffalo, and we'd send the meat out to the sites.

V. P. said no, the water buffalo had to be butchered where the men lived and worked. He cocked his head and knitted his brow as if confused about why I didn't understand this.

So we went to Greek and said V. P. has these water buffalo to move to the field.

"You don't mean live, do you?" asked Greek.

"Yea, we sorta do," Hog said.

"A water buffalo is bigger than a Volkswagen, weighs a ton. How are we going to get them to LS 15?" Greek asked.

"That's what Air Operations is supposed to know how to do. That's your job."

"You tell Vang Pao to go stick a water buffalo up his ass. We don't have any livestock facilities on our aircraft."

"Greek," Hog said with a meaningful look.

"Oh, shit, Hog, how do we move live water buffalo?" Greek asked rhetorically. "I reckon we have to sling them out."

It didn't work on the first try. The buffalo was fitted with a belly harness, and a helicopter came in and began to drop a weighted line for someone to attach to the harness. The water buffalo heard the helicopter and took off, dragging three or four Hmong behind him.

Tranquilizers were ordered from Udorn. The next buffalo was doped up for his sling ride. This time, the buffalo stood with his head down and allowed the helicopter to pick him up. In time, he was delivered to one of my positions near LS 15. For several days, Air America slung out water buffalo to the forward positions. An Air America helicopter coming in to a position with a doped-up buffalo was a strange sight—reminded me of the Brooks Brothers logo.

I had long since learned that the Hmong had better eyes than I did, even when I used binoculars. For instance, I might be waiting on a site for a helicopter, and the skies appeared empty. A Hmong looked in the distance, without squinting, and said, "Chopper." I looked up and didn't see a thing. Nhia said, "Yeap, sure is." When I took out my binoculars and scanned the sky, I might see a speck way in the distance. Maybe that was a helicopter, or it could be dirt on the lens. Once, the Hmong spotted a helicopter, but I could just make it out with the binoculars. Then they said it wasn't ours, that it wasn't coming our way. It took me another two or three minutes to see the speck moving laterally.

At one site, a helicopter arrived without its water buffalo. The kicker got on his stomach to guide the helicopter down so that the animal would have a soft landing, but there was no buffalo at the end of the sling.

The pilot said, "Shit, we had him just a moment ago."

"Nope," one of the Hmong said, "there wasn't a water buffalo there, at least since Sam Thong."

The Hmong had not only seen the helicopter ten miles out but had seen that it wasn't slinging anything. We often wondered if there were any Hmong along the way who saw that water buffalo fall from the chopper. "Why would Sky send the buffalo that way?" they might have asked. Or, if they didn't see the helicopter and suddenly a water buffalo dropped out of the sky at their feet, they would have said, "Damned thing was flying."

Greek's real problem came in getting water buffalo to Bouam Long. It was just too far to sling one buffalo at a time. Also, we were deep into the smoky season, and it was a constant struggle getting Air America pilots to fly helicopters through all that haze. Greek ordered up an Air America Chinook, a large transport helicopter with a sizable lift capacity. T. J. and Super Mex pitched in and worked on getting the buffalo ready for the flight.

"The plan here," T. J. explained, "is to dope these animals until they drop and then lift 'em onto pallets with a forklift, strap 'em down, and put 'em on the Chinook two by two. We can get eight on."

The water buffalo were led behind Air Ops where the tranquilizing and palleting was done. By the time the Chinook arrived from Udorn, the eight buffalo were on the ramp and lashed down to their pallets in neat rows. They looked like they were ready for mailing. Their legs were hog-tied, like rodeo animals. They were lying on their sides, strapped to the individual pallets with heavy webbing.

T. J. and Super Mex were justly proud of their cargo, but the Air America pilot said he wasn't carrying them to Bouam Long.

The Greek exploded. "You worthless, scum-sucking, overpaid bus driver, what do you mean you ain't carrying these pallets up to Bouam Long?" He took some antacid pills.

"I don't do animal acts," said the pilot. "How long are they tranquilized for? How long they going to lie there peacefully and sleep?"

"Hell, I don't know, we'll ask T. J.," Greek said. "Hey, T. J., how long have you got these cows tranquilized for? Long enough to get to Bouam Long, right?"

"Yeap," said T. J.

"How do you know, T. J.?" asked the pilot.

"Well, I've just been doing this air freight of water buffalo for a week and I know, or I knew before you two started arguing, that there was plenty of time to get to Bouam Long."

"OK," said the pilot, after consultation with his crew. "We will take your cows up to Bouam Long on two conditions. One, I use temporary, emergency chocks at the rear of the rollers (two tracks of rollers inside ran the length of the helicopter). If one of those animals so much as bats his eyes, shows any signs that he's coming off Dr. T. J.'s drugs, they're out the back door, all of them.

I do not want a half-crazy water buffalo loose inside my helicopter flying over clouds near the PDJ. You can understand that, can't you, Greek?''

"What's number two?" Greek asked.

"T. J. goes with us."

"Are you crazy?" T. J. exclaimed.

"Or you, Greek," the pilot said.

"Are you crazy?" the Greek said.

So Super Mex went.

Halfway to Bouam Long, one of the water buffalo blinked, but no one saw it. He blinked again, and still no one saw it. Then he must have realized that he was lying down in an unfamiliar place, and he wanted to get up and look around.

As he tried to get up, Super Mex and the crew said, "Holy shit."

They removed the chocks from the rear of the roller tracks. The buffalo, continuing to struggle on the pallet, kicked more violently. The pilot put the nose of the helicopter up in the air and dropped the rear. The buffalo began to go out the back, two at a time. The buffalo who had stirred was just getting on his feet and out of the webbing when he disappeared.

The North Vietnamese on the ground probably reported, "We were bombed by eight buffalo today."

V. P. decided to have a large baci at his Long Tieng compound during the Hmong New Year. He invited the Stick, Hugh T., the Ravens, all of Air America, and the Thai commanders. There was a big turnout.

Zack brought his wife and son up from Bangkok. The last to arrive, they came in over the valley about dusk on a Beach Baron aircraft. The valley was socked in. The pilot circled for several minutes, but his fuel was getting low. He either had to punch through and land or head back to Vientiane. Greek was working in Air Ops and noticed a small opening near the east end of the runway. He told the pilot that he could try to land, but it would require some quick turns around a karst to get in. The hole in the clouds was closing fast. The pilot guided the small plane down and around a karst. It landed first on one wheel and then came down hard on two wheels. Hog was there in a Jeep. As Zack's wife got into the Jeep, she said it was nice of Hog to come down and pick them up.

"Hell, ma'am," he said slowly, "I just came down to watch the crash."

Outside the assembly hall, Hmong girls in their colorful skirts tossed balls back and forth, a traditional courting gesture. If a Hmong boy broke in and started tossing a ball with one of the girls, it was taken as a serious show of affection and marriage often ensued. Inside, Hmong bands, with their flutes and drums, alternated playing. Tables displayed dishes of sticky rice, pork, peppers, greens, chicken, and water buffalo. Assorted bottles of liquor and tubs of beer sat on other tables.

And there were good, stouthearted men around—Thai, Hmong, and American.

At one point, Hog, Zack, the Stick, and Hugh T. were standing in a group. As I looked across the room, I thought that I had never worked for better men. Although unknown to the world outside, they had extraordinary character and well served the American public. The group broke up, and Zack came over to where I was standing with some Air America people. One pilot, who had flown up just for the baci, was well ahead of everyone else in drinks.

I said that Hugh T. was a fine man, a man of culture and education. "Look at his hair," I said, motioning over to Hugh. "I have seen that man get off a helicopter going full torq, and it didn't mess up his hair. Didn't put a hair out of place. That's class."

Slurring his words, the pilot said, "It'svsa a hairpiece, that's why it looks soo neat."

"No, it isn't," said Zack. "I don't know a lot, but I

know for sure that Hugh T. doesn't wear a hairpiece."

The pilot took a few steps back and looked wide-eyed at Zack. He kept repeating, "You don't believe me . . . you don't believe me. . . ."

"No," Zack broke in and grinned.

"I'll prove it tooo you," the pilot slurred. After putting his drink of local Mekong liquor on the floor, he staggered across the floor to a circle of men that Hugh had just joined. We thought he was going to look closely at the back of the station chief's head, but he moved beside the man standing to Hugh's left. He gave us an exaggerated wink and turned back to the circle. Slowly, he began to snake his right hand up behind the man standing next to Hugh. When his hand was about shoulder high, he leaned back so that he could see Hugh from the rear, then he quickly reached up and grabbed his hair.

The pilot might have honestly expected to come away with a hairpiece, but Hugh had a full head of hair and was almost yanked backward to the floor. He tried to get his balance, but the pilot continued to shake him by his hair. Hugh turned and said, "Ouch, goddamnit," and slapped the pilot's hand away.

16

THE POLITICS OF WAR

Soon after the baci we got the first message about the bomb damage assessment (BDA), an air force term. The air force wanted to know how effective its F-111s had been. A cable demanded BDA.

Previously, when we had received bureaucratic tasking up-country, someone got the word to the Stick in Udorn. The base either stepped in and took care of it or told the requester to go away.

This time, the Stick said he couldn't help. We had been penetrated by the U.S. Air Force and were part of its equation now. The air force office in Vientiane perhaps resented our direct targeting of its planes. The F-111 program did, in fact, obfuscate the need for so many air force bureaucrats in Vientiane, so proprietary interests were involved. For a bureaucrat, that is a life-and-death proposition. These detractors in Vientiane said the F-111 commitment to MR II was a misuse of air force resources. Our BDA was necessary to determine its cost-effectiveness.

But we didn't have BDA on all the strikes. We had sent the 474th F-111 squadron some damaged small-arms weapons from an air attack, and Zack had helped Vang Pao write a letter of appreciation that included the phrase "whispering death," a transliteration of the North Vietnamese term for the F-111s. We also knew that the North

Vietnamese were extremely hesitant about any massing of their forces, and we were not being pressed on Skyline or on any of our other positions as we had been in years past. To us, that was prima facie BDA evidence. The air force brass in Washington, possibly prompted by the air force bureaucrats in Vientiane, however, continued to hound us for more detailed reporting.

At times, we had necessarily diverted the planes to targets out of sight of the line troops and out of reach of the guerrilla patrols. We had no way to assess bomb damage other than through aerial reconnaissance. This required flying over old targets and enemy territory. It was dangerous and began to take up all our time, especially mine. I was doing most of the field BDA work.

The cables kept coming, asking for more BDA. We responded to most, but we felt like we were at the mercy of an insatiable animal. BDA for the F-111s was taking over our lives. We finally received a cable that said the air force had to go before a hostile U.S. Senate in a few days to justify spending a significant part of its budget on the F-111s, presently in use in our region. We were on the point. Give them BDA. We had been captured and mastered by our tools.

We renewed our field work and finally got together in the main room of the Long Tieng headquarters bunker to write the definitive BDA cable. Two weeks later, our words were delivered by U.S. Air Force brass before the Armed Forces Committee of the Senate. We read them, word for word, in *Stars and Stripes*, the military newspaper that we received several days late.

Times were changing. First, the Joint Chiefs of Staff, and now the U.S. Senate were getting involved in our work. It was reported in international newspapers. MR II had become a topic on the Washington political scene, and we knew in Long Tieng that the end of our secret war was near.

Resigned to our fate, we still marveled at the magical relationship between the Hmong talkers at Red Dog Control and the F-111 pilots. They never met. They used a total of about 150 words that communicated volumes—the mountain men and the astronauts. As Yer Pao Sher had said, the F-111s were worth everything else we had put together. Some felt that, if the war had gone on, the 474 TFW would have destroyed every sizable North Vietnamese unit in MR II, but Sky certainly would have lost its autonomy to run the war. We would have been engaged in bureaucratic battles, in which we had no experience. The F-111s came with a lot of baggage.

We thought it had been better with just the troops—our guys against their guys. Commandos lining up on some dirt strip in the rain during the middle of the night, their helmets tied down with old sheets, going off to jump into a little opening next to the PDJ if they could find it. Browbeating commanders to get their men out to patrol and engage the enemy. Firing our 105-mm howitzers and using strings and sticks for sighting. Moving our GMs out to high ground to entice the enemy into attacking. Getting live buffalo out to forward positions.

These were the things that Hog, Clean, Kayak, Greek, and I knew how to do. Zack was the only visionary in the group.

One foggy night, we received word that a Thai at a forward position had been severely wounded in an accident and would certainly die if he were not evacuated before morning. Al Cates, the senior pilot in the valley that night, volunteered his Twin Pack crew to go out on the evacuation. Charlie Basham was his first officer. As the helicopter was trying to make its way into the site, it crashed and came to rest between the Thai and North Vietnamese positions.

Cates came on his radio immediately and relayed back that no one was hurt, but the chopper was disabled. They would stay near the helicopter until morning.

Lumberjack contacted the Thais at one of the nearest friendly positions. He told them to go down to the crash site but not to try to make contact with the Air America crew until daylight. They were to surround the site to ensure that the North Vietnamese did not sneak in and take the crew as prisoners.

Cates's radio stopped working. Under the fog, he had no way to know that friendly Thais were coming down to cordon off the area. They heard the sounds of people surrounding them and expected an attack any minute.

Basham, the copilot, was a large man—about 290 pounds. He liked to say that if he was in a small helicopter with another large man as pilot, it would be so heavy that the only thing they could carry would be verbal messages. Sitting beside Cates, he leaned against their crashed helicopter and listened to the noises around them. He had his handgun at the ready—shivering and scared. When he got out of the plane, he had lost his watch. At one point, he asked Cates, "What time is it?"

Cates said, "1 A.M."

After what seemed like four hours, he asked Cates again, "What time is it?"

Cates, always the straight man, said, "Five after."

Brenda normally had the kids up eating breakfast before seven. One morning, Joseph heard a plane overhead as he was finishing. He yelled and ran outside through a door that led off the dining room. Before following Joseph outside, Brenda sent Mim back to her bedroom to change clothes. Mim was in her second year of kindergarten by this time. The wives in the area alternated in taking the neighborhood kids across town to the American school in the embassy housing compound. Sandy Wilson, who was driving that day, lived a couple of blocks away.

Joseph and Brenda sat on the back stairs and watched three bombers making practice runs near the Chainimo Army Garrison across a field behind the house. They had a front-row seat as the planes dived down, came up, circled around, and dived again. Finally, they dropped some bombs. Joseph clapped his hands as the planes came around and headed back to the airport. He jumped up and down and waved when the planes passed low over the house.

Mim came out, ready for school, and Brenda took the children to the car. Joseph stood on the floor in the back—his favorite riding position—and looked out between the two front seats they drove to Sandy's house.

Brenda blew her horn when she got to the front gate, but the guard was not around. She thought that strange but got out and opened the gate herself. As she drove through, Sandy came running out, screaming, "Brenda, Brenda, get inside the house. Get your children, get inside the house. Hurry, hurry. There's a coup."

Brenda scurried Mim and Joe inside. They joined Sandy and others under the dining room table—kids, maids, guards, everyone. Sandy tried to squeeze Brenda, Mim, and Joseph under, although, in truth, there were parts of people sticking out.

Sandy explained that some dissident Lao Air Force pilots were bombing the army camp behind our house. She was worried that our house was in the line of fire. She was so thankful that Brenda and the kids were OK.

"A coup?" asked Brenda. "Real bombs? Behind our house?"

Up-country, we began to plan our next dry season offensive but were not surprised to receive messages from Washington to stand down, hold our own, and put aside plans to go on the attack. Visitors from Washington speculated that our war was over. Vietnam had been conceded, they said. The United States no longer had a will to fight or to win there. A popular phrase was, "Let the Vietnamese fight their own war."

"Vietnamization" was, in fact, the U.S. government's fig-leaf means of extricating itself from South Vietnam. If the United States pulled out of the fight to protect

South Vietnam, there was no chance we would be allowed
to continue fighting in Laos. Our mission was in support of
overall U.S. objectives in Vietnam. The United States did
not come to this part of the world to protect Laos.

On the morning of 22 February 1973, an F-111, the
last to cross the river into Laos, delivered its ordnance
and was gone. All was quiet in MR II. The war had been
going on for a long time, but now it was quiet.

About this time in Vientiane, my wife faced the certain
prospects that a family member would die, for her a far
more serious matter than a cease-fire and peace negotiations.

Most American families in Vientiane had pets. We had
Harry, our lucky mongrel dog from Chapel Hill, who was
an adjunct to Brenda's everyday life. He slept on the foot
of the bed or on the floor at Brenda's side. During the
day, he followed her around from room to room. He sat
alertly at her feet when people came to visit and turned
occasionally to look into her eyes when she laughed or
called out to one of the children.

All of the pets in Laos lived under the threat of heartworms, which were prevalent in the tropics. Transmitted
by mosquitoes, heartworms entered an animal's blood-
stream and traveled to the heart, where they set up house-
keeping. They clogged the arteries and valves until the
heart stopped working. Few animals survived heartworm
disease.

A veterinarian, who came up to Vientiane every two
months, took blood samples of pets and had them tested
in Udorn. On his next trip he always had one or two
heartworm cases to report. Sometimes, the animals had
died in the interim. He often euthanized a pet, rather than
leave it to die gradually and painfully.

The vet used the gym of the American school for his
clinics. Some of the wives would arrive early to find out
which pets had tested positive for heartworms. If they

knew the owners, they would, out of a macabre sense of theater, wait until they came in to receive the bad news.

Brenda, accompanied by Mim, brought Harry to the gym during the April clinic. She noticed a group of women standing off to the side and waved. She greeted the young doctor warmly and said Harry was in for his blood test results.

The vet looked her in the eye and said Harry had tested positive for heartworms. Positive sounded good to Brenda. She said as much and asked the vet where he wanted to take Harry's blood this time.

"You don't understand," he said, "Harry has heartworms. I'm sorry."

Brenda stood very still for a moment. She turned and looked at the women standing nearby, suddenly aware of what was going on. Then, she turned back to the doctor. She was angry.

And she started crying, demanding that the doctor do something. He said there was nothing he could do. She said, "Please do something. Something!"

Her balled-up fist was pumping. "You will do something. Sorry is not enough!"

My wife had come a long way from North Carolina. She had not liked the Orient when she first arrived, but it had been very good to her and she was comfortable, happy. She had two children she loved very much, a good home, friends, a husband who enjoyed his work. She knew how to take care of things when I was away, which was most of the time. Thriving in the Lao culture, she was not easily intimidated or put off. She was not afraid of noises in the night. Like a pioneer woman, she had learned to look after herself and her loved ones.

This dog, who was looking up at her as she raged, was very precious to her, and she was not going gently into that quiet night suggested by the vet. She did not consider accepting this young doctor's decision that her dog was going to die. He did not understand that he had to do something.

"Do something. Do not touch me. Do something," she continued loudly. She was crying, but her voice was strong. Her eyes, through her tears, were intense and angry. She was breathing hard; she was afraid she was going to hit the man.

The vet said, "The only thing that can be done is to give the animal strychnine, but it has almost no chance of success. You try to kill the worms in the heart without killing the animal. It's a fine line, hair-thin. I don't know when it has ever been successful here in the Orient."

"Give me the medicine," Brenda said quickly, loudly.

The doctor gave her seven pills from his medical bag. He said, "Give the dog one pill a day, and then pray. If he begins to vomit, you have to stop, because he will discharge enough poison to kill other animals. You have to promise me if he upchucks that you will stop the medicine and accept his fate.

"And," he said, "you have to realize that there is almost no chance that it will be successful, that you might be giving him enough poison to kill him. Or that he will go through all this, and the heartworms won't die."

Brenda had not stopped crying, but she understood everything the vet had said.

She drove home with her dog, her daughter, and those seven pills. That night, she gave Harry pill number one.

The next day, she gave him pill number two. On day three, Harry was sick. He was in pain. His eyes were not clear, and he wobbled when he tried to walk. Brenda helped him get about, and she cried.

I had just left for up-country and didn't know what she was going through.

The next day Harry was so sick he could hardly get up. He fouled the rug by Brenda's bed. On day five, he vomited. Brenda held him and told him not to do that, please don't do that.

She had promised to stop the medication if he couldn't take it anymore, but she didn't. She gave him his sixth

and seventh pills, and Harry lay quietly, breathing irregularly.

There was no change on the eighth day when I returned from up-country. The next day, Harry was up and
moving around.

When the vet came back in two months, Harry was his
old self and tested negative for heartworms.

Brenda said she knew it would turn out that way.
''Harry's magic. He's a good dog, and he's lucky.''

''You're a pioneer woman,'' I said, feeling very proud
of my wife.

''Feel good about Harry,'' she told me. ''Don't think
about me.''

17

BRAGGING RIGHTS TO THE HMONG

The Laos cease-fire settlement finally took effect. Pathet Lao administrators eventually came to Vientiane to assist in running the country. Pathet Lao military forces, host to our North Vietnamese enemy for so many years, were garrisoned in the capital. It was strange to see my former enemies standing on the street corners of Vientiane when I came in from the valley.

We had been so intent on keeping them out in order to protect the local government. That had been our mission. I remembered Ambassador Godley standing in front of us and saying it was important to hold Skyline, to stop the Pathet Lao and the North Vietnamese from threatening Vientiane. He invoked the name of the president and spoke about what our efforts would mean to the overall U.S. position in this part of the world. Stop the Communists from moving south, he had said. And here they were. It was hard to understand how we could have worked so hard, been so successful, and yet we lost the country. It was as if the referees had decided the game.

June was approaching. The summer rotation was upon us again. Kayak, Bamboo, and Dutch left, as did many of the support people. They were not replaced. Zack, Hog, Clean, and I, plus administrative officers, were left to work with the Hmong. Most of the Thai mercenaries and their Sky advisers were sent south. We went from thirty-eight officers in MR II to eight.

With the war over, the tough, resilient Hmong fighters, who had supported American objectives for so many years and been in our employ for so long, were unsure about their future. The Hmong needed schools, hospitals, more chicken farms, and industry to generate cash. They needed alternatives to opium farming. We could make a difference. Zack, Hog, Clean, and I began looking at sites for different projects. Our daily routine changed from war mongering to social work.

Hugh T. was leaving Vientiane and being replaced by Dan A., a well-known manager in the CIA's East Asia Division. He had a reputation for being an effective station chief at his other postings, but he was ruthless in his dealings with subordinates. There were stories of agent operatives brought to tears by the man. He loved to intimidate, according to the rumors that preceded him, and he had no compassion for the feelings of those around him.

That did not bother us. What concerned us up-country was that Hugh T., who knew the sacrifices the Hmong had made, was leaving and a man who had no sweat equity with the program was going to be in charge. At the eleventh hour, we would have a new boss. It didn't seem fair.

In late July, we received a message from Dan A. in Vientiane, which had replaced Udorn as our principal correspondent. The message said that we were to facilitate the intent of the cease-fire by disarming the Hmong.

This was ludicrous. The Hmong were not going to give up their weapons. Without them, they would be slaughtered. We did not need to consider what would happen to them if someone took their guns, however, because we knew they would not give them up. They would disappear into the hills first; their society was primitive. The

Hmong were not going to give anyone their weapons, not to Sky, not to anyone.

Zack wrote a message back and said as much.

Soon, another message from Vientiane asked us to provide a timetable of departure for everyone in the valley, except for Hog and a support officer, who would be staying. Everyone else would leave. Vientiane station wanted to know when.

We got together and wrote a cable about chicken farms and schools and hospitals and why we were needed to assist the Hmong during this transition period.

The next cable did not mention our response. It asked for a timetable by the end of the week. Cold-hearted, insensitive bureaucrat, we thought. Vintage Dan A.

We didn't respond.

On Monday, we received a blistering message saying that we were to provide to the chief of station personally a list of our duties and the earliest dates we could leave.

Respectfully, we sent back a message talking about chicken farms and hospitals and schools.

Dan A. flew up the next day.

This business about our departure and our moral responsibilities to the Hmong was not the only item in our dialogue with Vientiane, Udorn, and CIA headquarters. We were involved in a variety of other activities: dismantling equipment, drawing boundaries on areas of Hmong control, wrapping up reports on subjects of intelligence interest. Ostensibly, the chief of station was coming up to discuss a host of issues, but we knew the main reason for his visit was to talk about our departure and our concerns about the chicken farms.

This was good, the small group of us agreed that night in the almost deserted bar. We were sure Dan A. was the problem. Hugh T. would have understood. We would have the chance to win over the new man when he got to the valley, educate him on the long history of the Hmong's close work with the Agency, and sensitize him to our residual obligations.

He was coming to us, which was a manly way to handle this. We had home field advantage, and we had him outnumbered.

Hog, Clean, and I, along with the Sky officers working with the Thais, were in the main room of the headquarters bunker when Dan A. came walking in the next morning. Zack, who had met him on the ramp, made the introductions.

He did not make much of an initial impact. He was slight and pale, someone who wouldn't get a second glance on the street. The altitude was having its effect, and he was breathing hard. He was dressed like a city dweller, like he belonged behind a desk—someone who did indoor work. He didn't appear to be the type of individual who could take on the Long Tieng garrison.

He began by saying that we had done a good job. Few people knew how well. He said it was expected, however; if we had not done a good job, we would have been replaced with people who could.

His mousy looks belied his tough language and the firmness in his voice.

"The war is over up here," he went on. "Your job is done. Time to get on with other things. It's like digging a ditch. When you're finished, you put down your shovels and you go home or to another job.

"Put down your Hmong. Go home. They have been well cared for these many years they worked for us. They can look after themselves now. Our job is finished here.

"You are public servants, employed by the CIA, but you work for the American people and you have a position of trust. You cannot afford to have divided loyalties. When there is some question about your loyalties, it's time to stop, step back, and have someone remind you of your obligations.

"You've gone native, some of you. You smell bad. You think your opinions are the appropriate ones here. You're a little lost in the forest, boys. No one forced the Hmong to fight for us. This is their homeland. We've helped them defend it all these many years. Our job's over, and we have to go. They got along without us for eons; they'll survive. There are professionals in other organizations who know more about chicken farms and schools and hospitals than you ever will and are itching to get up here. Leave your schools and chicken farms and hospital building to them. The Hmong will be OK. Go on to your next job.

"Anyone got any doubts on this, any questions?"

No one did. Clean left in the fall. I left on 3 December. Zack left the next summer.

I had received orders for Vietnam. Hog took me to Air Ops the last day. He told me that it was all over for us here and that I ought to return to North Carolina and maybe open up a Mule's Feed and Seed store. South Vietnam didn't have much of a future.

"No," I said, "you have it wrong. We haven't lost yet. It's to the barricades. Fight on. Do the job. Make the thing worthwhile. It's sorta my war now. Not too many good ol' boys left in South Vietnam. Have to stick around to maybe switch out the light when everyone else leaves. Mule's Feed and Seed can wait."

When I processed through Udorn after leaving Long Tieng and Vientiane, the base was almost deserted. In two years, it had gone from the nerve center of the private CIA war in Laos to a building of caretakers.

Air America drew down. All the Thai mercenaries who were returned to Thailand were discharged. The Hmong GMs were disbanded, and the irregulars, for the most part, returned to their villages. But they did not give up their weapons. Someone shot the Sky bear, and he was butchered for his meat, which was reportedly very tender after so many years of drinking beer.

The Stick retired, and so did Tony Poe. Hog and V. P. eventually left the valley, as did all the remaining Hmong ops assistants, T-28 pilots, and V. P.'s officers. Soon afterward, a Pathet Lao unit moved into Long Tieng and set up an office.

One of their first orders of business was to arrange the transfer of all the T-28s to the Pathet Lao headquarters at Phong Savan. Former pilots from the Lao National Air Force, which had worked with the United States, were located to move the planes. To ensure that these non-Communist pilots flew the planes to the Pathet Lao base and not into Thailand or to some Lao or Hmong hideout, a Pathet Lao guard, with a brace of pistols, was put in the backseat of each of the old fighters. The Lao pilots were told they would be shot if they tried to land at any base other than the one known to the guards.

One of the older pilots was the last to leave Long Tieng. His Pathet Lao guard sat behind him in the T-28 with drawn pistols. The pilot took off, made a low pass over the valley, and then, flying slowly, turned and headed north. As he gained altitude, with the PDJ in front of him, he came to the edge of the territory controlled by the Hmong.

And he punched out—leaving the young Pathet Lao guard in the rear seat of the open cockpit with no way to fly the plane.

The pilot drifted down in his parachute near a friendly Hmong village. The T-28 went out of sight as it headed north, eventually to run out of gas and crash.

With that final deed of derring-do, the pilot salvaged a piece of dignity for all of us and got bragging rights for the Hmong and the United States.

In the hearts and minds of Sky, we never lost.

EPILOGUE

This story about the last days of the CIA secret war in Laos describes CIA paramilitary forces in combat and the introduction of long-range artillery and sophisticated aeronautical fighting machines into a nonconventional mountain war. But as in all war stories, it is ultimately about people. I served with strong-willed men who knew exactly who they were and what they were doing. They believed in duty and forthright honesty, and those principles provided structure and purpose to their lives. Many are now dead. It is almost as if they were born to work in the Long Tieng valley. When they left, their characters, clearly defined in that unusual, insulated environment, were out of place—they weren't sure who they were anymore, what they were doing, where they were going. Confused but still charging windmills, many died. They were not sentimental, and they would not want your pity for dying young. "Proud 'Mericans," as Hog would say, and they got what they wanted out of life. They were not everyday people.

CAST OF CHARACTERS

Bag Deceased. He was killed when the aircraft he was piloting was hit by an antiaircraft missile in Zimbabwe.

Bamboo Died as the result of an automobile accident in Saudi Arabia.

Bear Retired from the CIA to a trout stream in Montana.

Father Luke Bouchard Serving the rural underprivileged in Indonesia.

Clean Deceased. He was disabled in a hang glider accident and died of cancer.

Jerry Connors Works with a private airline in Texas. His wife, Prou, is still one of the most beautiful women in the world.

Dan A. Retired from the CIA.

Dick J. Retired from the CIA.

Digger Served in the Middle East after Laos and then resigned from the CIA to return to active duty as a U.S. Marine officer. Now retired from government service, he skydives and surfs in southern California.

Dutch Retired from the CIA and living in Texas.

Izzy Freedman Night manager of the Royal Crown bar on Pat Pong II, Bangkok, Thailand. He had a cancerous growth removed from his chest, and his prognosis is good.

Greek Resigned from the CIA. He is now working in the Pacific Northwest.

Hardnose Resigned from the CIA after a tour in Cambodia. He is now a senior manager with a large American corporation.

Hog Deceased. After Laos, he returned to Montana, earned a college degree, and rejoined the Agency as a staff case officer. He was asphyxiated by a faulty gas water heater in Bangkok, Thailand.

Hugh T. Retired from the CIA and lives abroad with his second wife.

Jerry F. Still in the CIA and still a very funny man.

Jim G. Retired from the CIA. One of the most respected former officers in the clandestine service, he lives in the Washington, D.C., area.

Kayak Deceased. He resigned from the CIA after Laos

and was killed in an ambush on the Angola-Zaire border while working privately as a mercenary. One report was that, after initially sustaining multiple wounds from Cuban ambushers, he held his ground by the Jeep in which he was riding and returned point-blank fire until he was cut down. He died while still firing his assault rifle, probably with a toothbrush in his mouth.

Lao wife convicted of murdering her Air America administrator husband Living in the United States. After the Communists came to power in 1975, they reviewed the records of Laotian jail inmates in order to identify and release political, pro-Communist prisoners. This woman said, "Hey, I'm in here for killing an American, that should be worth something to you guys," and she was released. She went to the States, sued Air America for her husband's life insurance, and challenged U.S. government officials to prove she was guilty of any crime, a difficult proposition because all records from the former government of Laos were either destroyed or inaccessible. She won her case, received the insurance money, and settled permanently on the West Coast.

Lumberjack Retired from the CIA. He was indicted by the Walsh Commission for violation of the Bollings Amendment.

Nhia Lives in California. Now a U.S. citizen, he sells insurance and has six children.

H. Ownby Resigned from the U.S. Air Force. He now practices law in Plano, Texas.

Pao Vang U.S. citizen, married and has a family. After we left Laos, he lived with an Air America family. He escaped across the Mekong after all of the Americans had been expelled from the country and finally made his way to the United States. He lives in Detroit and works for a computer manufacturing firm.

Tony Poe Stayed roaring drunk, raising hell in Udorn, Thailand, until early 1993. He then moved back to northern California, where people look at him strangely.

Redcoat   Still employed by the CIA and working in his quiet, effective manner.

Shep   Still up to his old tricks as a smoke jumper.

Frenchy Smith   Deceased. He was killed in an automobile accident.

The Stick   Retired from the CIA. He now manages a host of joint ventures in Thailand.

The Sword   Deceased. He was captured by the North Vietnamese when Saigon fell in 1975 and, after six months as a POW, was repatriated. He was eventually assigned to Beirut, Lebanon, where he was killed.

Tahn   Deceased. He was killed in Laos.

George Taylor   Helicopter pilot for a hospital rescue unit in Montana.

T. J.   Actively employed by the CIA.

Va Xiong   Lives near Pinehurst, North Carolina. He manages a supermarket and owns twenty-two rental units in the Sandhills of North Carolina.

General Vang Pao   Living in Santa Anna, California, a leader-in-exile of the White Hmong.

Yer Pao Sher (alias), the Bouam Long Commander   Fled to a refugee camp in Thailand after the Communists took over in Vientiane but eventually returned to Bouam Long, where he now lives. He still fights the Communists with ammunition left over from the days of Sky. He insists that each bullet shot by his men kills one Communist. His clothes are held together by pins, and he has lost all of his teeth. The Communists have a price on his head, but he will not leave because of his "commitment of honor" to the Hmong of Bouam Long to stay with them and fight for their homeland. He commands the only outpost in Indochina that has never been captured by the Communists.

Zack   Retired from the CIA, presently playing golf in southern California.

Our son Joe   Served with the 82nd Airborne Division in Desert Storm. He now attends college in North Carolina.

Our daughter Mim   Left home after high school and had no contact with the family for seven years. She now lives and works in Beverly Hills, California.

Dad   Remarried at age 81, with homes in Hilton Head, South Carolina, and Aberdeen, North Carolina.

Brenda Joyce Denton Parker   Proprietress of the River Kwai Collection of fine gifts from the Orient in Pinehurst, North Carolina.

Mule   After Laos, I was assigned to the CIA unit in the delta of South Vietnam. The day before the U.S. Embassy in Saigon was evacuated in late April 1975, I led a group of sensitive CIA agents to a U.S. merchant ship lying off the delta coast. I spent the next two days evacuating other Vietnamese and finally left by landing craft from the port city of Vung Tau, the last American out of Vietnam. Back at CIA Headquarters in Langley, Virginia, I converted from SOG paramilitary contract to CIA staff and continued as an intelligence officer, working abroad in Africa and Asia. Now retired, I live in Pinehurst, North Carolina, with my wife and son.

GLOSSARY

ABCCC U.S. Air Force Airborne Control and Command Center. This 24-hour-a-day overhead air force platform coordinated air force support and provided radio relay services to Sky officers on the ground.

ADO Opération de L'Armée de Défense, the Hmong village militia originally organized by the French. General Vang Pao was chief of the ADO when he was initially contacted by the CIA.

Air Ops Air Operations. This term was commonly used to indicate (1) the building by the Long Tieng ramp where landings and takeoffs were coordinated and (2) the overall business of Air America and Continental Air Service support to the field.

ARCLIGHT Code word for the U.S. Air Force's B-52. Arclight Strike Zones were rectangular map grids passed to the Air Force (by the coordinates of the corners) for bombing.

ARMA Army Attache's Office in the U.S. Embassy. It provided ordnance, including T-28 bombs and fuses, to CIA forces.

Baci Hmong term for a party (welcoming baci, Hmong New Year baci, wedding baci, farewell baci). If the host could afford it, liquor was provided. Mekong, the local liquor, was usually the drink of choice, although Vang Pao served White Horse scotch. At some time during a baci, the host knelt in front of the guest of honor and tied a cotton string around the guest's wrist for luck and prosperity. Once the string was tied in a tight knot, the host usually downed a shot of liquor with the guest. The host then moved off, and other Hmong knelt to tie strings around the guest's wrist, followed by an exchange of drinks. If there was work to be done after the baci or the next day, Sky men usually insisted on a toast only with the host. Twenty, thirty, or forty Hmong could be waiting in line. Visitors from Washington, unsure of the custom and not wanting to offend anyone, would go shot for shot with the Hmong, until they toppled over. Though Sky officers often passed on the liquor, they appreciated the strings. They might have said, among themselves, that the strings were just Hmong hocus-pocus—had no actual bearing on a man's fate—but they never took them off.

BDA   Battle damage assessment, U.S. Air Force term for after-action reporting on the effectiveness of its bombing missions. This was an integral part of CIA duties associated with the employment of F-111s in MR II, Laos.

CASI   Continental Air Services International, a private airline that augmented Air America work in up-country Laos. It provided Twin Otter and Porter planes for field support work. The pilots were generally considered easy to work with.

Customer   Air America phrase for CIA case officers.

Dreaded   Hog term used in much the same way the British use "bloody." "The dreaded ramp," Hog might say, "is this war's bulls-eye."

E&E   Escape and evasion, a tactical process by which one tries to escape from an enemy-controlled area; also, the signature CIA paramilitary training course. In addition to a handgun or assault rifle, each CIA case officer and Air America pilot carried a military E&E kit when he was working in the field.

Exfil   Short for an exfiltration or egress.

Fast mover   Any military jet that delivers ordnance.

FNG   Fucking new guy. This military term did not originate in the Long Tieng valley.

Girl singer   Hog term used to describe a man who puts on airs and acts in a pretentious manner. It was taken from the visual image of an overdressed male lounge singer, strutting around on stage with half-closed eyes, who tried to appear romantic while warbling a love song to no one in particular. Hog said most politicians were girl singers.

GM   Groupe Mobile, a French military term for a regiment-size unit of approximately eight hundred Hmong. There were six Hmong GMs in MR II in 1971.

Hang   A term, as defined by CIA people in Washington, D.C., in the early 1970s, to describe people who could "hang in there" when the going got rough. "The man's got hang," was the most popular phrasing and, in SOG/Washington circles, was usually used in reference to Hog, who, by reputation, stayed in the thick of the fighting in Laos and never came out. According to old-timers at Long Tieng, however, the phrase came into the up-country language from the Lao word "hang" (phonetic), which means a man with a strong heart; a man who stays and fights. The Lao phrase "Lao me hang lie" (phonetic) means that he is a man with resolve and principle. The phrase Hog used most up-country was, "The man has no hang," a rough translation of the popular Lao phrase "bo me hang" (phonetic), which means he is not strong and cannot be depended on—he will not stay and fight.

Highly dangeral   Hog term used to indicate anything risky. It originated in a radio message from one of Hog's ops assistants who was describing a very dangerous field situation.

Hmong   One of several tribes who, over the course of several thousand years, drifted south out of China into the mountains of Laos. Other tribes include the Yao and the Kao. Because the rugged terrain of the mountains separated the Hmong, three dominant groups evolved in Laos. The Flower Hmong and Stripe Hmong, known as peaceful, agrarian hill people, lived in the western section of Laos. The White Hmong, who lived around the PDJ, were considered the least civilized and the most tenacious warriors. Vang Pao was military leader of the White Hmong from the late 1940s to the mid-1970s. Touby LyFong also had considerable influence in this clan, although he tended to focus his work on political and social programs. (Note: The name Hmong is used as both singular and plural.)

Hmong hocus-pocus Anything in the Hmong culture that Sky people did not understand.

Indoor work Bureaucratic nonsense.

Karst Rugged rock column that juts straight up in the air. It is found most often on valley floors.

Kicker Term used for flight mechanic on Air America rotary wing and for cargo master on fixed-wing planes. The word's origin is associated with the job on transport planes of pushing or "kicking" rice and other supplies out the side of air delivery planes.

Knuckle draggers Phrase used to describe SOGers, alluding to their possible close kinship with the gorilla family.

LS Abbreviation for Lima Sites, landing airstrips in Laos. Sometimes, the designation did not include the S; the airfield at Vientiane was designated L 08. The airfield in the Long Tieng valley was LS 20A. Although pilots and customers often said the whole phrase, Lima Site Twenty Alternate, it was most commonly referred to as Twenty Alternate or, more simply, the Alternate. When the Hmong civilians moved into a new area, they often built a Lima Site, and an Air America engineer had to fly up by helicopter and inspect it before a fixed-wing plane could land. The Lima Sites were often dug out of the sides of mountains; severe wind sheers and drafts affected take-offs and landings. There was little margin for error in landing.

LZ   Landing zones. The LZs by Hmong villages were cleared areas where fixed-wing pilots aimed air delivery of supplies, such as rice. By Hmong and Thai defensive positions, LZs were primarily landing areas for helicopters. They were usually designated by two-letter combinations of white cloth staked to the ground. The LZs on Skyline were in the C series: CA, CB, CC, and so forth.

Mekong   The river that separates Laos and Thailand. Also, a very inexpensive Thai liquor, not much different in taste from Southern mash bourbon. A few drinks can cause a normal-size Occidental man to fall over backward.

'Merican   American. This southern-accented word was initiated by Hog to describe any person or ideal that represents American common values. "Hard work's the 'Merican way. So is good pie."

MR   Military region. There were four MRs in Laos: MR I in the west, MR II in the northeast, MR III halfway down the eastern border, and MR IV in the south.

Ni Ban   Hmong village chief. Elected by the people, the Ni Ban decided when the village moved, ruled on domestic disputes, settled property rights, and selected the men to join the GMs.

Ni Khong   An official appointed by Vang Pao and Touby LyFong to coordinate activities of the various Ni Bans. Ni Khongs usually were former Ni Bans. They ruled on territorial matters and differences between Ni Bans. Disputes that they could not settle were passed on to Vang Pao or Touby LyFong.

Ops assistants   Hmong or Thai men who assisted Sky case officers in the field. They were used as interpreters, translators, area experts, radio operators, and bodyguards. A close bond always developed between a case officer and his ops assistant.

Pair of seconds   Hog phrase that meant a short period of time.

Pathet Lao   Lao hill people who supported the Communists and were hosts to the North Vietnamese in Laos. Predominantly from the Hmong and Kao tribes, they rarely became involved in confrontations with the Hmong GMs.

PDJ   Abbreviation for Plaine des Jarres, or Plain of Jars, a fifty-square-mile plateau in the mountains of Laos near the North Vietnamese border. It is named for the stone jars that litter the landscape; origin of the jars is unknown. As critical terrain in central Indochina, the PDJ is a trading center and often a battlefield. It is the homeland of the White Hmong.

Porter   Short takeoff and landing aircraft used for airdrops and to service Lima Sites throughout Laos. With a single engine and usually flown by a single pilot, the Porter was the civic affairs workhorse. Porters were flown by both CASI and Air America.

Ramp   The city block-size asphalt tarmac at the west end of the Long Tieng runway that was the hub of CIA activity in MR II.

Red Dog Control   Hmong radio hookup with the U.S. Air Force's F-111 bombers. Hmong talkers sat for hours in front of the dials on their radios—silently waiting for transmissions from the F-111 pilots and working on their messages to their heroes, to the "almost astronauts."

RTB   Returning to base, a phrase used by F-111 pilots to tell the Hmong talkers at Red Dog Control that they had dropped their ordnance and were returning to Thailand. The pilots often used the words, "I am RTB," and sometimes followed this phrase with "Good afternoon to you," or "Nice talking to you," or "Have a good day." The Hmong talkers seized on these farewells—they asked Sky officers hundreds of questions about the exact meaning of each phrase. At first, they usually repeated the farewell in signing off, but they eventually interchanged the phrases. When an F-111 pilot said, "Good afternoon to you," for example, the Hmong might sign off by saying, "Drive carefully. And thanks." The Hmong talker would then sit back, stare at the radio dials, and beam.

Sky   Term used by the locals for the CIA in up-country Laos.

Skyline   The towering ridgeline that guards the north side of the Long Tieng valley.

SOG   Special Operations Group of the CIA Directorate of Operation. It was responsible for staffing the Lao program. The CIA Special Operations Group should not be confused with the U.S. Army Special Operations Group, which saw extensive action in Vietnam. Although they had some similar paramilitary missions, they were two separate organizations.

SOGer   Any CIA case officer working in SOG. Also, see knuckle draggers.

Twin Pack   A Sikorsky S-58T used for heavy sling loads in support of field operations. It was usually flown by senior pilots.

INDEX

ABOUT THE AUTHOR

James E. Parker, Jr., was born in North Carolina in 1942. A graduate of the University of North Carolina at Chapel Hill, he served as a U.S Army Infantry platoon leader in South Vietnam in 1965–66.

In the summer of 1970 he was recruited by the Central Intelligence Agency's clandestine service. He spent most of his career in the Orient and Africa. Now retired, he lives in Pinehurst, North Carolina.

UNARMED, UNDERWATER, UNDER FIRE—THEY WENT TO WAR, AND BEGAN THE LEGEND OF THE NAVY SEALS.

Facing a fanatical, dug-in enemy in Europe and in the Pacific, U.S. planners turned to a new kind of warrior: daring swimmers who could knock out mines, map out enemy beaches, and pave the way for Allied naval assaults. With a few extraordinary and brave men, the U.S. Navy's Underwater Demolition Teams went to war.

Now, a founder and legendary commander of UDT-1 takes you into the world of the underwater soldiers. This is the inside story of a unique breed of warrior—and the bloody battles they helped win.

NAKED WARRIORS

Cdr. Francis Douglas Fane, USNR (Ret.) and Don Moore

NW 12/98

They go where no one else will go.
They do what no one else will do.
And they're proud to be called . . .

TWILIGHT WARRIORS

INSIDE THE WORLD'S SPECIAL FORCES

MARTIN C. AROSTEGUI

From deadly Scud hunts in the Gulf War to daring hostage rescue missions at London's Iranian Embassy, Special Forces go where no other army would dare—fighting for their countries and their lives on the world's most dangerous missions. Now, journalist and counter-terrorism expert Martin C. Arostegui tells their story—a fascinating true account of bravery, daring, and the ultimate risk.